Mrs. Hungerford

The Professor's Experiment

Vol. I

Mrs. Hungerford

The Professor's Experiment
Vol. I

ISBN/EAN: 9783337052799

Printed in Europe, USA, Canada, Australia, Japan

Cover: Foto ©ninafisch / pixelio.de

More available books at **www.hansebooks.com**

THE PROFESSOR'S EXPERIMENT

MRS. HUNGERFORD'S NOVELS

'Mrs. Hungerford has well deserved the title of being one of the most fascinating novelists of the day. The stories written by her are the airiest, lightest, and brightest imaginable, full of wit, spirit, and gaiety; but they contain, nevertheless, touches of the most exquisite pathos. There is something good in all of them.'—ACADEMY.

A MAIDEN ALL FORLORN, and other Stories. Post 8vo., illustrated boards, 2s.; cloth limp, 2s. 6d.

'There is no guile in the novels of the authoress of "Molly Bawn," nor any consistency or analysis of character; but they exhibit a faculty truly remarkable for reproducing the rapid small-talk, the shallow but harmless "chaff" of certain strata of modern fashionable society.'—*Spectator.*

IN DURANCE VILE, and other Stories. Post 8vo., illustrated boards, 2s.; cloth limp, 2s. 6d.

'Mrs. Hungerford's Irish girls have always been pleasant to meet upon the dusty pathways of fiction. They are flippant, no doubt, and often sentimental, and they certainly flirt, and their stories are told often in rather ornamental phrase and with a profusion of the first person singular. But they are charming all the same.'—*Academy.*

A MENTAL STRUGGLE. Post 8vo., illustrated boards, 2s.; cloth limp, 2s. 6d.

'She can invent an interesting story, she can tell it well, and she trusts to honest, natural, human emotions and interests of life for her materials.'—*Spectator.*

A MODERN CIRCE. Post 8vo., illustrated boards, 2s.; cloth limp, 2s. 6d.

'Mrs. Hungerford is a distinctly amusing author. . . . In all her books there is a "healthy absenteeism" of ethical purpose, and we have derived more genuine pleasure from them than probably the most earnest student has ever obtained from a chapter of "Robert Elsmere."'—*Saturday Review.*

MARVEL. Post 8vo., illustrated boards, 2s.; cloth, 2s. 6d.

'The author has long since created an imaginary world, peopled with more or less natural figures; but her many admirers acknowledge the easy grace and inexhaustible *verve* that characterize her scenes of Hibernian life, and never tire of the type of national heroine she has made her own.'—*Morning Post.*

LADY VERNER'S FLIGHT. Crown 8vo., cloth extra, 3s. 6d.; post 8vo., illustrated boards, 2s.; cloth limp, 2s. 6d.

'There are in "Lady Verner's Flight" several of the bright young people who are wont to make Mrs. Hungerford's books such very pleasant reading. . . . In all the novels by the author of "Molly Bawn" there is a breezy freshness of treatment which makes them most agreeable.'—*Spectator.*

THE RED-HOUSE MYSTERY. Crown 8vo., cloth extra, 3s. 6d.

'Mrs. Hungerford is never seen to the best advantage when not dealing with the brighter sides of life, or seeming to enjoy as much as her readers the ready sallies and laughing jests of her youthful personages. In her present novel, however, the heroine, if not all smiles and mirth, is quite as taking as her many predecessors, while the spirit of uncontrolled mischief is typified in the American heiress.'—*Morning Post.*

THE THREE GRACES. 2 vols., crown 8vo., 10s. net.

'It is impossible to deny that Mrs. Hungerford is capable of writing a charming love-story, and that she proves her capacity to do so in "The Three Graces."'—*Academy.*

LONDON: CHATTO & WINDUS, PICCADILLY.

THE
PROFESSOR'S EXPERIMENT

A Novel

BY

MRS. HUNGERFORD

AUTHOR OF
MOLLY BAWN,' 'THE RED-HOUSE MYSTERY,' 'THE THREE GRACES,'
'LADY VERNER'S FLIGHT,' ETC.

IN THREE VOLUMES
VOL. I.

London
CHATTO & WINDUS, PICCADILLY
1895

THE PROFESSOR'S EXPERIMENT

CHAPTER I.

'Thoughts are but dreams till their effects be tried.'

THE lamp was beginning to burn low; so was the fire. But neither of the two people in the room seemed to notice anything. The Professor had got upon his discovery again, and once there, no man living could check him. He had flung his arms across the table towards his companion, and the hands, with the palms turned upwards, marked every word as he uttered it, thumping the knuckles on the table here, shaking some imaginary disbeliever there—and never for a moment quiet—such old, lean, shrivelled, capable hands!

He was talking eagerly, as though the words flowed to him faster than he could utter them. This invention of his—this supreme discovery—would make a revolution in the world of science.

The young man looking back at him from the other side of the table listened intently. He was a tall man of about eight-and-twenty, and if not exactly handsome, very close to it. His eyes were dark, and somewhat sombre, and his mouth was thin-lipped, but kind, and suggestive of a nature that was just, beyond everything, if hardly sympathetic. It was a beautiful mouth, at all events, and as he was clean-shaven, one could see it as it was, without veiling of any kind. Perhaps the one profession of all others that most fully declares itself in the face of its sons is that of the law. A man who has been five years a barrister is seldom mistaken for anything else. Paul Wyndham was a barrister, and a rising one—a man who loved his profession for its own sake, and strove and fought to make a name in it, though no such struggle was needful for his existence, as from his cradle his lines had fallen to him in pleasant places. He was master of a good fortune, and heir to a title and ten thousand a year whenever it should please Providence to take his uncle, old Lord Shangarry, to an even more comfortable home than that which he enjoyed at present.

The Professor had been his tutor years ago, and the affection that existed between them in those far-off years had survived the changes of time and circumstance. The Professor loved him—and him only on all this wide earth. Wyndham had never known a father; the Professor came as near as any parent could, and in this new wild theory of the old man's he placed implicit faith. It sounded wild, no doubt—it was wild—but there was not in all Ireland a cleverer man than the Professor, and who was to say but it might have some grand new meaning in it?

'You are sure of it?' he said, looking at the Professor with anxious but admiring eyes.

'Sure! I have gone into it, I have studied it for twenty years, I tell you. What, man, d'ye think I'd speak of it even to you, if I weren't sure? I tell ye—I tell ye'—he grew agitated and intensely Irish here—'it will shake the world!'

The phrase seemed to please him; he drew his arms off the table and lay back in his chair as if revelling in it—as if chewing the sweet cud of it in fancy. He saw in his mind a day when in that old college of his over there, only a few streets away—in Trinity College—he should rise, and be greeted by his old chums and his new pupils, and the whole world of Dublin, with cheers and acclamations. Nay! it would be more than that—there would be London, and Vienna, and Berlin. He put Berlin last because, perhaps, he longed most of all for its applause; but in these dreamings he came back always to old Trinity, and found the greatest sweetness in the laurels to be gained there.

'There can't be a mistake,' he went on,

more now as if reasoning with himself than with his visitor, who was watching him, and was growing a little uneasy at the pallor that was showing itself round his nose and mouth—a pallor he had noticed very often of late when the old man was unduly excited or interested. 'I have gone through it again and again. There is nothing new, of course, under the sun, and there can be little doubt but that it is an anæsthetic known to the Indians of Southern America years ago, and the Peruvians. There are records, but nothing sufficient to betray the secret. It was by the merest accident, as I have told you, that I stumbled on it. I have made many experiments. I have gone cautiously step by step, until now all is sure. So much for one hour. So much for six, so much for twenty-four, so much'—his voice rose almost to a scream, and he thumped his hand violently on the table—'for seven days—for seven months!'

His voice broke off, and he sank back in his chair. The young man went quickly to a cupboard and poured out a glass of some white cordial.

'Thank you—thank you,' said the Professor, swallowing the nauseous mixture hurriedly, as though regretting the waste of time it took to drink it.

'Why talk any more to-night?' said the young man anxiously; 'I am going abroad in a few days, but I can come again to see you to-morrow. It is late.' He glanced at the clock, which pointed to ten minutes past eleven. The movement he made in pointing pushed aside his overcoat and showed that he was in evening dress. He had evidently been dining out, and had dropped in to see the Professor—an old trick of his—on his way home.

'I must talk while I can,' said the Professor, smiling. The cordial, whatever it was, had revived him, and he sat up and looked again at his companion with eyes that were brilliant. 'As for this pain here,' touching his side, 'it is nothing—nothing. What I want to say, Paul, is this'—he bent towards

Wyndham, and his lips quivered again with excitement: 'If I could send a human creature to sleep for seven months, then why not for seven years—for ever?'

Wyndham looked at him incredulously.

'But the last time——'

'The last time you were here, I had not quite perfected my discovery. But since then some of my experiments have led me to think—to be absolutely certain—that life can be sustained, with all the appearance of death upon the subject, for a full week at all events.'

'And when consciousness returns?'

'The subject treated wakes to life again in exactly the same condition as when he or she fell asleep—without loss of brain or body power.'

'Seven days! A long time!' The young man smiled. 'You bring back old thoughts and dreams. Are you a second Friar Laurence? Even he, though he could make the fair Juliet sleep till all believed her dead, could not prolong that unfortunate deception beyond a certain limit.

'"And in this borrowed likeness of shrunk death
   Thou shalt continue two-and-forty hours."

Less than two days—and yet, thou conjurer'—he slapped the Professor's arm gaily—'you would talk of keeping one in death's bonds for years!'

'Ay, years!' The Professor looked back at him, and his eyes shone. Old age seemed to slip from him, and for the moment a transient youth was his again. 'This is but a beginning—a mere start; but if it succeeds—if life can be sustained by means of this drug alone for seven days, why not for months and years?'

'You forget one thing,' said the young man. 'Who would care for it? Why should one care to lie asleep for years?'

'Many!' said the Professor slowly.

He ceased, and a strange gloom shadowed his face. His thoughts had evidently gone backward into a long-dead past—a past that still lived. 'Have you no imagination?' he said at last reproachfully. 'Think, boy—think! When affliction falls on one, when a grievous sorrow tears the heart, who would not wish for an oblivion that would be longer than a sleeping-draught could give, and less pernicious than suicide?'

'The same refusal in both cases to meet and face one's doom,' said the young man. 'You would create a new generation of cowards.'

'Pshaw! there will be cowards without me,' said the Professor. 'But here, again, take another case. A man, we will say, has had his leg cut off—well, let him sleep until the leg is well, and he will escape all the twinges, the agonizing pains of the recovery. This is but one instance; all surgical cases could be treated so, and so much pain saved in this most painful world.'

'Ah, I confess a charm lies there!' said Wyndham.

'It does. And yet it is to the other thought I lean—to the dread of memory where grief and shame lie.' The Professor's gaunt face lost again its short return of youth, and grew grim, and aged, and white.

'See,' he leant towards Wyndham, and pressed him into a chair beside the dying fire, 'to you—to you alone I have revealed this matter: not so much because you have been my pupil, as that you have a hold on me. You think me dry, and hard, and old. All that is true. But'—his voice grew if possible harsher than ever—'I have an affection for you.'

It seemed almost ludicrous to think of the Professor as having an affection for anything beyond his science and his discovery, with his bald head, and his bleared eyes, and his cold, forbidding face. The young man gazed at him with pardonable astonishment. That the Professor liked him, trusted him, was quite easy to understand—but the word 'affection'!

'It surprises you,' said the old man slowly, perhaps a little sadly. 'Yet there was a time——' He moved and poked the fire into a sullen blaze. 'I married,' he said presently. 'And she—well, I loved her, I think. It seems hard to remember now, it is so long ago, but I believe I had a heart then, and it was hers. She died.' He poked the fire again, and most of it fell into the grate—it was all cinders by this time, and the younger man shivered. 'It was well. Looking back upon it now,' said the Professor coldly, 'I am glad she died. She would have interfered with my studies. Her death left me free; but for that freedom, I should never have found out this.' He tapped some papers lying loosely on the table—three or four pages, no more, with only a line or two upon them—vague suggestions of the great discovery that was to shake the world, so vague as to be useless to anyone but himself.

'You had no children, then?' asked Wyndham, who had never even heard that he was married until now.

'One.' The Professor paused, and the silence grew almost insupportable. 'He, too, is dead. And that, too, is well. He was of no use. He only burdened the world.'

'But——'

'Not a question——' The old man silenced him. 'I cast him off.' There was something terrible in the indifference with which he said this. 'He was a fool—a criminal one. I heard later that he had married—no doubt as great a fool as himself. I hope so. Set a thief to catch a thief, you know.'

He laughed bitterly—the cruel, mirthless laugh of the embittered old. 'For the rest, I know nothing,' he said.

'You made no inquiries?'

'None. Why should I?'

'He was your son.'

'Well, does that make a black thing white? No—no! My son—my child is here!' He touched the loose papers with a loving hand.

Wyndham did not pursue the subject further, and as if to show that it was ended, he stooped and threw some coals upon the fire that now seemed to be at its last gasp. A tiny smoke flew up between the fresh lumps, and after that came a little uncertain blaze. The fire had caught the coals.

The Professor had gone back to his heart's desire.

'To see the blossom of my labour bear fruit—that is my sole, my last demand from life. I have so short a time to live that I would hasten the fulfilment of my hopes.'

'You mean——'

'That I want to see the drug used on a human being. I have approached the matter with some of the authorities at Kilmainham, with a view to getting a condemned criminal to experiment upon; but up to this I have been refused, and in such a presumptuous manner as leads me to fear I shall never receive a better answer. Surely a man respited for seven days, as has been the case occasionally, might as well risk those seven days in the cause of science.'

Wyndham shrugged his shoulders. 'I have never met that man,' said he. But the Professor did not hear him.

'The most humane people in the world,' said he, 'refuse help to the man who has devoted twenty years of his life to the cause of humanity. Such an anæsthetic as mine would work a revolution in the world of medicine. As I have told you, a man might not only be unconscious whilst a limb was being lopped off, but might remain so until the wound was healed, and then, made free of pain and perfectly well, be able to take his part in the world again.'

'It sounds like a fairy-tale,' said Wyndham, smiling. 'You have, I suppose, made many experiments?'

'On animals, yes—and of late without a single failure; but on a human body, no. As yet no opportunity has been afforded me. Either jealousy or fear has stopped my march, which I feel would be a triumphal one were the road made clear. I tell you I have addressed many leading men of science on the subject. I have asked them to be present. I would have everything above board, as you who know me can testify. I would have all men look on and bear witness to the splendour of my discovery.' Here again the Professor's strange deep eyes grew brilliant, once again that queer flash of a youth long ago departed was his. 'I would have it shown to all the world in a blaze of light. But no man will take heed or listen. They laugh. They scoff. They will not countenance the chance of my killing some-one; as if'—violently—'the loss of one poor human life was to be counted, when the relief of millions is in the balance.'

He sank back as if exhausted, and then went on, his tone hard, yet excited:

'Now it has come to this. If the chance were given me of trying my discovery on man, woman, or child, I should take it, without the sanction of the authorities, and with it that other chance of being hanged afterwards if the experiment failed.'

'You feel so sure as that?' questioned Wyndham. The old man's enthusiasm had caught him. He too was looking eager and excited.

'Sure!' The Professor rose, gaunt, haggard, and with eyes that flashed fire beneath the pent brows that overhung them. 'I would stake my soul—nay, more, my reputation—on the success of my discovery. Oh for a chance to prove it!'

At this moment there was a low knock at the door.

CHAPTER II.

'Of all things tired thy lips look weariest.'

* * * * * *

'What shall I do to be for ever known?'

THE handle was turned, and the door opened with a considerable amount of caution (the Professor did not permit interruptions). It was evidently, however, the caution of one who was suppressing badly a wild desire to make a rush into the room, and presently a man's head appeared round the corner of the door, and after it his body. He came a yard or two beyond the threshold, and then stood still. His reddish hair was standing out a little, and his small twinkling Irish eyes were blinking nervously. He looked eagerly first at the younger man, who was his master, and then at the Professor, and then back again at Wyndham.

'Well, Denis?' said the latter, a little impatiently.

'If ye plaze, sir, there's an unfortunate young faymale on the steps below.'

The Professor frowned. As if such an ordinary occurrence as that should be allowed to interfere with a discussion on the great discovery! Wyndham spoke.

'If she is noisy or troublesome, you had better call a policeman,' he said indifferently.

'Noisy! Divil a sound out of her,' said Denis. 'She looks for all the world, yer honour, as if there wasn't a spark o' life left in her. Sthretched in the hall she is, an' the colour o' death.'

'In the hall?' said Wyndham quickly. 'I thought you said she was on the steps.'

'She was. She' — cautiously — 'was. But——' He paused and scanned anxiously the two faces before him. 'It's bitther cowld outside to-night, so I tuk her in.'

And, indeed, though the month was May, a searching wind was shaking the city, and biting into the hearts of young and old. As often happens in that 'merrie month,' a light fall of snow was whitening the tops of the houses.

'I had better see to this,' said the young man, rising. He left the room, followed by Denis (who had stopped to throw a few more coals on the now cheerful fire), and went down to the cold, bare, hideous hall below. The light from the solitary gas-lamp scarcely lit it, and it took him a few seconds to discern something that lay on the worn tarpaulin at the lower end of it. At last he made it out, and, stepping nearer, saw that it was the figure of a young and very slight girl. She was lying on the ground, her back supported against a chair, and Wyndham could see that Denis had folded an old coat of the Professor's that usually hung on the hat-stand, and placed it behind her head.

The light was so dim that he could not see what she was like; but stooping over her, he felt her hands, and found that they were cold as ice. Instinct, however, told him that life still ran within her veins, and lifting her quickly in his arms, he carried her upstairs to the room he had just left, and where the Professor still sat, so lost in fresh dreams of the experiment yet to be made that he started as Wyndham re-entered the room with his strange burden; it was, indeed, with difficulty that he brought his mind back to the present moment. He had forgotten why the young man had left the room.

'She seems very ill,' said Wyndham. His man had followed him, and now, through a sign from his master, he pulled forward a huge armchair, in which Wyndham placed the unconscious girl.

The Professor came nearer and stared down at her. She was very young—hardly eighteen —but already Misery or Want, or both, had seized and laid their cruel hands upon her, dabbing in dark bistre shades beneath her eyes, and making sad hollows in her pallid cheeks. The lips, white now, were firmly closed as if in death, but something about the formation of them suggested the idea that even in life they could be firm too.

It was a face that might be beautiful if health had warmed it, and if joy had found a seat within the heart that now seemed at its last ebb. The lashes lying on the white, cold cheek were singularly long and dark, and Wyndham roused himself suddenly to find himself wondering what could be the colour of the eyes that lay hidden behind that wonderful fringe.

Her gown was of blue serge, neatly, even elegantly made, and the collar and cuffs she wore were quite primitive in their whiteness and simplicity. She had no hat or cloak with her, but a little gray woollen shawl had been evidently twisted round her head. Now it had fallen back, leaving all the glory of her rich chestnut hair revealed.

Involuntarily the young man glanced at her left hand.

There was no ring there. An intense wave of pity swept over him. Another!

Dear God! what cruel sorrows lie within this world of Yours!

The face was so young, so free of hardness, vice, or taint of any kind, that his very heart bled for her. Misery alone seemed to mark it. That was deeply stamped. Looking at her, he almost hoped that she would never wake again—that she was really dead; but even as this thought crossed his mind, she stirred, sighed softly, and opened her eyes.

For awhile she gazed at them—on the Professor, impassive, silent; on the younger man, anxious, pained—and then with a sharp, quick movement she released herself from the arm Wyndham had placed round her, and raised herself to a sitting posture. There was such terror in her eyes as she did this that the younger man hastened to reassure her.

'You are quite safe here,' he said kindly. The girl looked at him, then cast a frightened glance past him, and over his shoulder, as though looking fearfully for some dreaded object. 'My man found you on the steps outside. You were ill—fainting, he said—so he brought you in here to'—with a gesture towards the Professor—'this gentleman's house.'

The girl looked anxiously at the Professor, who nodded as in duty bound, but who seemed unmistakably bored, for all that, and angry enough to frighten her afresh.

'If you will tell us where you live,' said Wyndham gently, 'we shall see that you are taken back there.'

The girl shrank visibly. She caught the little shawl that had slipped from her, and drew it round her head once more, almost hiding her face.

'I can find my own way,' she said. The voice was low, musical; it trembled, and as she moved forward to pass Wyndham, so did she. She even tottered, so much, indeed, that she was obliged to catch hold of a table near to keep herself from falling.

'It is impossible for you to walk to-night,' said the young man earnestly. 'And there is no necessity for it. My servant is at your disposal : he can call a cab for you, and he is quite to be trusted ; he will see you to your home.'

The girl hesitated for a moment, then lifted her heavy eyes to his.

'I have no home,' she said.

It was a very forlorn answer, and it went to Wyndham's heart. God help her, poor girl ! whoever she was. He glanced again at her clothes, which were decidedly above the average of the extremely wretched, and he was conscious of a certain curiosity with regard to her—a distinctly kindly one.

The girl caught the glance and turned away her head.

'You can at least say where you want to be driven,' said he gravely, but with sympathy ; he hesitated for a moment, and then went on. 'No questions will be asked,' he said.

She made no answer to this, and while he waited for one the Professor broke in impatiently :

'Come, girl, speak ! Where do you want to go ? Where do you live ?'

On this followed another shorter silence, and then at last she spoke.

'I shall not go back,' she said. Her tone was low, but defiant, and very firm.

'That means you will not tell,' said the Professor. 'Then go—do you hear—go! You are interrupting us here.' He motioned towards the door, where Denis stood mute as a sentinel; he was, indeed, an old soldier, for the matter of that.

The girl stepped quickly, eagerly forward, but Wyndham stopped her imperatively, and standing between her and the door, he spoke to the Professor.

'It is impossible to turn her out at this hour—in this weather.' He stopped, and now looked at the girl and spoke to her.

'Why can't you trust us?' he said, with angry reproach. 'Why can't you let us do something for you? You must have a home somewhere, however bad.'

The girl thus addressed turned upon him suddenly with miserable passion shining in her large, dark eyes.

'I have not,' she said. 'Under the sky of God, there is no creature so homeless as I am.'

Her passion was so great that it struck the listeners into silence. She made a little gesture with her arms suggestive of awful weariness, then spoke again:

'There was a place where I lived yesterday. It was not a home. I shall not live there again. I have left it. I shall not go back.'

'But where, then, are you going?' asked Wyndham impulsively.

'I don't know.' She drew her breath slowly, heavily. It was hardly a sigh. There was enough misery in it for ten sighs. But her passion was all gone, and a terrible indifference had taken its place; and there was such consummate despair in her tone as might have touched even the Professor. But it did not. He had begun to study her. He was always studying people, and now a curious expression had crept into his face. He leaned forward and peered at her. There was no compassion in the glance, no interest whatever in her as a suffering human thing; but there was a sudden sharp interest in her as a means to a desired end. Thought was in his glance, and a wild longing that was fast growing to a hope.

'Have you no plans, then?' asked the young man. His tone was sad. He had looked into the depths of her dark eyes, and found there no guile at all.

'None!' She was silent awhile, and then very slowly she raised her head; her brows contracted, and she looked past them both into vacancy. If she was communing with her own heart, the results were very sad. Despair itself gathered in her eyes. She turned presently and looked at Wyndham. 'I wish,' said she, with a forlorn look, 'that I had the courage to die.'

It was unutterably sad, this young creature, with all her life before her, praying for courage to end it; craving for death in the midst of life, wishing she had the courage to escape from a world that had evidently given her but a sorry welcome.

Wyndham looked round at the Professor as if expecting him to join in his commiseration for this poor, unhappy child, but what he saw in the Professor's face checked him. It startled him, and stopped the tide of sympathy for a time—as great floods will for the moment always catch and carry with them the milder rushes of the rivers near.

The Professor's face was indeed a study. It was radiant—alight with a strange and sudden hope. His piercing eyes were fixed immovably upon the girl. They seemed to burn into her as though demanding and compelling an answering glance from hers.

She obeyed the call; slowly, languidly she lifted her head.

'So you would die?' said he.

'Yes.' The word fell listlessly from her lips; but she stared straight at him as she said it, and her young unhappy face looked nearly as gray as the old merciless one bending over it.

'Then why live?' pursued he. 'Death is easy.'

'No, it is hard,' she said. 'And I am afraid of pain.'

'If there were no pain, you would risk it, then?'

She hesitated. His glance was now, indeed, so wild, so full of frantic eagerness, that it might readily have frightened one older in the world's ways. To Wyndham, waiting, watching, it occurred that the Professor was like a spider creeping towards its prey. He shuddered.

'Speak, girl, speak!' said the Professor. His agitation was intense, and almost beyond control. Here—here to his hand was his chance. Was he to have it at last, or lose it for ever? Wyndham could stand it no longer; he went quickly forward, and, standing between the Professor and the girl, took the former by the shoulders and pushed him gently backwards and out of hearing.

'If this drug of yours possesses the life-giving properties you speak of,' said he sternly, 'why speak to her of death? Do you honestly believe in this experiment? Or do you fear it—when you suggest this sort of suicide to her?'

'I fear nothing,' said the old man. 'But we are all mortal. We can all err, even in our surest judgments. The very cleverest of us can be deceived. The experiment—though I do not believe it—might fail.'

At the word 'fail' he roused.

'It will not! It cannot!' he cried, with vehemence. 'But in the meantime I would give her her chance, too. She shall know the worst that may befall her.'

'Why not tell her all?' said the young man anxiously. 'It'—he hesitated and coloured faintly—'it would give her her chance perhaps in another world if your experiment failed. It would take from her—in part—the sin of deliberately destroying herself.'

The Professor shrugged his shoulders. He thought it waste of time, this preparing for another world—another Judge.

'You think, then, that I should tell her?'

'I do. I think, too,' said Wyndham strongly, 'that if your experiment succeeds you should consider yourself indebted to her for ever.'

'I shall see to her future, of course.'

'If,' said the young man gloomily, 'anyone could see to the future of such a one as she is!'

The Professor looked at him.

'You are out of sorts to-night,' he said. 'Your natural instinct is deadened in you. That girl does not belong to the class of which you are thinking. Whatever has driven her to her present desperate state of mind, it is not impurity.'

'You think that?' Wyndham looked doubtful, but was still conscious of a faint wave of relief; and the Professor, watching him, smiled, the tolerant smile of one who understands the cranks and follies of poor human nature.

'If so,' said Wyndham quickly, 'she should surely not be subjected to this experiment at all. She——'

'For all that, I shall not lose this chance,' said the Professor shortly. He turned and went back to the girl.

She was sitting in the same attitude as when he left her—her hands clenched upon her knees, her eyes staring into the fire. God alone knew what she saw there. She did not change her position, but sat like that, immovable as a statue, as the Professor expounded his experiment to her, and then asked her the cold, unsympathetic question as to whether, now she knew what the risk was, she would accept it. It might mean death, but if not, it would mean safety and protection in the future.

When he had finished, she turned her sombre eyes on his.

'I will take the risk,' she said.

Wyndham made a movement as if to speak, but the Professor checked him.

'Of course, if the experiment is successful,' he said, 'I shall provide for you for life.'

'I hope you will not have to provide for me,' she said.

At this, a little silence fell upon the room, that seemed to chill it. The Professor broke it.

'You agree, then?'

'I agree.' She rose, and held out her hand. 'Give me the draught.'

Wyndham started, his voice vibrating with horror.

'No, no!' he cried. 'She does not understand; and'—to the Professor—'neither do you. If this thing fails, it will mean murder. Think, I entreat you, before it is too late to think. That girl'—pointing to the young stranger, who was standing regarding him with a dull curiosity—'she is but a child. She cannot know her own mind. She ought not to be allowed to settle so stupendous a question. Look at her!' His voice shook. 'Many a happier girl at her age would still be in her schoolroom. She is so young that, whatever her wrongs, her sorrows may be, she has still time before her to conquer or live them down. Professor, I implore you, do not go on with this.'

The Professor rested a contemptuous glance on him for a moment, then swept it from him, and addressed the girl.

'You are willing?' he said.

'Yes.' She spoke quite firmly, but she was looking at Wyndham. It was a strange look, made up of surprise and some other feeling hardly defined.

'She is not all,' broke in Wyndham again, vehemently. 'There is you to be considered, too. If this sleep of your making terminates fatally, have you considered the consequences to yourself?'

The Professor smiled. He pointed to the girl, who stood marble-white beneath the dull gaslight.

'Like her, I take the risk,' he said. 'I think I told you a little while ago that I would chance the hanging.' His smile—a very unpleasant one—faded suddenly, and his manner grew brusque and arrogant. 'There—enough,' he said. 'Stand aside, man. Do you think that now—now when at last my hour has come—I am likely to let it slip, though death itself lay before me?'

'For God's sake, Professor, think yet a

moment!' said the younger man, holding him in his grasp. 'She is young—so young!... To take a life like that!'

'I am going to take no life'—coldly. 'I see now that you never had any faith in me at all.'

'I believe in you as no other man does,' rejoined Wyndham hotly. 'But surely at this supreme moment a doubt may be allowed me. If this thing were done openly in the eye of day, in sight of all men, it were well; but to try so deadly an experiment here, at midnight—with no witnesses, as it were— great heavens! you must see the pitfall you are laying for yourself. If this experiment fails——'

'It will not fail,' said the Professor coldly. 'In the meantime'—he cast a scornful glance at him—'if you are afraid of being called as a witness, it is'—pointing to the door—'still open to you to avoid such a disagreeability.'

Their eyes met.

'I don't think I have deserved that,' said the other proudly, and all at once in this queer hour both men felt that the tie that had bound them for years was stronger than they knew.

'Stay, then,' said the Professor.

He went into an inner room and returned with a phial and glass, and advanced towards the girl with an almost buoyant step. There was, indeed, an exhilaration in his whole air, that amounted almost to madness. He looked wild—spectral, indeed—in the dim light of the solitary lamp, with his white hair thrown back and his eyes shining fiercely beneath the rugged brows.

'Are you ready?' he asked.

She made a slight gesture of assent, and went a step or two to meet him. She was deadly pale, but she stood without support of any kind. The Professor poured some of the pale fluid from the phial into the glass with a hand that never faltered, and the girl took it with a hand that faltered quite as little; but before she could raise it to her lips, Wyndham caught her arm.

'Stop!' cried he, as if choking. 'Have you

thought—have you considered that there is no certainty in this drug?' Her eyes rested for a moment on his.

'I thought there was a certainty,' she said slowly.

'A certainty of death, perhaps,' said he, poignant fear in his tone. 'At this last moment I appeal to you, for your own sake. Don't take it. If you do, it is doubtful whether you will ever come back to life again.'

She looked at him steadily.

'I hope there is no doubt,' she said. She raised the glass and drank its contents to the dregs.

As she did so, some clock in the silent city outside struck the midnight hour.

CHAPTER III.

'A land of darkness, as darkness itself, and of the shadow of death; without any order, and where the light is as darkness.'

Morning had broken through the sullen gloom of night, and still the two men watched beside the couch on which the girl lay, seemingly, in all the tranquillity of death. The Professor's drug had been calculated to keep her asleep for exactly six hours. So long a time would be a test. If she lived, and woke at the right time, then he would try again. He would make it worth her while. For the younger man, during this anxious vigil, there had been passing lapses of memory, that he, however, would have disdained to acknowledge as sleep; but with the old man there had been no question of oblivion, and now, as the vital moment drew near that should test the truth of the great discovery, even Wyndham grew abnormally wide-awake, and with nervous heart-sinkings watched the pale, death-like face of the girl.

Could it be unreal? Wyndham rose once and bent over her. No faintest breath came from her lips or nostrils; the whole face had taken the pinched, ashen appearance of one who had lain for a full day dead. The hands were waxen, and the forehead too. He shuddered and drew back. At that moment he told himself that she was dead, and that he had undoubtedly assisted at a form of murder.

He turned to the Professor, who was sitting watch in hand, counting the moments. He would have spoken, but the old man's grim face forbade him. He was waiting. At twelve o'clock the girl had sunk into a slumber so profound, so representative of death, that Wyndham had uttered an exclamation of despair, and had told himself she was indeed struck down by the Destroyer, and now when six o'clock strikes she ought to rise from her strange slumbers if the Professor's drug possessed the powerful properties attributed to it by its discoverer.

As Wyndham stood watching the Professor, a sound smote upon his ear. One! Again the city clock was tolling the hour. The Professor rose; his face was ghastly. One, two, three, four, five, six!

Six! The Professor bent down over the girl, and Wyndham went near to him, to be ready to help him when the moment came—when the truth was made clear to him that his discovery had failed. Wyndham himself had long ago given up hope, but he feared for the old man, to whom his discovery had been more than life or love for over twenty years.

The Professor still stood peering into the calm face. Six, and no sign, no change!

Already the sun's rays were beginning to peep sharply through the window; there was a slight stir in the street below. Six-thirty, and still the Professor stood gazing on the quiet figure, as motionless as it. Seven o'clock, and still no movement. The face, now lovely in its calm, was as marble, and the limbs lay rigid, the fingers lightly locked. Death, death alone could look like that!

Half-past seven! As the remorseless clock recorded the time, the Professor suddenly threw up his arms.

'She is dead!' he said. 'Oh, my God!'

He reeled forward, and the young man caught him in his arms. He was almost insensible, and was gasping for breath. Wyndham carried him into an adjoining room and laid him on a bed, and, finding him cold, covered him with blankets. This, so far as it went, was well enough for the moment, but what was the next step to be? The old man lay gasping, and evidently there was but a short step between his state and that of his victim outside. Yet how to send for a doctor with that victim outside? To the Professor, whose hours were numbered, it would mean little or nothing; but to him,

Wyndham, it would mean, if not death, eternal disgrace. He drew a long breath and bent over the Professor, who was now again sensible.

'Shall I send for Marks or Drewd?' he asked, naming two of the leading physicians in Dublin.

The Professor grasped his arm; his face grew frightful.

'No one—no one!' he gasped. 'Are you mad? Do you think I would betray my failure to the world? To have them laugh—deride——' He fell back, gasping still, but menacing the young man with his eye. By degrees the fury of his glance relaxed, and he fell into a sort of slumber, always holding Wyndham's arm, however, as if fearing he should go. He seemed stronger, and Wyndham knelt by the bed, wondering vaguely what was going to be the end of it all, and whether it would be possible to remove the corpse outside without detection. There was Denis—Denis was faithful, and could be trusted.

Presently the Professor roused from his fit of unconsciousness. He looked up at the young man, and his expression was terrible. Despair in its worse form disfigured his features. The dream of a life had been extinguished. He tried to speak, but at first words failed him, then, 'All the years —all the years!' he mumbled. Wyndham understood, and his heart bled. The old man had given the best years of his life to his discovery, and now——

'I have killed her!' went on the Professor, after a minute or two.

'Science has killed her,' said Wyndham.

'No; I, with my cursed pride of belief in myself—I have killed her,' persisted the old man. 'I would to God it were not so!' He did not believe in anything but science, yet he appealed to the Creator occasionally, as some moderns still do to Jove. His lean fingers beat feebly on the blankets. 'A failure—a failure,' he kept muttering, his eyes fixed on vacancy. 'I go to my grave a failure! I set my soul on it. I believed in it, and it was naught.' He was rambling, but presently he sprang into a sitting posture, his eyes afire once more. 'I believe in it still!' he shouted. 'Oh, for time, for life, to prove . . . O God, if there is a God, grant me a few more days!' He fell into a violent fit of shivering, and Wyndham gently laid him back in his bed, and covered him again with the blankets, where he lay sullen, powerless.

'Try not to think,' implored the young man.

'Think—think—what else is left to me? Oh, Paul!' He stretched out his arm and caught Wyndham. 'That it should be a failure after all. I wish——' He paused, and then went on: 'I wish I had not tried it upon her; she was young. She was a pretty creature, too. She was like . . . someone——' He broke off.

'She was a mere waif and stray,' said Wyndham, trying to harden his voice.

'She was no waif or stray of the sort you mean,' said the Professor. 'Her face—was not like that. There'—pointing to the room outside—'go; look on her for yourself, and read the truth of what I say.'

'It is not necessary,' said the young man, with a slight shudder. And again a silence fell between them. It was again broken by the Professor.

'She was full of life,' he said; 'and I took it.'

'She wished you to take it,' said Wyndham, who felt choking. Her blood seemed to lie heavily on him. Had he not seen, countenanced her murder? The Professor did not seem to hear him; his head had fallen forward, and he was muttering again.

'She is dead!' he whispered to himself. He made a vague but tragic gesture; and then, after a little while, 'Dead!' he said again. His head had sunk upon his breast. It was a strange scene. Here the Professor dying—out there the girl dead—and between them he, Paul Wyndham. What lay before him?

He roused himself with an effort from his

horrible thoughts, and made a faint effort to withdraw his hand from the Professor's; but though the latter had fallen into a doze, he still felt the attempt at withdrawal, and tightened his clutch on Wyndham; and all at once it seemed to the young man as though the years had rolled backward, and he was still the pupil, and this old man his tutor, and the days were once more present when he had been ordered here and there, and had taken his directions from him, and loved and reverenced him, stern and repellent as he was, as perhaps no tutor had ever been reverenced before.

After a little while the Professor's grasp relaxed, and Wyndham rose to his feet. A shrinking from entering the room beyond was combated by a wild desire to go there and look once again upon the slender form of the girl lying in death's sweet repose upon her couch. He went to the door, hesitated involuntarily for a second or two, and then entered.

How still is death! And how apart!

Nothing can approach it or move it. He looked at her long and earnestly, and all at once it came to him that she was beautiful. He had not thought her beautiful last night, but now the dignity of death had touched her, and her fear and her indifference and her despair had dropped from her, and the face shone lovely—the features chiselled, and a vague smile upon the small, closed lips. He noticed one thing, and it struck him as strange—that pinched look about the features that he had noticed an hour ago was gone now. The mouth was soft, the rounded chin curved as if in life. Almost there seemed a little bloom upon the pale, cold cheeks.

With a heavy sigh he turned away, and, leaning his arm upon the mantelshelf, gave himself up a prey to miserable thought. The fire had died out long ago, and the morning was cold and raw, and from under the ill-fitting door a little harsh wind was rushing. The Professor, though actually a rich man, had never cared to change the undesirable house that had sheltered him when first he tried a fall with fortune, and, conquering it, came out at once to the front as a man not to be despised in the world of science.

What was to be done? The Professor would have to see a doctor, even if the medical man were brought in without his knowledge. Would it be possible to remove the—that girl —and trust to to-night for her removal to—— To where? Again he lost himself in a sea of agonized doubt and uncertainty.

Denis would still be here, of course; but what could Denis do? He fell back upon all the old methods of concealing dead bodies he had ever heard of, but everything seemed impossible. What fools all those others must have been! Well, he could give himself up and explain matters; but then the Professor —to have his great discovery derided and held up to ridicule! The old man's look, as he saw it a little while ago, seemed to forbid his betrayal of his defeat. Great heavens! what was to be done?

He drew himself up with a heavy sigh, and passed his hand across his eyes, then turned to go back to the inner room to see if the Professor was still sleeping. As he went he tried to avoid glancing at the couch where the dead form lay, but when he got close, some force stronger than his will compelled him to look at it. And as he looked he felt turned into stone. He seemed frozen to the spot on which he stood; his eyes refused to remove themselves from what they saw. Staring like one benumbed, he told himself at last that he was going mad. How otherwise could he see this thing? Sweat broke out on his forehead, and a cry escaped him. The corpse was looking at him!

CHAPTER IV.

'Look, then, into thine heart and write!'

VERY intently, too, and as if surprised or trying to remember. Her large eyes seemed singularly brilliant, and for a while the only thing living about her. But all at once, as though memory had returned, she sprang to her feet and stood, strong, and utterly without support, and questioned him with those eyes silently but eloquently. The queerest thing about it all to Wyndham was that, instead of being enfeebled by the strange draught she had drunk, she looked younger, more vigorous, and altogether another person from the forlorn, poor child of eight hours ago. Her eyes were now like stars, her lips red and warm ; the drug had, beyond doubt, a property that even the Professor had never dreamt of; it gave not only rest, but renewed health and life to those who drank it.

Seeing Wyndham did not or could not speak, she did.

'I am alive—alive!' she cried, with young and happy exultation. Where was the desire for death that lay so heavily on her only a few hours ago? It was all gone. Now it was plain that she desired life—life only. Her voice rang through the room fresh and clear, filling it with music of a hope renewed, and so penetrating that it even pierced into the room beyond. And as it reached it, another cry broke forth—a cry this time old and feeble.

Wyndham rushed to answer it, taking with him his last memory of the girl, as she then stood, with her arms thrown out as if in quick delight, and her whole strange, beautiful face one ray of gladness.

The Professor was sitting up in bed a mere wreck, but with expectation on every feature. He was trembling visibly.

'That voice!' he whispered wildly—'that voice! I know it. Long years ago I knew it. Boy, speak—tell me, whose voice was that?'

Wyndham knelt down beside him, and took his hand in his. He, too, was trembling excessively, and his eyes were full of tears.

'Sir,' he said softly, 'she is alive.'

'She—she—who?' asked the Professor. He bent forward; his features were working.

'That girl . . . last night . . . She lives, sir. Your experiment has not failed, after all.'

He feared to look at the Professor when he had said this, and bent his head, leaning his forehead on the wrinkled hand he held. It quivered slightly beneath him, but not much, and presently the old man spoke.

'She lives?' His voice was stronger now. Wyndham looked up, and found the Professor looking almost his normal self, and with that expression in his eyes that the young man knew as meaning a sharp calculation.

'Yes; I have spoken to her. Will you see her?'

'No.' The Professor silenced him by a gesture. He was evidently in the midst of a quick calculation now.

'The hour she woke?' he asked presently, with such a vigorous ring in his tone that Wyndham rose to his feet astonished.

'Two minutes ago.'

'Hah!' The Professor went back to his calculations. Presently a shout broke from him. 'I see it now!' he cried victoriously; 'I see where the mistake lay! Fool that I was not to have seen it before! It was a miscalculation, but one easy to be rectified. An hour or two will do it. Here, help me up, Paul.'

'But, Professor, it is impossible; you must rest; you——'

'Not another moment, not one, I tell you!' cried the Professor furiously. He lunged out of bed. 'This thing must be seen to at once. What time can any man be sure of, that he should waste it? The discovery must be assured. And what time have I?'

He fell forward; he had fainted. Wyndham laid him back, and rushed frantically into the next room.

The girl was standing just where he had left her. But her arms were outstretched no longer; they were better employed—they were doing up her hair.

There was a glass on a wall opposite to him, and by this she was trying to bring herself back to as perfect a state of respectability as circumstances permitted her.

'You must go,' said Wyndham, 'and at once. Do you hear—at once?'

And, indeed, it was imperative that she should be out of the house before the arrival of the doctor, for whom he was now about to go.

She rose. And suddenly gladness died from her face, her arms dropped to her sides; something of the old misery, but not all, settled down on her once more.

'I can go,' she said. 'I—I am not so afraid now, when it is day; but—he said——'

Poor child! she had remembered the bargain of the night before. She had not thought it worthy of thought then, believing Death indeed lay before her when she drank that draught; but when she woke, when memory returned to her (and it always came quickly after such a draught as that), she had gladly told herself that now all her troubles were at an end, that the old man would provide for her, protect her. And now this young man, so forbidding, so unkind, with his harsh voice and ways; and yet last night he had seemed so kind!

'He is dying!' said Wyndham shortly. 'A doctor must be summoned without delay. I shall arrange for your going—for your safety; but you must be quick.' He rang the bell for Denis, who was waiting for him below. The Professor's only servant was a charwoman, who left nightly at ten, and did not return till the same time next morning.

'You need provide for nothing,' said the girl. She caught up the little shawl that had been wrapped round her last night, and moved towards the door.

'Stay a moment; you can't go like this,'

said the young man distractedly. 'I have a servant who will take you to some place of safety. It is impossible that you should go like this. Why'—awkwardly—'you haven't even got a bonnet.'

She stopped and looked at him.

'It is not you who are responsible,' she said. 'And'—she drew her breath quickly—'after all, no one is. I took that drug of my own accord, of my own will, but he did promise to—to—— But if he is dying?' She looked at him anxiously, making the last speech a question.

'I am afraid so.'

'Then that is at an end.' She went towards the door.

'Wait for my servant,' entreated he, following her and laying a hand upon her arm. 'I cannot allow you to go like this.'

'I don't see what it is to you,' said she.

'It is much—a great deal. For one thing, the Professor, if he recovers, would never forgive me for letting you go out of his life without reparation—without the fulfilment of his promise to you. He is indebted to you, remember. It'—eagerly—'was a bargain. And, after all, if you throw off his responsibility now, where will you go? You say you have no home—no——'

'Nothing! nothing!' she said. He could see her face pale again, and again that dreadful look of despair, of hopelessness, that had crowned her last night, aged and made miserable her face.

He turned gladly from the sad contemplation of it to address Denis, who had entered the room, his small twinkling eyes as bright as ever; but, then, he had slept tranquilly the whole night through by a kitchen fire that would have been hard to rival in heat and brilliancy. Amongst all Denis's many virtues, one stood out: he could always be depended on to look after himself. And really that is a great thing in a faithful servant; so many of them like to pose as martyrs in the cause.

Wyndham led his servant a little aside.

'You see this——' He hesitated for a

word, and then said, 'young lady; you will take her away at once. There is not a moment to be lost. Get her out of the house directly. I am going for a doctor. The Professor is seriously ill. Do you understand? You are to lose no time. You must take her away at once.'

Denis stared at him in the appallingly non-understanding way that belongs, I believe, to Irish servants alone. It doesn't mean that they don't understand; it only means that they are taking it all in, with a cleverness that few other servants can show at a moment's notice.

'An' where, yer honour?'

'Anywhere out of this!'

This struck him as abominably unfeeling, and he added hastily: 'To the safest place you know—the very safest. I depend upon you, Denis. Treat her as you would your own daughter.'

CHAPTER V.

> 'For the shades are about us that hover
> When darkness is half withdrawn,
> And the skirts of the dead Night cover
> The face of the live new Dawn.'

THE doctors when they came could do nothing for him. The Professor, though hardly an old man as the ordinary acceptation of the word goes, being still within the seventies, had so burnt out his candle at both ends that all the science in Europe could not have kept him alive for another twenty-four hours. A spice of gruesome mirth seemed to fall into the situation when their declaration was laid bare and one thought of the great discovery.

Wyndham was the one who thought of it, and a wild longing to rouse the old man, who was now sunk into an oblivion that presaged death, and compel him even in his death-throes to reveal the secret that might bring even him back to life, seized upon him. But he felt it was impossible, and presently the two great men went downstairs to consult each other, and he was left alone with his dying friend.

They had hardly gone when, watching as he incessantly did the face of the Professor, he noticed a change. He bent over him.

'Why doesn't she speak now,' said the Professor. He was thinking of the girl's voice—a voice that had taken him back to his early days in some strange way.

'Master,' said Wyndham—he, too, had gone back to the old days—'you are thinking——'

'Of her. They said she was dead.'

'Who was dead?' asked Wyndham.

At this the old man roused. He had not known Wyndham's voice the first time, but now he did, and he turned and looked at him; and presently consciousness once more grew within his eyes.

'It is you, boy. And where is she?'

'She? The girl, you mean?'

'Yes. ... I promised her. You remember ... It is late now, very late ... and I must sleep. But ... a word, boy ... I have left you all, and she ... out of it ... you must give her ... give her ...' He sank back.

'All—all,' said Wyndham eagerly.

'No ... no'—he rallied wonderfully—'three hundred a year—that for a girl. ... The rest is yours. ... But see to her. ... I can trust you. You are a good boy. But your Greek, boy—your Greek is bad—your aorists are weak. You must mend—you must mend. ...'

His dying eyes tried to take the old stern look as they rested on Wyndham, the look he used to give the boy when his Greek or his Latin verses were hardly up to the mark, but presently it changed and softened into a wider light. 'The boy,' in the last of all moments, was forgotten for the love that was strongest of all.

'She was very like my wife,' he gasped faintly, and fell back and died.

* * * * *

It was all over. The doctors had taken their departure, and the old dismal house was very still. The Professor had died in the morning, and it was quite night again before Wyndham had time to think of ordinary matters. It was the presence of Denis, who had come up to see, probably, how his master had continued to live so long without him, that brought back the thought of the girl to Wyndham's mind.

'Where did you take her?' he asked listlessly. Even as the words passed his lips he knew it was most important that she should be found again. She was now the inheritress of three hundred a year—no mean thing for a girl who only last night was ready and willing to die of want, amongst other things, no doubt.

'To the Cottage, sir.'

'To——' Wyndham gazed at him as if too astonished to give way to the words that evidently lay very near to his tongue.

'The Cottage, sir. Yer own place, sir.'

'The Cottage,' repeated Wyndham, now breaking forth in earnest. 'What the devil did you take her there for?'

His extreme anger would have cowed perhaps any other servant in Europe save Denis. That good man stood to his guns without a flinch.

'Fegs, sir, 'tis you can answer that,' said he, with quite an encouraging air.

'What d'ye mean, Denis?' demanded Wyndham almost violently.

'I'm manin'—what I'm manin',' said Denis, who certainly was not violent at all. 'Ye know yourself, sir, that the first thing ye said to me about the crathur was to take her to the safest place ye knew.'

'Well?' said Wyndham, with anger he tried hard to stifle.

'Faix, yer honour, it seemed to me that

the safest place I knew for the young lady was the house that belonged to yer honour.'

This no doubt was distinctly flattering, but at the moment the flattery did not appeal to Wyndham. The girl down there—and what the deuce was he to do with her? And what would all the people round be thinking?—for the most part country folk. The Cottage lay twenty miles outside Dublin. The Rector, Mr. Barry, would for one be positively enraged. He would require all sorts of explanations.

Denis had waited for a reply, but finding none, now went on :

' Anything wrong, sir ?'

' Anything !' said Wyndham. ' Were you mad that you should take a—a person like that down to my house ? A girl found lying on the Professor's doorstep ! Good heavens, man ! what could you mean by it ?'

He exaggerated a little when he said ' my house.' As a fact, he lived very little in the Cottage, only using it when he felt tired and overdone by work. His real home was to be found in rooms in Dublin—pleasant rooms in Upper Merrion Street. There he entertained his bachelor friends, and was highly regarded by his landlady. He was one of those men—more usual than the coming young lady believes—who thought a great deal more of their work, and their reading, and their golf, than of the opposite sex.

'Well, sir, there's this,' said Denis, who had remained beautifully calm. 'Besides tellin' me I was to take her to a safe place, ye specially said as she was to be thrated as me own daughter. I remimber the words well. Now, ye know well, sir, havin' bin intimate with me an' Bridget since ye wur in yer first throusers, that we haven't a child between us; an' yet for all that I tuck it for manin' that the young lady was to be given to Bridget.'

'You took a great deal upon yourself then,' said Wyndham.

'Maybe so,' said Denis, pursing up his lips. 'But ye said as how she was to be thrated like that; an' if a girl was my daughter—why, I'd take her to Bridget.'

It was impossible to go into this involved affair. Wyndham dismissed him with a gesture; but Denis dallied at the door.

'I suppose there's something wrong, sir?' persisted he.

'Nothing,' said Wyndham, putting a match to his cigar, 'except that you are the most infernal ass I ever met.'

With a heavy heart Wyndham, assisted by a physician of great note, had gone through the Professor's papers. There were few of them, and with regard to the experiment only a few useless notes here and there, principally written on the backs of envelopes. There was nothing connected—nothing that could be used. The Professor, it seemed, had been in the habit of writing on his brain, and on that only. Alas! there was nothing left wherewith to carry on the great discovery.

Wyndham abandoned his search with a sigh. There was no doubt now that the wonderful experiment was lost to all time. With this sad ending of it he told himself he had closed one chapter in his life, but he made a mistake there; the chapter was only beginning.

CHAPTER VI.

> 'In her is highe beauty without pride,
> And youth withoute greenhood or folly.
> To all her workes virtue is her guide.
> Humbless hath slain in her all tyranny:
> She is the mirror of all courtesy,
> Her heart a very chamber of holiness,
> Her hand minister of freedom for almess.'
> —CHAUCER.

'No!' says Susan. The word is not a denial; it is merely an ejaculative expression of the most extreme astonishment, largely mingled with disbelief.

The sun is glinting through the trees in the old orchard right down on her head, striking a light from the glancing knitting-needles she has now let fall into her lap. This old orchard is the happy hunting-ground of the Barry children old and young—the place which they rush to in their joyous moments, the place which they crawl to with their griefs and woes. To-day neither joys nor griefs are near them, and it is out of sheer love alone for its mossy old apple-trees and its sunlit corners that Susan had tripped in here a while ago with a dilapidated old novel tucked into her apron pocket, and the eternal sock with the heel half turned between her pretty fingers. After her had straggled Betty, a slender creature of sixteen, and Tom, the baby. Tom was five, but he was always the baby, there having been no more babies after him, principally because his mother died when he was born. And last of all came Bonnie, the little cripple, hopping sadly on his crutches, until Susan saw him, and ran back to him and caught him in her arms, and placed him beside her on the warm soft grass, putting out her much-washed cotton skirt that he might sit upon it, and so be protected from even an imaginary damp, and had cuddled him up to her, to the many droppings of the stitches of the long-suffering heel.

Carew, who came between Betty and Susan, was away, fishing somewhere in the Crosby river, and Jacky had not put in an appearance since breakfast. How on earth his lessons are going to be prepared between this —two o'clock—and five, makes Susan wonder anxiously. Why doesn't he come home? What can he be doing?

She has hardly got further than this in her thoughts of the truant, when suddenly he appears upon the scene, a very rosy, bright-eyed rascal, big with news. Indeed, it was the coming of Jacky, and the astounding revelation in his opening sentence—that he had sprung upon them in a most unprincipled way, without a word of warning—that had drawn from Susan that heavily emphasized 'No!'

She speaks again now.

'I don't believe it,' she says.

'Oh, Susan, why not?' asks Betty, who is sitting with her hands folded behind her head, perhaps because if she brought them forward she might find some knitting to do, too. Idle hands they are, only made for mischief; so is the face to which they belong.

'Because it's nonsense,' says Susan, shrugging her shoulders, and drawing Bonnie closer to her. 'And, besides, I don't want to believe it.'

'Oh, I do!' says Betty, with a little grin from under her big sun-hat. 'Go on, Jacky.'

'I saw her, I saw her plain,' says Jacky, his rosy round face fired with joy at the thought of being for once the bearer of important news. 'She was walking about in the garden.'

'In,' from Susan, in a severe tone, 'Mr. Wyndham's garden?'

'Yes, in there.' Jacky now looks as though he is going to burst. 'Why don't you believe me? I saw her, I tell you. I saw her quite plain. An' her hair is dark, a lot darker than yours, an she's got a blue frock like your Sunday one, only better.'

Susan interrupts him with dignity.

'I don't see how Mrs. Denis's——' Denis's wife was always called Mrs. Denis; if she had any other name, it was sunk beneath insuperable barriers. Mr. and Mrs. Denis she and her husband had been since the priest poured his blessing down upon them and made them one in the old chapel built on the rock at the end of the village. This rock gave the parish priest a distinct crow over the Protestant clergyman.

'Ye would quote me the Scriptures, would ye?' Father McFane would call to Mr. Barry as the latter drove by the chapel in his Norwegian on his way to the church beyond. 'An' what did St. Paul say? "Like a house founded upon a rock." Why, here's the rock, man. Come in! come in! where are ye going?'

It occurred every Sunday, and Mr. Barry would smile back at Father McFane, and nod his head, for the two, indeed, were great friends, as the Protestants and Roman Catholics often are in small places, until someone comes in to them with wild news and absurd tidings from incendiaries outside to upset the loving work of years.

'I don't see how Mrs. Denis's niece or cousin, or whatever she is, should have a better gown than mine,' says she.

'But she isn't Mrs. Denis's cousin, she's too young,' says Jacky. 'She's a girl, and she was pulling the flowers like anything, and if she belonged to Mrs. Denis she wouldn't be let do that.'

Jacky's English is always horrible.

'Oh, you've dreamt the whole thing!' says Susan contemptuously. 'Run away and play.' She has forgotten about the lessons.

'Oh, you are a marplot! I am going to believe in Jacky for once in my life. Don't go, Jacky! Jacky, come back! If you don't, Aunt Jemima will make you do your lessons.'

This has a magical effect. Jacky swerves round.

'She is there,' says he indignantly. 'I did see her.' He seems to dwell on this fact with gusto. 'An' she's not Mrs. Denis's niece. An' old Meany down by the mill says she's been there for four weeks.'

'The plot is thickening,' says Betty lazily. ''Tis a clever villain, whoever she is; fancy her being here for four weeks without the very size of her shoes being known throughout the length and breadth of Curraghcloyne! Four days ought to have done it. Go on, Jacky! Had she a cloven foot by any chance?'

'No; but'—and Jacky's eyes widen, and he seems to swell—'Meany says she's a prisoner.'

'A what?'

'Yes, a real prisoner. She's not let go out of the place. Mrs. Denis never opens the front-gate now, but comes out by the little green one we can see from the hall-door, an' even that's locked when she comes out an' goes back again, Meany says.'

'Mrs. Denis very seldom comes out by any other,' says Susan.

'But she doesn't always lock it behind

her,' puts in Betty, who is evidently beginning to enjoy herself.

'Now she locks the front-gate too,' says Jacky triumphantly.

'It's perfectly thrilling,' declares Betty, sitting up and growing openly interested. Betty is frivolous. 'A prisoner, and a young girl. Can she be the long-lost princess of our infancy? And imprisoned by Mr. Wyndham! Oh, the terrible man!'

'She is of course a friend of Mrs. Denis's,' says Susan, with the grand air of one who will have the truth at any price, and who is bent on dismissing all theories save the practical one. 'It's the most natural thing in the world. We all know Mr. Wyndham told her he wouldn't come down for a month or two, and so she is entertaining a niece or a cousin, or something.'

'She isn't a niece of Mrs. Denis's, any way,' persists Jacky obstinately; 'she'—with a hopeful, yet doubtful glance at Betty, whose latest idea has struck him—'she is much more like a—a princess.' Again he looks at Betty, as if expecting her to bring him through this difficulty of her own making; but Betty fails him, as she fails most people.

'After all, I dismiss the romantic element,' says she, nursing her knees and swaying herself indolently to and fro in the warm sunshine. 'I incline now towards the supernatural. Susan,' addressing her elder sister with due solemnity, 'perhaps she is a ghost.' Her face thus uplifted is sufficiently like Susan's to let all the world know they are of kin; but Betty's face, piquante, provocative, as it is, lacks the charm of Susan's. Betty is pretty, nay, perhaps something more, for the Barrys are a handsome race; but Susan —Susan is lovely. It is useless saying her nose is not pure Greek, that her mouth wants this or that, that her forehead is a trifle too low. Susan, when all is said, when long argument has been used, remains what she was before — lovely. The smiling, earnest lips, the liquid eyes, the rippling, sunny hair— all these might be another girl's, but yet that other girl would not be Susan. Oh, beauteous

Susan! with your youthful, starry eyes and tender, mirthful, timid air, I would that a brush, and not a pen, might paint you!

'A ghost! Nonsense,' says she, now contemptuously. 'But'—thoughtfully—'what a queer story!' And again, with a wrathful glance at Jacky: 'After all, I don't believe a word of it.'

'Oh, I do! I want to,' says Betty, who revels in sensations. 'And the ghost development is beautiful. I'd rather see a ghost than anything. As you looked, Jacky, did she vanish into thin air?'

'No; only round the corner,' says Jacky reluctantly. He would evidently have liked the vanishing trick.

'Very disappointing! But perhaps that's her way of doing it. Corners are always so convenient.'

'If the gates are all locked,' says Susan, turning suddenly a magisterial eye upon her brother, 'may I ask how you saw her?'

'Ah, that's part of it! That,' says Betty,

'is where the fire and brimstone come in. That's what makes her a ghost. It isn't everybody can see through stone walls,' says she, lowering her voice mysteriously, and glancing at the staring Jacky. 'She had evidently the power to turn Mrs. Denis's walls into glass! It's very unlucky, Jacky, for ghosts to fall in love with people, and I'm sorry to say I think this one has developed a mad fancy for you.'

'She hasn't!' says Jacky, who is now extremely pale.

'Circumstances point to it,' says Betty, who is nothing if not a tease. 'And when ghosts fall in love, they do dreadful things to people. Things like this!' She has risen, and is now advancing on the stricken Jacky with her slender arms uplifted, and long fingers pointed downwards and arranged like claws. She has taken to a sort of prance, a high-stepping walk that brings her knees upwards and her toes outward, and she has worked her face out of all recognition in an abominable grin. All this taken together proves too much for Jacky, who, his face now visibly paler, descends precipitately upon Susan.

Susan has been seeing to the comfort of her little Bonnie, and has therefore been ignorant of Betty's flight of fancy until the moment when Jacky stumbles somewhat heavily against her, and looking up, she sees Betty's diabolical pose.

'Betty, don't!' says she, glancing back to Jacky's face, which is, indeed, a mixture of pluck and abject terror.

'Would you not warn him, then?' says Betty reproachfully, returning, however, to her ordinary appearance, and making an aside at Bonnie, a pretence at shooting him with her first finger and thumb, that sends the delicate little creature into fits of laughter. 'Poor old Jacky!' returning to the charge. 'It isn't for nothing that ghosts reveal themselves. It is easy to see that this one has her eye on you!'

'She hasn't,' says Jacky again, who is on the point of tears. He is evidently not partial to ghosts. 'And it wasn't through a glass wall I saw her—it was——' He stops dead short.

'Yes?' says Susan, still severely. 'Do be quiet, Betty, and let him speak. It was——'

'Through the hole in the wall near the garden,' confesses Jacky doggedly, but somewhat shamefacedly.

'You see, it was through the wall, after all!' says Betty, breaking into a delighted laugh. 'She'll get you, Jacky—she'll get you yet.'

'I don't think it is a very nice thing to peep through other people's walls into their grounds,' says Susan, more from the point of view that she is the eldest sister, and bound to say a word in season now and then, than from any feeling of horror at the act. All boys peep through holes in walls, when lucky enough to find them. 'How would you like it,' says she, 'if you were found doing it?'

'But I wasn't found,' retorts Jacky sulkily.

'Susan,' Betty breaks into the argument with a vivacity all her own, 'you have no more morality than a cat. You are teaching him all wrong. It isn't the not being found out, Jacky, that is of importance, as Susan is most erroneously bent on impressing upon you; it is the fact of peeping in itself that makes you the'—shaking her finger at him— 'miserable sinner that you are!'

'Sinner yourself!' says Jacky, now driven to desperation and the most unreserved impertinence. 'I often saw you look through the hole in the wall yourself.'

At this, instead of being annoyed, both Susan and Betty give way to inextinguishable mirth; whereupon Jacky, who had, perhaps, hoped that his shot would take effect, prepares once more to march away. But Betty, making a sudden grab at him, catches him by his trousers.

'Wait awhile,' cries she, still shaking with laughter. 'Susan, seize his arm. Tell us the rest of it. Was she——'

'I won't tell you anything; and I'm sorry I told you a word at all. Let me go, Betty. D'ye hear? You are tearing my breeches.'

'And you are tearing our hearts,' says

Betty, 'Jacky darling. Go on; don't be a cross cat, now. Was she——'

'Twice as pretty as you, any way,' says Jacky, with virulence.

'Is that all? Poor girl!' says Betty, who is very hard to beat. 'Prettier than Susan?'

'Yes, lots.'

'She must be a real princess, then, and no ghost. I'd like to leave a card upon her. Perhaps you would kindly push it through the hole in the wall, Jacky.'

This is adding to the insult, and Jacky, with the loss of a button or two, and serious injury to his suspenders, breaks away.

'There now!' says he, beginning to cry. 'Look what you've done; and no one to mend it; and Aunt Maria will be angry, and father will give me twenty lines——' Sobs check his utterance.

Susan rises hurriedly, and, with a whispered word to Bonnie, she passes him on to Betty, who, in spite of her carelessness, receives the little fragile creature with loving arms, hugging him to her, and beginning to ransack her memory for a story to tell him, such as his soul loveth; then Susan, slipping her arm round Jacky's shoulder, whispers soft comforts to him. He shall come in now and do his lessons with her, so that father shall not be vexed this evening, and after dinner (the Rector's family dined at two, and had high tea at seven) she would take him with her up to Crosby Park.

Jacky's recovery is swift; his sobs cease, and he graciously allows himself to be kissed. To go to Crosby Park is always a joy—the big, huge, handsome place, with its long gardens and glass houses, and, best of all, its absentee landlord.

It is, indeed, quite ten years since George Crosby has been at the Park, and in all probability ten more years are likely to elapse before he comes again. The last accounts of him were from Africa, where he had had a most unpleasantly near interview with a lion, but had got off with a whole skin and another not quite so whole: the lion had come to grief.

CHAPTER VII.

'Where there is mystery, it is generally supposed that there must also be evil.'

IT is three o'clock as Susan, with Jacky in tow, leaves the Rectory gate and goes up the village towards the broad road beyond that mounts steepwards to Crosby Park. Curraghcloyne possesses but one street, and a very small one, too; but as a set-off to that it teems with interest.

This morning a pig-fair was held in the 'fair-field,' a square mass of beaten earth, anything but 'fair,' and as unlike a field as possible; and now that the 'payers of the rint' have been mercifully removed, bought, or sold, the unsightly patch is covered by young colts, that are being ridden up and down by their owners, with a view to showing them off; whilst in the far part of the field, over there, cows, sheep, and donkeys are changing owners.

Here, in the main street, much lively conversation is going on. On the right, Salter, the hardware man—a virulent Methodist, who calls himself a Protestant—is retailing to a hushed and delighted group the very latest ritualistic news of the curate just lately imported, and who, if a most estimable man, is undoubtedly abominably ugly. Short and stout and ill-made, poor Mr. Haldane has not proved a success amongst the Protestants of the parish. His views are extreme, and so are his looks, and, as Betty most unkindly put it, he should, on his ordination, have been at once despatched by the Bishop of the diocese as a missionary to the Cannibal Islands, with a view to getting rid of him as quickly as possible. He is a sore trial to Mr. Barry, the Rector of the parish, and Susan's father. But he had to replace the last curate in a hurry, that young man having resigned his charge at a moment's notice, because the Rector would not give his sanction to having matins at six a.m., he said; but in reality because Susan had, the evening before, rejected him with a haste that deprived him of all hope.

Just now the excitement amongst the groups at Salter's is growing intense. The curate had been knocked down. No! But he had fallen—and so on, and so on. A few shops lower down comes Mr. Murphy, the undertaker's. He, too, as indeed do all the shopkeepers in Curraghcloyne, stands in the front of his shop-door, chatting to all who come and go. A little, fat, jolly man, rather useless you would think in a solemn business like his, and yet the best undertaker, for all that, in the seven parishes round. Perhaps it is well to have a cheerful person of that sort to dispel the dreadful gloom of death. However it is, he is a universal favourite, and no wonder, when I tell you he is the man in all Curraghcloyne who can tell you most about the babies!—the ones come, the ones to come immediately, and those in the middle distance! The gayest, happiest little man in the town, with a wife as rosy as himself, and quite a crowd of embryo little undertakers swarming round his knees. But these, and many more of the Curraghcloyne celebrities, sink into insignificance before Ricketty, the proprietor of the Crosby Arms Hotel. This name is painted on a swinging signboard, with a huge boar beneath, the crest of the Crosbys from all time.

Ricketty—his name was once Richards, but time and many devoted friendships has brought it down to Ricketty—is a huge benign Irishman, with the biggest jaw in Europe and the smallest eyes. To his bones flesh has grown, until now he might have exhibited himself in the most fastidious show in New York as the 'Last of the race of Anak,' or some such attractive title.

And as most big men are, so is he—the mildest-mannered man on earth; who would have run away if he had been asked to scuttle a ship, and who would have fainted if the idea of cutting the throat even of a mouse had been suggested to him. One side of his hotel has the usual bar blind up in it, behind which is a parlour, where on special occasions the politicians congregate to air their eloquence. The other side is given up to a fancy shop, kept by his sister, Miss Ricketty.

Miss Ricketty is the wit, and therefore the scourge, of the village (very little wit suffices for a village such as Curraghcloyne), and though nearly stone-deaf, knows more of the 'goings on' of her neighbours than anyone else in the small town.

Of course there is a bank and a post-office in Curraghcloyne. And a town-hall, where the future tenors and sopranos of the world sometimes 'kindly consent' to sing to the poor people round them. And there is the draper's shop called 'The Emporium,' very justly, of course; and there is a market-place too, where everyone says the beef and mutton are both bad and dear. But even the interest of all these fails before the caustic tongue of Miss Ricketty.

Just as Susan reaches the window of the hotel that holds Miss Ricketty's show of note-paper, ballads, bull's-eyes, woollen mufflers, the latest thing in veils ten years old, and the flotsam and jetsam of various seasons past, she finds herself face to face with Wyndham.

'You have come back!' says she involuntarily. She is glad to see him. He is—well, scarcely an old friend, because the distances between his comings and goings to the Cottage make such broad margins on the leaf of time that he has hardly come into quite close contact with the family at the Rectory. But they have known him for a long time, and they have liked him, and there is a good deal of soft, pleasurable welcome in the glance that Susan gives him. He has been away now, she tells herself, quite two months.

'Yes,' says Wyndham, smiling. His smile is a little preoccupied, however. 'And how are you, Jacky? My goodness, how we are grown! You'll be as big as Ricketty presently if you don't put a weight on your head.'

Jacky sniggles, but, like Wyndham's smile, his sniggles are a little preoccupied. Having shaken hands with the latter, he retires behind Susan, and wonders if Wyndham is going up to the Cottage, and if he is, will the ghost catch him? He rather hopes it. It would leave him—Jacky—free, any way, and Mr. Wyndham is a big man and would be a better match for her.

Susan, too, is thinking of the ghost. As Wyndham is facing now, the Cottage lies before him. Is he going to see the mysterious 'prisoner'? Perhaps he is married to her! This seems delightful—like an old romance, so much nicer than the commonplace marriages of to-day. She scans Wyndham's face swiftly with a view to saying something nice and kind to him, if she sees anything there to help her to believe in this sentimental marriage. But evidently she sees nothing, because she says nothing. After all, she tells herself, it is of course a secret.

'I hope you will come in and see father,' she says presently, when she and Wyndham have discussed the town and its inhabitants, and she has told him all the news. He is in the habit of sleeping at the Cottage whenever he does come down, and in the habit, too, of spending his evenings at the Rectory, which is only just over the way from the Cottage.

'Not to-night, I'm afraid,' says Wyndham. 'I must go back to town by the evening train.'

A slight frown gathers on his brow, but he dismisses it as he bids her good-bye.

'Remember me to him,' he says quickly, absently. He pinches Jacky's ear, and is gone.

Susan, who has been inveigled into a promise concerning bull's-eyes, is now led triumphantly into Miss Ricketty's shop, where that spinster is discovered in an Old English attitude, her body being screwed out of all shape in her endeavour to catch sight of someone going down the street. Her window is quite blocked up by her shoulders, and her deafness prevents her from knowing of Susan's coming until Jacky, falling over her left leg, which is sticking out behind in mid air, brings her back to the perpendicular and a view of Susan.

She is a small woman, thin to a fault, and shrewd-visaged, with a quizzical eye and a bonnet. The latter is of the historic coal-scuttle shape, and must have been a most admirable purchase when bought—'warranted to wear,' in the truest sense of the word, as it has lasted without a break for at least fifty years. As no one in Curraghcloyne ever saw her 'outside of it,' and as she is popularly supposed to sleep in it, it may safely be regarded as a sound article; even her worst enemy had once been heard to say that, 'no matther how great an ould fool she was wid her tongue,' she had made no mistake about ' the bonnet.'

' An' is that you, Miss Susan, me dear?' says she, when Jacky has picked himself up, and she has ceased to rub her ankle. ' Ye're as welcome as the flowers in May, though divil a flower we had this year, wid the rain an' all. Ye're not in a hurry, miss, are ye, now? Ye can spare a minute to the ould maid? Come in, then.'

She opens the little gate that hinges on to her little counter, and draws Susan inside, to her 'parlour,' as she calls the tiny space within—a cosy spot in truth, where in the winter a fire burns briskly, and with a wall lined with bottles that make glad the souls of children. To Susan Barry the old maid has given all the heart that remains from her worship of her giant brother. Perhaps it is the almost childish sweetness of her manner that has won the old maid's heart, or else the young unconscious beauty of her—beauty being dear to the Irish heart. However it is, she has a warm corner in Miss Ricketty's.

'An' how's your good aunt?' says the spinster, adjusting the bonnet with one hand, whilst with the other she pulls out from under the counter a huge ear-trumpet, half a yard long, and big enough at the speaking end to engulf Susan's small and shapely head. 'She's been expectin' that clutch o' eggs I promised her, no doubt; but them hens o' mine might as well be cocks for all the eggs we get out of them.'

'Aunt Jemima knows that eggs are scarce now,' cries Susan, softly, into the gulf.

'Scarce! 'Tis nothin' them ungrateful hens is doin' for us now, an' we who coddled 'em up all the winther. The saints forgive thim! Miss Susan'—leaning towards the girl, and speaking with the suppressed emotion of the born gossip—'was that Misther Wyndham as wint up the street just now?'

'Yes,' says Susan. 'I was talking to him just before I came in here.'

'No! Blessed Vargin!' says Miss Ricketty, recoiling; she had, of course, been the first to hear of the mysterious stranger at the Cottage, and had, indeed, told the news to her brother, under promise of secrecy, that she knew he would not keep. Nor did she want him to keep it. How can you gossip unless you have someone to gossip with? That is why people spread scandals.

'And what was he saying?' asks she presently, when she has produced a little box of figs and given them to Jacky, with a view to keeping him quiet until she has got the last word of news out of Susan.

'Nothing, I think,' says Susan, running over mentally her late conversation with Wyndham. 'He won't have time to see father to-night, because he is going back to town by the evening train.'

'Is that what he says?' Miss Ricketty gives her bonnet a push. 'Faith, he's full of smartness. An' did he tell ye nothin' at all?'

'Oh, it was I who told him everything,' says Susan. 'He wanted to know how the new curate was going on, for one thing, and——'

'If 'twas Misther Haldane he was askin' afther so kindly, I could a' tould him somethin',' says Miss Ricketty. 'But never mind him! What else was Misther Wyndham sayin'?'

'There was not time to say anything,' says Susan, laughing. 'He was in a hurry, and so was I—at least, Jacky was; he wants you to give him two pennyworth of bull's-eyes. Though, really, after those figs——'

'Miss Susan'—the old maid puts Susan's last remark aside with an eloquent gesture—'have ye heard anything sthrange about the Cottage lately?'

Susan starts, and Jacky comes to a dead set, the last fig between his finger and thumb. Jacky must be far gone indeed when, having anything edible between his fingers, he delays about putting it between his lips.

'Ye have, I see,' says Miss Ricketty. 'I'm tould, me dear,' looking behind her, and beside her, and to the door, and now, for even better security, putting up her opened palm to one side of her mouth, 'that there's a young—a'—she hesitates as if to choose a word, then comes to a safe conclusion—'a faymale there,' she says.

'There's a girl there, I think,' says Susan nervously. 'At least'—here Jacky looks at her appealingly, and she changes her sentence —'someone says there is. A niece, or a friend of Mrs. Denis's, I suppose.'

'Arrah! Suppose!' says Miss Ricketty with considerable eloquence, but without committing herself.

'Well, if not that,' says Susan, who is full of her late romantic idea about a secret marriage between the unknown and Wyndham, 'perhaps — perhaps Mr. Wyndham knows something about her.'

Miss Ricketty turns sharply, and looks at her. But the girl's lovely, open, tranquil face betrays nothing but a soft enthusiasm. A sense of amusement fills Miss Ricketty's breast.

'Fegs, I'm thinkin' ye're on the right thrack,' says she evenly.

'You won't say it again, Miss Ricketty, will you?' says Susan; 'but I have thought —at least, it has occurred to me—that perhaps she's Mr. Wyndham's wife.'

This is a little too much for Miss Ricketty. She gives way suddenly to a fit of coughing, and, turning her back to Susan, dives under the counter, whether to recover from a very proper confusion, or to indulge in very improper laughter, can now, alas! never be known. When she emerges, however, her face is a fine crimson.

'That would be very romantic, wouldn't it?' says Susan, looking at her and speaking softly, yet with a pretty delight. 'A marriage like that, with nobody knowing anything except they two, you know; and I feel sure she is lovely, and Mr. Wyndham is very nice-looking too, and after awhile perhaps we shall know her. He will introduce us to her, and we shall be friends, and——'

''Tis a beautiful story,' says Miss Ricketty, breaking in with unction. 'An' beautiful stories, we all know, come thrue. I wish ye joy o' the bride at the Cottage, Miss Susan; but I wouldn't be for intherferin' wid the young married people too soon if I were you, me dear.'

'Of course, I shouldn't do that,' says Susan hastily, her fair face growing earnest. 'But I thought that if——'

'Well, ye'd betther wait, I think,' says

Miss Ricketty. ' 'Tis bad bein' in a hurry, as Misther Haldane found out last night.'

' Mr. Haldane ! What has happened to him ?'

' Fegs, miss, it seems that last night, as he was descendin' the steps from the vesthry, he thripped, God help us ! an' fell on his ugly mug an' broke his front teeth.'

' Oh, how dreadful !' says Susan, real compassion in her tone, though the new curate is rather farther beyond the range of her sympathy than even the old. ' I wonder father hasn't heard of it.'

' It seems the poor gintleman is keeping it dark,' says Miss Ricketty, ' wid the thought of gettin' thim put in agin widout anyone knowin'. But'—wrathfully—' 'twill be no use for him. I see that villain of a Salther down there'—with a glance out of the window —' tellin' every wan of it. Why, ye must have seen him yerself, miss, as ye come by.' And suddenly Susan does remember the crowd round Salter's shop-door, with Salter himself in its midst. ' He's got hould of it, for sure, and if he has 'twill be short shrift for Misther Haldane.'

'But why?' asks Susan.

'Why, this, miss! He hates your clergy because he's not in wid ye, like. A Methody he is; an' Mr. Haldane goes agin his grain, wid the candles an' the flowers an' that, an' he says how that Mr. Haldane had a dhrop too much last night when he thripped on the vesthry stairs.'

'What a shame!' says Susan indignantly. 'I know for a fact that Mr. Haldane is——'

'Yes, of course, miss. But that's how thim Methodys does. An' as for that Salther himself, I don't believe in him. 'Tis a power o' whisky he can get undher his own belt widout bein' found out, until his timper is up. I know for a fact that 'twas only a week ago that he bate his poor wife until she let a screech out of her that would have waked Father D'Arcy himself, only that the seven sleepers aren't a patch on him.'

It appears she cannot even spare her parish priest! Susan, who has risen, and who is now dragging Jacky from under the counter, where he has been in hot pursuit of a kitten, bids her old friend good-bye for the present.

'You'll tell Miss Barry about the clutch,' says the spinster; and 'Yes!' shouts Susan into the terminus, a little louder than usual, perhaps, because Miss Ricketty lifts up her hand and shakes it at her reproachfully.

'Wan would think I was deaf,' says she tragically, whereupon both she and Susan laugh together. The girl's happy mirth—seen if not heard—delights the old maid behind the counter.

'Good-bye, me dear, an' God bless you!' says she, and, disdaining to even see Susan's pennies, she thrusts a big parcel of sweets into Jacky's small hands.

'Keep a few for Masther Bonnie,' whispers she, as she kisses him and sends him after his sister.

At the door, however, Susan turns back, and once more calls down the trumpet:

'You will contradict that thing about Mr. Haldane, won't you?' says she; 'surely it is bad enough that he should have lost his front teeth, without having scandalous stories spread about him. Besides, they will make father very unhappy.'

'I'll look afther him,' says Miss Ricketty, 'if only to oblige ye, me dear; though, I think, I'm not wantin'. Providence seems to have his eye on that young man.'

'Oh, poor man! I'm afraid not,' says Susan; 'he was ugly enough before, and now his front teeth are gone!'

'That's it,' says Miss Ricketty; 'whin next ye look at him, ye'll see what a fine openin' the Lord has made for him.'

The last vision Susan has of Miss Ricketty shows her leaning back in her chair, with her apron over her bonnet, convulsed with joy at her own wit.

CHAPTER VIII.

'Nature often enshrines gallant and noble hearts in weak bosoms—oftenest, God bless her! in female breasts.'

QUITE close to the gardens Susan meets one of the under-gardeners at Crosby Park.

'I suppose Master Jacky and I can go in and see the gardens, Brown?'

'Oh yes, miss, o' course. But I'm afraid there's no one there. As it happens, no one's working there to-day. 'Tis a holiday, you know, miss. An' the gates are locked.'

It happens, indeed, to be a saint's day, or holiday—one of the innumerable saints' days that are held sacred in Ireland, and on which no man will work, if he is a Roman Catholic labourer, though the loss of the day's hire is a severe strain upon his slender resources. And the funny part of this arrangement is that, though they are too religious to support their families by working on these days, they never know what saint's day it is, or anything in the world about him—or her.

'Oh!' says Susan; she had forgotten about its being a holiday, though both the maids had gone to chapel in the morning, leaving her and Betty to make up the many beds. Her tone is so disappointed that Brown drags out a key from his trousers pocket.

'If ye'll take this, miss, ye can let yoself in, an' ye can lave it at the lodge wid Mrs. Donovan whin ye're goin' back.'

'Oh, thank you, Brown!' says Susan joyfully; and diving into her pocket, she produces twopence (it is quite a sum for Susan, whose pennies are very scarce), and gives it to him, an instinct born with her—a sort of pride—compelling her to reward the underling. And yet she had refused to give Tommy—the baby, the youngest of all, and the **dearest** to her of the children after Bonnie—a halfpenny out of that twopence only this morning.

'Thank you, miss,' says Brown, with considerably more gratitude than he would have shown another if she had given him half a crown, and Susan, who had paid for the key quite as much for her own sake as for Jacky's, goes on her way rejoicing.

Yes, the gate is locked. Susan, having unlocked it, carefully removes the key, locks it on the other side, and goes down the broad, beautiful, scented path with Jacky beside her. Some of the houses are near, but not so worthy of notice as those that come after, and through these they hurry to the great glass ones beyond—where the roses are all a-growing, all a-blowing, in magnificent profusion—that are always kept up in a very perfect state, though the master of them be in the Soudan or North America, or among the highest peaks of the Andes.

Between these two sets of houses runs a wall, now laden with cherry-trees in full fruit, and as Susan and her brother emerge from the seedling-house into the freer air, she catches sight of something that brings her to a standstill.

Against the wall where the cherries are growing stands a ladder, and on the top of it —a man.

Now, Susan knows all the gardeners at Crosby Park, and even those beneath them, and certainly this man is not one of them.

She turns and retreats on Jacky, who is just behind her, and for a moment fear covers her. She has never been brought face to face with a thief before — few girls have been—and a desire to fly is the thought uppermost in her breast. She glances upward fearfully to the figure on the top of the wall, who is hastily pulling off the cherries and dropping them into the basket he has slung on to the top of the ladder. She draws her breath quickly. Could anything be more premeditated—could anything show more plainly what a determined rogue he is? And to-day of all days! A holiday, when, of course, he knew that all the gardeners would be away, and the place safe to him! No doubt he had climbed the outside wall—thieves can do anything—and had found the ladder inside with which to rob poor Mr. Crosby, who is now goodness knows how many miles away.

Susan stands rooted to the ground, not knowing whether to stay or fly. Old stories of heroines return to her, and it seems to her that it would be base to steal away now and say nothing; even if she happened to gain the walk outside, it is doubtful whether she should meet any servant, this being a saint's day; and if she did, would he be willing to tackle a real live thief single-handed? As she hesitates, she again looks at the man, and notices that he is glancing from right to left, hesitating, as if either uneasy or else with a view to choosing the best fruit. Both ideas anger her, but the second more than the first. Uneasy? of course he is! And no wonder, too! A thief must necessarily be uneasy. And to attempt to steal here, in this lovely secluded place!

The owner of Crosby Park has been so long away that Susan has almost adopted his place as her own. Many years ago Mr. Crosby, who had been a pupil of Mr. Barry's, had given directions that every member of the Barry family should have free right to his grounds, and Susan, once come to years of discretion—not so long ago—has taken great advantage of this kindly permission. It is so near to the Vicarage, and so lovely! All its walks and pretty windings are so well known to her. They have been much to her, indeed, during all these years, though so little to the actual possessor of them, who has evidently found more pleasure in shooting grizzlies than in cultivating cherries.

That now someone has come to steal these cherries seems dreadful to Susan. With that poor man away, too—at the end of the world probably, shooting, or being shot by, some of those awful Indians! Again she casts her frightened glance at the thief, still high on his ladder and secure from detection now that all the servants are away; and something in his air—an insolent security, perhaps—drives her to action.

No, she will not fly! She will tell him, at all events, what she thinks of him before flying. She makes her way straight to the foot of the ladder, wrath in her bosom, and addresses him.

'I wonder you aren't ashamed of yourself!' cries she, righteous indignation in her tones and in her lovely uplifted eyes.

The sweet voice rings up the ladder. The start that the thief on the top of it gives, when he hears her, condemns him to all eternity in Susan's eyes. 'No one,' argues Susan to herself, 'ever starts unless he is guilty.' Susan is very young.

The man casts a sidelong glance at her. It is so one-sided that Susan hardly sees him, but evidently he is trembling, conscience-stricken, because he makes no reply.

'Come down!' says Susan again, her courage mounting with the occasion. Her tone is now severely calm, and without a vestige of fear. After all, he is a poor creature whom even a girl can frighten, so small is the courage of the unrighteous! 'Do you know what you are doing? You'—with accumulated scorn—'are stealing!'

This terrible charge brings the culprit round. He sinks upon the topmost rung of the ladder, as if overcome, and pulls his cap over his eyes, evidently to avoid recognition. Says Susan to herself: 'He is ashamed, poor creature!' and seeing the abject attitude of the wretch, she grows bolder, and presses the wondering Jacky to her side, and tells him to take courage. This poor man will not kill them. No—no, indeed.

'Yes, stealing,' repeats she, her fair, beautiful face uplifted to the sinner's above her. There is a second pause, during which, perhaps, the sinner takes note of it.

'I——' begins he, then pauses. Susan's eyes are looking into his, and Susan's face, implacable and austere, no doubt has daunted him. But Susan tells herself that conscious guilt has rendered him silent. After awhile, however, he makes another attempt.

'I——' says he again, and again stops. It is contemptible! Susan turns a scornful glance upon him.

'It is not to be defended,' says she. 'To steal from a garden like this! From a garden that the owner has so kindly left open to many people—who has besides been so kind, and who has helped all the poor in the district. He has given forty blankets where another has given ten, and coals without restriction everywhere. And these beautiful gardens, too—he has given these as a recreation to some who have no lovely gardens of their own; and now you take advantage of a day like this, when all the servants are away, to defraud this kind, kind man and steal his cherries. Oh, how can you bear to be so bad?'

'If you would hear me!' begins the man on the top of the ladder, in a low tone. He is evidently immensely touched by the scorn of the young evangelist below, because his voice is very low and uncertain.

'There is nothing to be said,' says Susan, her eyes gleaming with honest disgust. 'There is no excuse for you. You are here stealing Mr. Crosby's cherries, and, as I said before, you ought to be ashamed of yourself.'

'Still, miss, if you would listen a moment!' He has pulled his cap even closer over his brows.

'You needn't do that,' says Susan. 'Poor creature! you need not be afraid of me; I will not give you up to justice!'

'Thank you kindly, miss,' comes from the wretched creature behind the cap. He is evidently struggling with emotion.

'I don't want you to thank me,' says Susan, who is feeling inclined to cry. She has often read of thieves, but never met one until now, and it seems to her, all at once, that they are decidedly interesting, so ready to hear—to receive admonition, too. 'I want you to promise me that for the future you will abstain from—from thieving of any sort.'

'I'll promise you, miss—I will indeed. I'd promise you anything.' Poor thing! he seems quite overcome. 'But, miss, I wasn't really stealing just now.'

'Oh, nonsense!' says Susan; a revulsion of feeling makes her once again hard to him. Confession is good for the soul, but denial—and such a useless denial, too, caught in the act as he is—savours of folly, that worst of all things, for which there is no forgiveness.

'Do you think I did not see you? Why, look at that basket; it is nearly full. How can you say you were not stealing those cherries? Better to show some regret than to carry off your crime in such a barefaced way.'

It is hardly barefaced, the unhappy culprit's face being now quite hidden by his cap.

'Just think,' says Susan, her clear, sweet voice trembling with grief because of this sinner; 'if you had a garden, would you like people to come into it and steal your fruit?'

The poor thief is evidently beginning to feel the situation acutely. He has taken out his handkerchief in a surreptitious fashion, and is rubbing his eyes with it.

'I shouldn't mind if it was you, miss,' says he, in a stifled tone.

Poor thing! he is evidently very sorry.

'You won't give me up, miss?'

'No, no!' cries Susan hastily. 'But I do hope you see and are grieved for what you are doing. When people are so good and so generous as to let other people go through their grounds and get a great deal of enjoyment out of them, I think the least those others may do is to respect them, and their shrubs, and fruit, and flowers.'

'You're right, miss. I seem as if I never saw it like that till now.'

'Ah! that's what they all say,' says Susan sadly, and with a sigh. She has a good deal to do with her father's impenitent penitents. 'But you are no doubt from some distant parish. A tramp, I suppose,' says Susan, with another sigh. 'At all events, I am sure you do not belong to this part of the world, as your voice is strange to me.'

'I've come a long way, miss, indeed.'

'Poor man! Perhaps you are hungry,'

says Susan. Again she searches her pocket, and produces the last coin in it—the last coin she has in the world, for the matter of that—and lays a sixpenny bit on the lowest rung of the ladder.

'Perhaps this may help you,' says she. 'I'm sorry I haven't any more, but I haven't. And now remember I expect you to keep your promise. I shall not report you, or get you into trouble of any sort; in fact, this'—gently—'shall be a secret between you and me; but I do expect you to go away without those cherries, and with the promise never to steal again.'

'I promise you that, miss, most gratefully. I'll never steal again. But, miss, might I give the cherries to you or the young gentleman?'

'No, no!' says Susan in horror. She catches Jacky's hand and draws him away from temptation. After going a yard or two, however, she looks back; and the thief, who has been looking after her, again pulls his cap hurriedly over his guilty face.

'The gate is locked,' says she; 'how will you get out?'

'The way I came, miss,' says the bad man, with open signs of contrition.

'I see—yes,' says Susan sadly. 'But go at once. I trust you—remember.'

'I'll never forget it, miss,' says the unhappy man, sinking down upon the ladder and covering his face with his hands.

'Jacky,' says Susan, when they have left the garden and locked the door carefully behind them, 'if you ever say a word about that poor creature, I'll never think the same of you again. Do you hear? He is a wretched thief; but I have given my word not to betray him, and you must give your word too. Poor man! I think he was sincerely sorry. You won't say a word at home or anywhere, Jacky?'

'No,' says Jacky. He looks at her. 'Why couldn't you have taken the cherries?' says he.

It takes the entire remainder of the walk home to make the 'why' clear to him.

CHAPTER IX.

*'He knew not what to say,
And so he swore!'*

WYNDHAM, when he met Susan, had been in rather a disgusted mood. Shortly after the Professor's death he had gone to Norway for a month with the friend whom he had arranged to go with on the morning following the luckless night that had seen the last of the Professor's experiment. He had induced his friend to wait for him—the latter consenting with rather a bad grace—until the Professor's funeral was over and his affairs looked into. He had had a last conversation with Denis about the uninvited guest whom the latter had taken to the Cottage, and had told him to find a suitable home for her at once, comfortable—luxurious even, if necessary, as she was now undoubtedly the possessor of three hundred a year—but, at all events, to get her out of the Cottage without further delay. He spoke peremptorily, and Denis promised all things; yet only yesterday, on his return, he had heard from Denis's own lips that still that girl was located in the Cottage.

'Didn't I tell you to get her a home somewhere else?'

'Ye did, sir—ye did. Faix, I don't wondher ye're mad, but 'twasn't aisy to do it.'

'To do what?'—firmly.

'To get her to go.'

'What nonsense! A girl like that—as if she could resist! Why, one would think there wasn't a policeman anywhere. Do you mean to tell me she refused to go?'

'No, sir; that's not me manin'. 'Tis that ould fool of a wife o' mine. It seems she got set upon her wan way or another, an' do all I could I couldn't git her to turn the young lady out. "There's room for us all here," says Bridget. "But that's not his ordhers," says I—manin' you, sir. "But whin is she to go?" says she. "That's nothing to me," says I. "'Tis so," says she. "A comfortable home he tould ye to git for her, and where'll she find wan but here?" An' divil a fut I could move her from that. Don't you iver get married, Misther Paul; it will be the undoin' o' ye. Ye won't have a mind o' yer own in six months.'

'I've a mind now, any way,' says Wyndham, still swearing, 'and that is to get rid of you without another second's notice.'

'An' I'm not surprised, sir,' says Denis, drawing himself up and saluting. He is an old soldier. 'It was most flagrant disobadience. But what can ye do wid a woman, sir? Fegs, nothing—nothing at all. They carries all before thim—even a man's conscience. When Bridget refused to let her go, what could I do?' He pauses satisfied, having put the blame upon his particular Eve. 'Is it yer wish that I tackle Bridget agin, sir?'

'No; I shall go down to Curraghcloyne myself to-morrow,' says Wyndham, getting rid of him with a gesture.

He had gone down, had met Susan, had read something in her face that seemed to him (whose senses were very much alive to impressions on the subject) to be studying him—wondering at him. It was with a still more enraged feeling he left her, and went on to the Cottage, where, to his supreme indignation, he found, for the first time on record, the entrance-gate locked.

Good heavens! What could be the meaning of this? Were they determined to compromise him in the eyes of the world? When he has rung the bell until it is hopelessly smashed, someone comes to the gate, and without opening it says, in a voice evidently meant to alarm any unwelcome intruder:

'Who's there?'

'Only the master of this place,' says Wyndham grimly, who has recognised Mrs. Denis's handsome brogue even under these new conditions. Indeed, it would be hard to mistake it anywhere; as Fitzgerald, who knows her, says, 'you could sit on it at any moment without the slightest chance of a breakdown.'

'Glory be!' comes in a muffled tone from Mrs. Denis, and, with tremendous fuss and flurry, she draws the bolt, unlocks the gate, and opens it wide to Wyndham.

'Oh, yer honour, who'd a' thought to see yerself this day! Faix, I thought 'twas still in thim haythin countries ye were. Sure, if I'd known I'd have had the gates open to yer honour; and I hope ye'll forgive me cap, sir—I've another wan just ironed, an'——'

'Are you preparing for a siege?' demands Wyndham grimly; 'or what may be the reason of this "barring out" on your part? Anything threatening on the part of the Land Leaguers or the Home Rulers round here?'

'Oh, law, sir! How could ye think o' sich a thing? It was only that the young lady, sir, was a trifle nervous.'

'She will have to take her nerves somewhere else,' says the barrister. 'Now, Mrs.

Denis, I hear from your husband that it is your fault that this—this distinctly undesirable person is still a resident in my house.'

Mrs. Denis, who has been bowing and scraping up to this, now grows suddenly alert.

'Arrah, what are ye sayin' at all?' says she. 'D'ye mane to tell me that Denis knew ye were come back, and niver give me tale or todin's of it?'

'That is altogether beside the question. The thing is——'

'Faix, the raal thing is this,' says Mrs. Denis, 'that I'll break ivery bone in that thraitor's skin the next time I see him! Why,' says she, squaring her arms and growing so wrathful that the questionable cap on the top of her head begins to quiver, 'sixpence would have brought any boy down from Dublin wid the news of yer return, and'—with a truly noble declaration of an innate dishonesty—'I could thin have'—she stops herself, happily, at the last moment—'made mesilf clane to meet ye,' says she.

Wyndham, who is sufficiently Irish himself to put in the broken paragraph, smiles coldly.

'I am not going to discuss Denis with you,' says he. 'What I want to know is why these gates are locked.'

'Well, sir, there was this: when the young lady came she was that upset wid bad thratement of wan sort or another that she seemed to be tremblin' all over. But whin I questioned her as to what ailed her, not a word could I git out of her. I put her to bed, an' she just clung to the wall like, turnin' an' twistin' her purty head, an' always keepin' away from me, an' refusin' the tay even, till the night came down upon us. Ye will remimber, sir, that it was in the airly mornin' that Denis——' At this word she breaks off, and grows again intensely angry.

'That varmint,' says she, 'what did he mane by not tellin' me? Wait till I get me hands on him!'

'Yes, the early morning,' says Wyndham, bringing her back somewhat impatiently to the place where she had broken off.

'Well, yes, sir. I beg yer pardon. She come in the airly mornin', an' I could see at once that she was very sad at her heart, an' so I just tuk her in as I tell ye, for Denis, though a divil all out in most ways'—here again a most ominous frown settles on her forehead—'is still a man to be depended on where a woman is concerned. And so I tuk her in to oblige ye, sir.'

'To oblige me!' says Wyndham.

'Well, sir, I thought so thin. An''—she pauses, and looks straight at him—'an' ye'll nivver regret it, sir. If ye saw her a bit afther she came, an' her delight at yer purty place! "Why, there's flowers growin'," she'd say, as if she never see them before, except whin sellin'! "And, Mrs. Denis," says she, "I like these walls," says she. "They is so high," says she. "An' it would be very hard for anyone," says she, "to git through thim, or even to look over thim." Faith, 'tis little the crayture knows of the boys round here, I said to meself whin she said that. But I declare to ye, sir, it went to me heart whin she said it, for it made it plain to me like that there was someone in her life that she was thinkin' of, that she didn't want to get through these walls or over thim aither. If he did, I could gather from what she said that it would be wid no good intintions towards herself.'

'Has she said anything as to where she came from or who she is?' asks Wyndham, with most disgraceful want of sympathy for this moving story.

'No, sir, sorra a word, barrin' that she was very unhappy until yer honour sint her here.'

'Till I sent her here! What on earth do you mean?' says Wyndham indignantly. 'You must know very well that it was that blundering idiot of a husband of yours that brought her here.'

'Fegs, 'tis plain that ye know Denis, any way,' says Denis's wife complacently. 'Idjit is the word for him, sure enough! But however it is, sir, the poor young lady is very continted here entirely, an''—waxing enthusiastic—''twould do your heart good to hear her singin' about the garden, for all the world like wan o' thim nate little thrushes.'

This expectation on Mrs. Denis's part, that he will find delight in the thought of the unwelcome stranger making herself at home in his garden and singing there like a 'nate little thrush,' naturally adds fuel to the fire that already is burning vigorously in Wyndham's breast.

'Look here,' says he, so fiercely that Mrs. Denis starts backwards, 'you've taken a wrong impression of me altogether, if you think I shall for one moment sanction the presence of that girl here. Your husband has got me into this mess with his confounded stupidity, but I can trust myself to get out of it—and I expect you to understand at once that your "thrush"'—scornfully —'will be out of this within twenty-four hours.'

With this he brushes by her, his temper —never very sweet—now considerably the worse for wear.

Nice situation, by Jove! If it comes to

the old man's ears there will be the devil to pay; and it's sure to. He had felt there was something queer in his aunt's and Josephine's manner yesterday when he called at their house in Fitzwilliam Square. Why, if it gets about, there isn't one in forty amongst his acquaintances who will believe in the real facts of the case. . . . It is a most confounded affair altogether. If he hadn't gone abroad, trusting—like the fool that he was—in Denis's ability to get her out of the Cottage at once, he could have done it himself, and so speedily that no one would ever have been the wiser about it. But now it has gone a little too far; people, no doubt, are beginning to talk. Well, it shall go no farther. He will put an end to it at once —this moment.

CHAPTER X.

> ' My heart is sad and heavy,
>   In this merry month of May,
>   As I stand beneath the lime-tree
>   On the bastion old and gray.'

'This moment' has come. As Mrs. Denis, routed, but by no means vanquished, disappears hastily round one corner of the pretty cottage, someone else comes round the other. A young girl, singing sweetly, merrily, though in a subdued voice. Just as she reaches her corner she looks behind her; her singing ceases, and an amused look brightens her face—a face that has known much sadness. Again she looks behind her, as if expecting something, this time turning her back on Wyndham; and now, a moment later, a huge dog tears across the grass and literally flings himself upon the girl, whose tall but slender frame seems to give way beneath his canine embraces. For a second only; then she recovers herself, her pliant body sways forward, and, catching the dog's handsome head in her arms, a merry tussle ensues between them. It is almost a dance, so agile is the girl, so bent is the dog on entering into the spirit of the fun with all his heart.

Wyndham, watching, feels no sense of amusement. Indignation is still full upon him, and now it grows more intense as he sees the dog—his dog—a brute hitherto devoted to himself, lavishing its affection upon an utter stranger.

He makes an impatient movement, which the dog's quick eye sees, and, bolting from his late companion, he comes bounding towards Wyndham, from whom, it must be confessed, he gets but a poor welcome.

The girl, turning, surprised at the dog's desertion of her, becomes suddenly aware that there is someone beyond, and as Wyndham emerges into sight she makes a movement to fly, then stands stricken, as if turned to stone.

It is impossible, under the circumstances, but that she should be known to Wyndham; but as he looks at her he tells himself that, if he had not known that Denis had brought her down here on the morning of the Professor's death, he would never have recognised her. Her dress, for one thing, is so different. Of course he had found time to send a cheque to Mrs. Moriarty before going abroad for the use of the 'waif,' as he had somehow called the girl to himself, not knowing her name—a sum handsome enough to dress her as the young heiress of a most unexpected three hundred a year should be dressed—and it comes to him now that the 'waif' had not been slow in the spending of it. No doubt Mrs. Moriarty had been the 'middle man,' but the 'waif' had known what she was about, or else some well-born instinct had directed her.

'Well born!' Pah! A poor, miserable girl like that, with a shawl thrown over her head when first he saw her—and yet, her face, her feet——

He can see them from beneath her petticoats. They are not like mice, by any means, but they are of the proportions usually assigned to those who have many grandfathers, and they are very delicately clad.

If he had not recognised her at all at first, she had barely recognised him. That was because of the surprise—the shock, perhaps. She had almost come to believe in the possibility of living here always and alone, never seeing anyone except kind Mrs. Moriarty and Nero, the dog.

She has turned as white as death; and Wyndham, looking at her, tells himself it is the memory of that last dreadful night, when she had accepted death as her portion, rather than the life that lies behind her, that has blanched her cheeks and brought that terror into her eyes.

But in a minute all these theories of the

clever barrister are distilled and float into air.

Having seen him, and dwelt upon his face, the colour in her own face has crept back, and with a sharp sigh of relief she draws nearer to him slowly, the dog, who has gone back to her, following, his muzzle in her hand.

'I—I thought you were a stranger,' says she faintly.

It is an odd sentence. A stranger! What else is he to her? Her manner, however, makes it clear to him that she has lived, since her entrance into the Cottage, in constant dread of being discovered by someone, and of being dragged back to a former existence—to which death, as she had proved to him that night, seems far preferable.

This accounts for the locked gates, and the girl's admiration for the walls—an admiration that no doubt has but little to do with the ivy and the Virginian creeper, now throwing out its palest leaves of green, and the other trailing glories that have lifted them into a dream of beauty.

'Your thought was very nearly right,' says Wyndham, with a cold smile; he is quite unmoved by the nervous pallor and the frightened expression on the young face before him. Barristers after a while get accustomed to young, frightened faces, and lose their interest in them. 'But, no doubt, you remember me?'

He pauses, and the girl looks at him for a moment.

'Yes,' says she slowly, her eye sinking to the ground. That last dreadful scene, in which he had played so conspicuous a part, and when in the sullenness of her despair she had welcomed death, lies once again clear as a picture to her eyes. She shudders, and a faint moisture breaks out upon her forehead.

'I am glad to see you quite recovered,' says he in a tone which belies his words. 'If you will be so good as to come indoors, I should like to speak to you for a few minutes about your future.'

His tone is so curt, so positively unpleasant, that the girl, colouring deeply and without another word, moves towards the hall-door of the charming cottage, and leads the way through the porch—so exquisitely festooned with delicate greeneries—into the long many-windowed room beyond. This room runs the entire length of the house, and overlooks the garden. As she goes a deep melancholy falls upon her. What has he come to say? Why is his manner so unkind? That night—that awful night—he had seemed to befriend her —to take her part—and now——

'You are of course aware,' says Wyndham formally, when they have reached the drawing-room—the drawing-room that used to be his, but that now seems to slip out of his possession, as he sees the slender figure of the girl turn after his entrance, as if to receive him. 'You are of course aware that the late Professor, Mr. Hennessy, left you three hundred a year?'

The girl, standing midway between one of the windows and Wyndham, makes a slight affirmative movement of her head. She would have spoken, but words failed her.

'That was in accordance with his promise to you. If the experiment failed, well'—with a careless shrug—'there was nothing. If it was successful—you were to be the gainer by it.'

His voice is clear, unemotional; there is a sort of 'laying down the law' about it that takes every spark of sympathy that there might have been quite out of it.

'Yes.' This time she manages to speak, but she colours as she speaks, and blushes very painfully; and now her eyes seek the ground. If one were to exactly describe her, one would say—but very reluctantly, I think—that she looks ashamed.

'With three hundred a year you should be able to——'

She interrupts him.

'It is too much—far too much,' says she, with an effort. 'I don't want so much as that. Fifty pounds a year would be enough; I am sure I could——'

She stops.

'All that is beyond question,' says the

barrister coldly. 'It was the Professor's wish that you should have three hundred a year, and now that he is gone, there can be no further argument about it. He has no near relations so far as I can make out, so that there is no reason why you should not accept the money left to you by him. What I came to-day for was, not about the Professor's gift to you, but to know what you intend to do with it.'

'With it?'

'Yes; what, in fact, are you going to do?'

'What am I going to do?' She looks up at him for the first time; a startled expression grows in her large dark eyes.

'We all have a future before us,' says Wyndham, 'and you——' He hesitates here, hardly knowing how to go on with those earnest eyes on his. 'Of course I feel that, for the time being, I am in a sense bound to look after you, the Professor being an old friend of mine, and you——' Again he stops. It seems impossible, indeed, to refer to that strange scene where he had had so prominent a part. 'You will understand,' says he, 'that the Professor wished you to be placed in an assured position, and he left me to see to that.'

Here the girl makes a sharp movement of her hands descriptive of fear.

'Naturally,' says Wyndham, in answer to that swift movement of the pretty hands, 'you object to my interference. But I must ask your forbearance in a matter that'—with a steady look at her—'does not concern me in the slightest degree. You must really forgive me if I seem impatient; but, as you are aware, I know nothing about you, and to look after you as the Professor asked me to do requires thought. I am in complete ignorance about you. I can see that you are educated, but beyond that I know nothing.'

'Ah! you know nothing indeed,' says she quickly. 'I am not educated. I know hardly anything. I am one of the most ignorant people alive.'

'And yet——'

'I have read anything I could find to read,'

interrupts she; 'and at one time I went to a day-school, but that is all.'

'I see,' says Wyndham. His tone is indifferent, but, inwardly, curiosity is stirring him. So little education, and yet so calm, so refined a manner! Who is this girl, with her well-bred air, but with, too, the little touches here and there that betray the fact of her having lived not only out of the fashionable world, but very far from even the outskirts of it? What whim of fate has given her that shapely head, those shell-like ears and pointed fingers, yet given her into the clutches of the middle classes?

'You would wish to enlarge your studies?' asks he presently.

For the first time since she came towards him, in the garden outside, she now lets her eyes rest frankly upon his.

'Oh, if I could!' says she.

'That is very easily to be managed, I should think. You have three hundred a year of your own, and can command advantages that hitherto, I imagine, from what you say, have been withheld from you.' He waits a moment, as if expecting her to speak, to make some comment on his words, but she remains mute.

'If you could tell me something of yourself—your history—what brought you to this,' says Wyndham, 'it might make matters simpler for both you and me.'

The girl shrinks backwards as though he had struck her.

'No, no!' cries she quickly.

CHAPTER XI.

> 'I wept in my dream, for I fancied
>   That you had forsaken me;
> I woke, and all night I lay weeping
>   Till morning, bitterly.'

WYNDHAM lifts his brows.

'Pray do not distress yourself,' says he. 'It is a free country; you can speak or be silent, just as you wish. It had merely occurred to me that there might be friends of yours naturally very anxious about you, and that I might convey to them a message from you.'

The unsympathetic nature of his tone has restored the girl to her usual manner more than anything else could have done. She glances at him.

'Friends!' says she bitterly.

'At all events,' says Wyndham, who has now begun to acknowledge his curiosity with regard to her even to himself, and is determined on pushing the matter as far as possible, 'there must be someone on the lookout for you.'

At this she turns as white as death.

'Is there? Have you seen—have you'—she looks as though she is about to faint—'heard anything?'

'Nothing—nothing at all!' exclaims he quickly, a little shocked at her agitation, that seems excessive. 'Do not be frightened; I assure you I know as little of anyone connected with you as I know of yourself.'

Here again he gives her an opening, if she wishes to make a declaration of any sort, and again she remains mute. There is something even obstinately silent in her whole air.

Her hands in her lap are tightly clasped, as though to help her to keep her secret to all eternity.

'You will not confide in me, I see,' says

he, with a little contemptuous shrug; 'and, after all, there is no earthly reason why you should. I am as great a stranger to you as you are to me, and if I spoke at all it was, believe me, because I fancied I might be of some assistance to you. But women nowadays have taken the reins into their own hands, and I have no doubt that you will be able to manage your own affairs to perfection. In the meantime, however, if I can be of the slightest use to you in looking out a suitable home, for instance, I hope you understand I shall be delighted to do all I can.'

The girl has drawn nearer during this speech, and is now standing before him, the frightened eyes uplifted and her breath coming short and fast. 'You mean—but here—can I not—might I not—a home, you said——'

'Well, yes,' says Wyndham. 'A home where you might have a companion and be very comfortable; but not here, you know.'

'But——'

'You can't stay here, I'm afraid,' says Wyndham, who, between his anger and his suspicions of her, is beginning to wish he had never been born.

The girl turns away from him, in so far that only her profile now can be seen, whilst her right hand has caught hold of the back of a chair near her, as if for support.

'But why?' asks she, in a low tone. 'Mrs. Moriarty likes me to be here.'

'But, you see,' says Wyndham gravely, 'it is my house, and not Mrs. Moriarty's.'

'Yes.' She looks at him as if hardly understanding, but presently an expression grows upon her face that gives him to know that she thinks him churlish.

'It is quite a big house,' says she.

There is a pause—a pause in which he tells himself that evidently up to this she had been accustomed to houses of very cramped limits. The Circular Road in Dublin would supply such houses, built for respectable artisans and clerks in commercial places, and the best of the decent strata that cover the earth and are of the earth earthy. The Circular Road, or some other road, has no doubt supplied the kind of house to which the girl has been accustomed—this girl, with her pale patrician face and her singular strength of mind. It is she who at last breaks the silence. 'There is plenty of room for me,' says she.

'I know—of course I know that,' says Wyndham hurriedly. 'But then, you see, it—it wouldn't do, you see.'

He looks deliberately at her, as if to explain his meaning, but, nothing coming of the look, he falls back once more upon facts.

'I come here sometimes,' says he.

'Yes; Mrs. Denis told me that,' says the girl. 'But'—eagerly—'I shouldn't be in the way at all. I could stay in that little room belonging to Mrs. Denis—that little room off the kitchen.'

'Oh, that isn't it,' says Wyndham, frowning in his embarrassment. How the deuce is one to say it plainly to a girl who can't, or won't, or doesn't understand! 'The fact is——' He has begun with the greatest bravery, determined to explain the situation at all hazards; but, happening to meet her eyes, this clever barrister, who has faced many a barefaced criminal victoriously, breaks down. The eyes he has looked into are full of tears.

'Look here,' says he almost savagely, 'it's out of the question! Do you hear?' His tone is so terribly abrupt that it strikes cold to the heart of the poor girl looking at him. If he is going to turn her out of this house, this haven of refuge, where—where can she go?

She struggles with herself, some touch of dignity that belongs to her—wherever she came from or whoever she is—giving her a certain strength.

'Of course—I see——' She is beginning to stammer dreadfully. 'I am sorry about it; but I thought—I fancied I could stay here. But now I can go—I can go somewhere. There must be other places, and, indeed, just now you told me there were other places, and that I could go to——'

She struggles with the word 'them,' the last of her sad sentence, but can't speak it; and now all her hard-found dignity gives way, to her everlasting shame, and to Wyndham's terrible discomfiture she bursts into a passion of tears.

'Don't do that,' says Wyndham gruffly. It is impossible to conceal from himself the fact that he is frightened out of his life. Fear because of her tears is nothing, but it is with ever-increasing self-contempt that he knows that he is going even so far as to give in and let her stay at the Cottage. After all, there are many other places for him in this big world, but for her, perhaps, not so many; and she seems to have set her heart on this little spot, and, hang it all! why can't she stop crying?

'Oh, I'm sorry,' says she at last, trying passionately to stifle her sobs. She has turned away from him to the window, and there is something in her whole attitude so descriptive of despair, and fear, and shame, that, in spite of his anger, pity for her rises in his heart. 'I don't know why I'm crying; I don't often cry. But if I leave this, where shall I go? where shall I hide myself?'

What on earth has she done? Her words denote fear—a guilty fear. What if he should be about to take as a tenant for the Cottage a well-known and hardened criminal, for whom, perhaps, the police are even now on the look-out? Her face, however, belies her tone; and, for the rest, he has not the courage to face again a flow of those pitiful tears. Stay she must.

One last protest, however, he makes as a salve to his conscience.

'What do you see in this place that so attracts you?' asks he, with ever-increasing grumpiness. The girl turns to him a flushed and tearful face.

'I never knew what a home could be like till I came here,' says she. 'Never, never! You have had one—all the world has had one except me. It means new life to me. Oh'—bitterly—'it is the only life I have ever known—the only happiness. If, sir'—she comes towards him and with a little impulsive action holds out her hands—'if I might stay——'

'Well, you can,' says he ungraciously.

He gives in so suddenly, and she is naturally so unprepared for so quick a surrender, that for a moment she says nothing. Her eyes are fixed on him, however, as if trying to read him through; they are beautiful eyes, and Wyndham, his professional instincts on the alert, finds himself wondering what lies behind them in that brain of hers.

'Do you mean it?' says she at last breathlessly; 'if you do, I cannot thank you enough. Oh, to stay here within these lovely walls!' Instinctively she glances out of the window to the ivy-clad walls, as if in their protection she finds great comfort. A moment later a cloud gathers on her forehead. 'But you don't like me to stay,' she says.

'It doesn't matter what I like,' says Wyndham, who certainly does not shine on this occasion. 'The arrangement we have come to now is that you are to rent this cottage from me, at what sum we can agree about later on.'

'To rent it? I shall, then, be—— It'—

she tries to hide the joy in her eyes, feeling it to be indecent—'it will belong to me?'

'Yes,' says Wyndham. At this moment he feels very little more will make him positively hate her.

'It will no longer be yours?' Her voice is trembling.

'In a sense, no.' He turns and takes up his hat; this interview is getting too much for him. There will be an explosion shortly if she goes on like this.

'It seems very selfish,' says the girl. She is looking at him, though for the last three minutes he has refused to look at her. 'I am taking your house away from you.'

'There are other houses.' He is now putting on his gloves.

'Ah! that is as true for me as for you.'

'We have come to an agreement, I think'—grimly. 'Let us keep to it.' He turns to the door.

'You are going?' says she nervously. She follows him. 'You——' She stops, and courtesy compels him to look back. Two troubled eyes meet his.

'When——' stammers she.

'I shall come down some day next week to make final arrangements,' says he impatiently, and again takes a step or two away, getting so far this time as to turn the handle of the door. Here, however, again he glances back. She is standing where he last saw her, her young face looking troubled, frightened, and uncertain.

'Next week,' repeats he jerkily. It is disagreeable to him to think that it is through his fault that the nervous anxiety has crept into her eyes. 'And—er—good-bye.' He certainly had not meant to do it, but he now holds out his hand to her, and with a little swift, eager movement she comes to him and slips her own into it.

A slim little hand, and beautifully shaped, but brown, and looking a little as though it had done some hard work in its time, yet the grace with which she gives it to him is exquisite.

* * * * *

Just at the gate he meets Mrs. Denis again.

'This young lady,' says he abruptly, 'seems to have set her heart upon living here. It is extremely unpleasant for me, but she appears to have no other place to go to. She will therefore become my tenant. She will, you understand, take the Cottage from me.'

'Bless us an' save us!' says Mrs. Denis. 'An' yer honour—what will you do?'

'Keep out of it,' says Wyndham coldly. 'I suppose she will arrange to keep you on. She—— What's her name?'—sharply.

'I don't know, sir; she don't seem to like to spake about it. Miss Ella I calls her.'

'Ella? Did you say her Christian name was Ella?'

'Yes, sir.'

'Ah!'—thoughtfully. 'Well, good-bye.'

'But, sir, you'll be coming again?'

'Yes, next week, to arrange about the rent; not after that.'

He strides through the gate and up the road.

'Faix, and I'm thinkin' ye will,' says Mrs. Denis, watching him with her arms akimbo till he disappears round the corner. ''Tis mighty purty eyes she's got in that mighty purty head of hers. An' so he's not goin' to turn her out, after all! Didn't I tell you, Bridget Moriarty,' rubbing her chin, on which a very handsome beard is growing, 'that he'd soften whin he put his glance upon her?'

CHAPTER XII.

'Jest and youthful jollity,
  Quips and cranks, and wanton wiles,
  Nods and becks, and wreathed smiles.'

'WHERE'S our beloved auntie?' asks Mr. Fitzgerald, looking generally round him from his seat on the tail of Betty's gown.

It is the evening of the same day, and still divinely warm. Not yet has night made its first approach, and from bush to bush the birds are calling, as if in haste to get as much merriment out of the departing day as time will give them. From here—in the bushes round the tennis-ground, the one solitary court that Carew Barry and his cousin, Dom Fitzgerald, have made with their own hands, after a hard tussle with the Rector for the bit of ground, that seemed to him quite a big slice off his glebe—to the big syringa-tree beyond, the sweet, glad music of the birds swells and grows, filling the evening air with delicate throbbings. Ever the little creatures seem to call one to another; passionately sometimes, as if bursting their little throats in their wild joy, and anon softly, pleadingly, but always calling, calling, calling.

From the old-fashioned garden beyond comes the scent of the roses—all old-world roses, as befits the garden, but none the less beautiful for that. The rose céleste and the white rose unique, the cabbage rose and the perfect rose of a hundred leaves, all lend their sweetness to the air; indeed, on this June evening the place is 'on fire with roses.'

The little group sitting on the edge of the tennis-ground seems very happy and contented—lazy, perhaps, is a better word. Susan, as usual, has Bonnie in her lap, and Tom, the baby, has fallen asleep with his head on Betty's knee. Jacky, still full of memories of the awful burglar he had interviewed in the morning, is wondering whether he will raid the village to-night, and if so, whether he will carry off Aunt Jemima; whilst Carew, the eldest son, who is seventeen, and therefore a year younger than Susan, is lazily dwelling on the best choice of a stream for to-morrow's fishing.

His cousin, Dom Fitzgerald, is the first to break the lovely spell of silence that has fallen on them. He is a cousin of the Barrys, and a nephew of their father and of Miss Jemima Barry also, the Rector's sister, who, since the death of her sister-in-law, has always lived with them, and who, if a most exemplary person, is certainly what is commonly described as 'trying.'

The parish of Curraghcloyne is small, the income even smaller. But if Providence, in giving Mr. Barry this parish as his special charge, had been niggardly to him in money matters, it had certainly made up to him lavishly in another respect—it had given him, for example, a large, and what promised to be an ever-increasing, family, so increasing, indeed, that it would ultimately have beaten the record but for the untimely death of Mrs. Barry, who had faded out of life at Tom's birth. She was then just thirty-two, but she looked forty.

To her husband, however, gazing at her dead face, surrounded by its lilies and white roses, she looked seventeen again—the age at which he had married her—and though he was a man entirely wrapped up in his books and theories, it is an almost certain thing that he never forgot her, and that he mourned and lamented for her as few men whose lives are set in smoother places do for their beloved.

Miss Barry, his sister, came on the death of his wife and took possession of the house, Susan being then just thirteen. She had but a bare sum wherewith to clothe and keep herself, and was therefore of little use in helping the household where money was concerned; and it was therefore with a sense of thankfulness that the Rector four years ago accepted the charge of Dominick

Fitzgerald, an orphan, and the son of a stepbrother of his wife.

The poor, pretty wife was then a year dead, but he knew all about Dominick's people. The Rector himself came of a good old Irish family, and his wife had been even more highly connected. Indeed, the lad who came to Mr. Barry four years ago, though he had inherited little from his father, would in all probability succeed to his uncle's title and five or six thousand a year—a small thing for a baronet, but, still, worth having. Of course, there was always a chance that the uncle, a middle-aged man, might marry, though he was consumptive and generally an invalid; but all that lay in the future, and at present it was decided that the boy should be given a profession; but having proved remarkably idle and wild at school—though nothing disgraceful was ever laid to his charge—his uncle in one of his intervals of good health had desired that he should be sent down to Mr. Barry, for whom Sir Spencer Fitzgerald had an immense respect and a little fear, for a few reasons that need not be specified, though, if Sir Spencer only knew it, the Rector was the last man in the world to betray the secrets of anyone.

The Rector accepted the charge gladly. He had passed several young men (who had been private pupils of his before his marriage) very successfully for the Civil Service, and he was doing his best for Dominick now, whom from the very first he liked, in spite of the reputation for idleness that came with him.

Indeed, Dom Fitzgerald had fallen into the family circle as though it had been made for him, and had grown to be quite a brother to his new-found cousins. He at once grew fond of Susan, and became on the spot a chum of Carew's, who was reading with his father for the army and expected to pass next year. And he quarrelled all day long with Betty, who accepted him as a 'pal' from the moment of his appearing. Betty inclined towards slang.

As for the children, they all loved him;

and, indeed, it must be said that he loved them, and spent a considerable amount of the fifty pounds allowed him for yearly pocket-money upon them.

'Well, where is she?' persists he, turning a lazy eye from one to another, at last resting it on Susan.

'She has gone down to Father Murphy's about Jane,' says Susan reluctantly. 'You know Jane is always breaking everything, and to-day she broke that old cup of our great-grandmother's, and Aunt Jemima was very angry. She has gone to tell Father Murphy about it, and to say she will never take a Roman Catholic servant again unless he punishes Jane severely.'

'And Father Murphy will laugh,' says Carew, with a shrug. 'He knows she must take Catholic servants or do without them. All the Protestant girls of that class here are farmers' daughters, and either won't go into service at all, or else only to Lady O'Donovan's or the O'Connors'.'

'Oh, you should have heard Jane!' cries

Betty, going off into one of her peals of laughter. 'When Aunt Jemima had reduced her to a rage, she came in weeping to me. All the forlorn hopes fall back upon me.'

'True, even this poor old forlorn one,' says Dom promptly, seizing his opportunity to lift his head from her gown to drop it upon her lap.

After which there is a scuffle.

'Oh, never mind Dom!' says Susan impatiently. 'What did Jane say to you about the cup?'

'She said—— Go away, Dom.'

'I'm sure she didn't,' says Dom, with an aggrieved air. 'It's an aspersion on my character, Susan. You don't believe this, do you?'

'She said,' goes on Betty, very properly taking no notice of the interruption: '"Law, Miss Betty, miss, did ye iver hear the like o' that? Did ye iver hear such a row about nothin'?"'

'"It wasn't about nothing," I said; "because you know how even father valued that cup, though an uglier thing I never saw in my life."'

'"Fegs, I don't know what ye call anythin'," said Jane (she was crying all the time; you know how she can roar); "but yer aunt herself tould me that that cup is a hundhred years ould if a day, an' wid that to make sich a screech over it! Faix, it must have bin rotten wid age, miss; an' no wondher it come to bits in me hands."'

They are all delighted with the story.

'I don't think Aunt Jemima would have been so cross with poor Jane,' says Susan, in a low tone and with a glance round her to make sure of no one's being within hearing, 'but for those eggs this morning.'

'The eggs under the speckled hen?' asks Jacky; 'I heard her speaking about them. Won't they come out?'

Susan shakes her head, and Carew and Dominick edge a little out of sight. The latter, under a pretence of feeling too warm, hides his face under the big straw hat that Betty has thrown upon the grass beside her.

'They should have come out ten days ago,' says Susan; 'but they'—she casts an uncertain glance at Carew, who has turned over and is now lying with his face upon his arms, and is evidently developing ague-fever—'but they didn't.'

'Were they all addled?' asks Jacky, with amazement.

'No; they were all boiled,' says Susan.

'Boiled!' says little Bonnie, sitting up with an effort. 'Who boiled them—the hen?'

At this there is a stifled roar from under Betty's hat, whereupon the owner of it lifts it and discovers Mr. Fitzgerald plainly on the point of apoplexy.

'Just the sort of thing one would expect from you,' says she scornfully. 'No wonder you want to hide your face; but you shan't do it under my hat, anyhow.'

'Oh, Carew, think of that poor hen waiting and waiting for three weeks, and then for ten days more; I call it horrid,' says Susan. 'I really think you ought to be ashamed of yourselves, you two.'

'Ought we? Then we will be,' says Dom; 'never shall it be said that I shirked my duty, at all events. Carew, get out of that, and be ashamed of yourself instantly.'

'Oh, that's all very fine,' says Betty, 'trying to get out of it like that; but let me tell you that I think——'

However, what Betty may think of people who put boiled eggs under sitting hens is for ever lost to posterity, because at this moment Jane, with red eyes and a depressed demeanour, comes hurrying up to them across the small lawn, a covered basket in her hand.

CHAPTER XIII.

'O, coward conscience, how dost thou afflict me!'

'For you, miss,' says she, handing the basket to Susan.

Susan turns crimson. That basket! She knows it well.

'For me?' stammers she.

'Yes, miss.'

'Who'—nervously—'who brought it?'

'A boy, miss.' For an instant Susan's heart feels relief, but for an instant only.

'Whose boy?' falters she.

'I don't know, miss. He came an' wint in a flash like. I hope, miss, as there isn't anythin' desthructive in it,' says Jane, whose misfortunes of the morning have raised in her a pessimistic spirit. 'They do say thim moonlighters are goin' about agin.'

'Do you mean to say the—the messenger said nothing?'

'No, miss, except that it was for you. That was all, miss; and I'm not deaf, though I wish I was before I heard all that was said to me this mornin' about an ould cup that——' Here she lifts her apron and sniffs vigorously behind it.

'Oh, it can't be for me,' says Susan, with decision; 'take it away, Jane. There has been some mistake, of course. Take it away at once. Do you hear? The—the boy will probably call for it again in a little time.'

'I don't think he will, miss; he looked like a runaway,' says Jane.

'Good heavens! how interesting,' says Mr. Fitzgerald, breaking at last into the charmed silence that has held them all since the advent of Jane and the mysterious basket. 'Who can this unknown admirer be? No doubt it contains roses'—staring at the basket—'or heliotropes—heliotrope in the language of flowers means devotion! Susan, are you above a peep?'

'Yes, I am,' says Susan hastily.

'I am not,' says Betty, springing forward and pulling open the cover. 'Oh, I say, cherries! and such beauties, too! Susan, you are in luck!'

'And so are we,' says Fitzgerald, putting a hand lightly over her shoulder and drawing up a bunch of the pretty fruit between his fingers.

'Oh, I think we ought not to eat them—I do indeed,' says Susan, in a small agony. There can be no doubt now about the fact that the thief, repentant and struck to the very soul by her eloquent pleadings, had sought to redeem himself in her eyes by sending the stolen cherries to her. Whether with a view of giving her the pleasure of eating them, or with the higher desire of proving to her that he hadn't devoured them, must, she feels and hopes (because to meet him again would be very unpleasant to her), for ever remain unknown.

'Poor fellow!' thinks she, regarding the cherries with mixed emotions that are not altogether devoid of admiration for her own hitherto unimagined powers of persuasion; 'he was certainly and sincerely penitent. One could see that.' She feels quite an uplifting of her soul. Perhaps, who knows? she has been born as a worthy successor to Mrs. Fry, or some of those good people! But then, after all, it is, undoubtedly, to Mr. Crosby he should have made restitution, not to her. It is, however, difficult to restore Irish cherries—a rather perishable commodity—to an owner who happens to be at the moment in the middle of Africa, or America, or China, for all she knows.

'Not eat them!' says Betty indignantly. 'Why, what else are you going to do with them—make them into jam?'

'They are not mine—I'm sure they are not mine,' says Susan. 'Who, for instance, could have sent them?'

Here Jacky makes a movement.

'Jacky, you know nothing!' cries Susan,

turning indignant, warning eyes upon him; whereupon Jacky, remembering his promise, subsides once again into dismal silence.

'Jacky, I smell a conspiracy,' says Dominick, who has caught the look between them; 'and you are the head-centre. Speak, boy, whilst yet there is time!'

'I've nothing to say,' says Jacky sulkily; he is naturally of a somewhat morose disposition, and now feels positively ill at not being able to divulge the delightful story of which these glowing cherries are the result.

'Susan, I do believe you have at last got an admirer,' says Carew, in the complimentary tone of the orthodox brother, who never can understand why on earth any fellow can admire his sister. 'Come! out with it; he seems a sensible fellow, any way. Flowers are awful rot, but there's something in cherries.'

'Betty, when I fall in love with you I'll present you with a course of goodies,' says Dominick, regarding that damsel with an encouraging eye.

'I have no admirers, as you all know,' says Susan, her pale and lovely face a little heightened in colour. She is thinking with horror of what would have happened if that poor awful thief had brought them in person. But, of course, he was afraid.

'Perhaps Lady Millbank sent them,' suggests Betty, after a violent discussion with Fitzgerald on the head of his last remark. 'I saw her in town yesterday.'

'So did I,' says Carew. 'Like a sack—not tied in the middle.'

Susan feels almost inclined in the emergencies of the moment to say 'Perhaps so,' and let it stand at that, but conscience forbids her.

'She would have sent a footman and her card,' says she dejectedly. 'No'—decidedly, and preparing to close up the basket—'they are not meant for me, and even if they were, I could not accept them, unless I knew where they came from.'

'Do you mean that you are not going to give us some?' says Betty, rising, not only figuratively, but actually, to the occasion, and standing over Susan. 'I never heard anything so mean in all my life.'

'Susan,' says Fitzgerald mildly but firmly, 'if you think to escape alive from this spot with these cherries, let me at once warn you of a sense of impending danger.'

'Oh, I say, Susan, don't be a fool!' says Carew, turning his lazy length upon the grass, a manœuvre that brings him much closer to Susan and the cherries.

'It's a beastly shame!' says Jacky, in a growl. And at this little Tom, as if moved to the very soul, or stomach, sets up a piteous howl.

Susan, with all the 'young martyr' air about her, looks sternly round. No; she will not give in, and it's perfectly disgusting of them to think so much of eating things. Her glance finishes at Jacky, who is scowling and threatening her with the fellest of all fell eyes, and then descends at last on Bonnie—Bonnie, who is lying in her arms, his pretty, thin, patient little face against her shoulder. Poor little Bonnie! darling little Bonnie! who has said nothing—not a word —but whose gentle eyes are now resting on the fruit; Bonnie, whose appetite is always miserable—so difficult to please. Susan, seeing that silent, wistful glance, feels her heart sink within her.

Must she—must she deny him, her poor little delicate boy, her best beloved of all the many that she loves? Oh, she must! she will be firm. These cherries really are not hers. Even for Bonnie she——

The child stirs in her arms and sighs, the faintest, gentlest little sigh—only one who loved him could have heard it; but with that little sigh went out all Susan's stern resolutions. Almost unconsciously her hand goes towards the basket that holds the cherries. Slowly, slowly at first, as if held back; but as it nears the glowing fruit it makes a rush, as it were, dives into it, and in a second more Bonnie's thin little paws are filled with a huge and crimson bunch of the sweet cherries.

Alas for Susan's principles! They have

all vanished away like snow in the sun, beneath two little pain-filled eyes.

Alas for Susan's principles again! As Bonnie's white little face lights up as he catches the pretty fruit, and bites one of them in two with his sharp childish teeth, and as after that he lifts the other half of it to Susan's mouth, and presses it against her closed but smiling lips, she does not refuse him. She opens her lips, and, against all her beliefs, lets the stolen thing glide between them. The happy laughter of the child as she takes the fruit is nectar to her, and in a little joyous way she hugs him to her, catching him against her breast; and though she does not know it, her one thought is this: 'Let all things go so long as this one is happy.'

And certainly Bonnie for the moment is happy with his cherries. But the cherry he gave her is the first and only one out of her basket that passes between her lips. And that is self-denial, I can tell you from experience, for a girl of eighteen.

After this there is a general raid upon the

basket, Betty and Fitzgerald being quite conspicuous in their efforts to secure the largest cherries, whilst Jacky runs them very hard. And Susan, afraid lest the supply should fail before Bonnie gets a handsome share, pulls him to her and fills his little hands. But her own hands? Never! Stern is her youthful virtue. Those stolen cherries! No, no, she could not touch them, and, besides, to watch Bonnie's delight in them is enough for her.

Bonnie! It seems such a sad critique upon the little fragile child racked with rheumatism and so sadly disabled by it.

In happier days, when he was, in truth, the bonniest little being of them all, his poor mother — now mercifully in heaven — had given him the dear pet name. And of course it had clung to him through all the ills that followed.

The beginning was so simple, so easy to be described. A wet day when the child had escaped from home and had been forgotten until the early dinner reminded them of him. There were so many to remember, and they all ran so loosely here and there, that up to that hour no one had missed him. His mother was dead. The keynote of course lay there. She was dead and lying in her grave for a year or more, and the young things who tried to take her place, when they had asked a question or two, never thought of Bonnie again. Carew, the eldest boy, then only twelve, did not appear at dinner either, and it was naturally and carelessly supposed that Bonnie was with him.

Alas for little Bonnie! Late that night he was discovered and brought home, saturated to the skin, and almost lifeless. Asleep he had been found beneath the shade of a big beech-tree; and sleep eternal he would have known indeed had he not been discovered before morning by the frightened people from the Vicarage, who, when night set in, had gone hunting for him far and near. The Rector himself, roused from his notes and papers by Susan's terrors, had joined in the search; but it was Susan who found him, tired, exhausted (after a ramble in which he had lost himself, poor little soul!), and wet through from the rain that had fallen incessantly since three o'clock in the afternoon.

It was Susan who carried him home, staggering sometimes beneath the weight, but strong in the very misery of her fear. When at last home was reached, it was Susan who undressed him, and lay awake the long night through with him, holding him in her warm arms to heat his shivering little body. And, indeed, when the morning came he seemed nothing the worse for his exposure.

But towards the evening he began to shiver again, and next day he was lying prone, racked with all the pangs of rheumatic fever. They twisted and tore his little frame, and though at the last the doctor pulled him through, and he rose again from his bed, it was but as a shadow of his former merry self—a stricken child, a cripple for life.

Poor Susan—then thirteen—took it sorely to heart. Her mother in heaven—had she looked down that night when Bonnie lay under the dripping tree, and seen her pretty lamb alone, deserted?—the mother who had left him to Susan to look after and care for. She had seemed to think more of Bonnie in her dying moments than of the baby who had brought death to her with his own life. Susan had been left in charge, as it were—sweet Susan, who was barely twelve, and who, with her soft, shy ways and lovely face, should have been left in charge herself to someone capable of guiding her tender footsteps across earth's thorny paths.

Her remorse dwelt with her always, and became a burden to her, and made havoc of her colour for many a day. Of course she grew out of all that—youth, thank God, is always growing—and at last, after many days, joy came to her again, and all the glorious colour of life, and all the sweetness of it. But she never lost a little pulsing grief that came to her every now and then, telling her how she ought to have seen that Bonnie had not wandered so far afield.

Oh, if only he could be made strong and

well again. This was the heart of the sad song that she often sang for herself alone, when time was given her in her busy life.

She had dreamed dreams of how it would be with the little lad if he could have been sent abroad. She had heard of certain baths, and of wonderful cures worked by them. If he could go abroad to one of them he might recover. But such baths were as far out of her reach as heaven itself. It seemed hard to Susan, to whom life was still a riddle. And she reproached herself always, and always mourned that there would never come a time when Bonnie would be strong again, as he was when his mother left him, and when she might meet that dear mother in heaven without fear of reproaches.

All this lay in the background of Susan's life, and now, as years grew, seldom came to the front. But the child was ever her first thought and her dearest delight, and the fact that he was not as his brothers were was the one little blot on the happiness of her young life.

CHAPTER XIV.

> ' O that this calculating soul would cease
>   To forecast accidents, Time's limping errors,
> And take the present, with the present's peace,
>   Instead of filling life's poor day with terrors.'

About seven o'clock, Wyndham (who had come up to Dublin by the afternoon train), going down Nassau Street, finds hmself face to face with a tall, big, good-humoured-looking man of about thirty-two.

'Hallo! that you?' cries the latter, stopping Wyndham, who, in somewhat preoccupied mood, would have gone by without seeing him. The preoccupation disappears at once, however, and it is with genuine pleasure that he grasps the hand held out to him.

'You, Crosby, of all men!'

'Even so.'

'Why, last week, when we met in Paris, you told me you were going to Vienna to see a friend there.'

'The friend came to me at Paris instead the very day after you left.'

'But I thought you had arranged with him to go on an expedition to some unpronounceable place in Africa?'

'So I had, but he proved disappointing. Hummed and hawed, said he couldn't go just now, but perhaps a little later on. One saw through him at once. I told him I never travelled about with fellows' wives, and that settled it.'

'He was going to be married?'

'Of course. Love was writ large all over him—in huge capitals. And he was in such a hurry over everything. People in love are always in a hurry—to get back. So I dismissed him with my blessing, and a bauble for the venturesome young woman he has chosen to explore life's boundless ways with him. R.I.P. He's done for; and a right good fellow he was, too! Well, what's up with you?'

'With me?'

'Think I can't see? You're out of your luck in some way.'

'Nothing much, any way,' says Wyndham, with an involuntary smile.

'Too vague—too vague by half,' says Crosby, laughing. It is the happiest, heartiest laugh. 'Come, what's the matter? Out with it. Money?'

'No, no,' says the barrister, laughing in turn.

'Still, there is something.'

'Is there? I don't know,' says Wyndham, in a tone half comical, half forlorn.

At this Crosby thrusts his arm into his, and wheels him down the street.

'It must be hunger,' says he gaily, seeing the other is not ready for confession yet. That the confession will come he knows perfectly well. Ever since they were boys together, Wyndham, whose brain was then, as now, very superior to Crosby's, had still always given in to the personal attractions of the stronger and older boy, whose big fists often fought Wyndham's battles for him on the public playground.

Crosby had been a big boy then; he is a big man now, and, in spite of his adventurous wanderings by land and sea, looks younger than Wyndham, though he is actually four years older. A splendid man, bronzed, bearded, and broad-shouldered, with the grand look of one who has been through many a peril and many a fight, who has led a cleanly life, and can look the world in the face fearlessly. His eyes are large and blue, and full of life and gaiety. He has a heart as true as gold, and a strong right arm, good for the felling of a foe or the saving of a friend.

'For my own part, I'm starving,' says he. 'Come along; we're near our club, and you'll dine with me. Considering what a stranger I am in my own land, you'll be able to help me out a bit. I feel as if I did not know anyone—that is, if you are not going anywhere else. There's a wandering look about you. No? No other engagements? That's good.'

They have reached the steps of the Kildare Street Club by this time, and presently are in the pleasant dining-room.

'By the way, talking of engagements,' says Crosby, between the soup and fish, 'I have one for to-night, at your aunt's—Mrs. Prior's In some odd fashion she heard I was in Dublin, and sent a card to the Gresham for me. You'—glancing at Wyndham's evening dress—'are going somewhere, too, perhaps?'

'There, too,' says Wyndham. 'I've got out of it a good deal lately; but it doesn't do to offend her overmuch. She's touchy. And the old man, my uncle, Lord Shangarry —you remember him, how he used to tip us at school long ago?—makes quite a point of my being civil to her.'

'To her, or——'

'My cousin?' Wyndham lifts his brows. 'I feel sure my cousin is as indifferent to me as I am to her.' He pauses. 'Still, I will not conceal from you that my uncle desires a marriage between us.'

'Is this the cause of your late depression?' asks Crosby, with a quizzical expression.

'Not it,' says Wyndham. 'By-the-by'— a little hurriedly—'what of that late adventure of yours in Siam? You were just telling me about it when——'

Crosby at once plunges into the interrupted anecdote, bringing it, however, to a somewhat sharp close.

'You know what life is!' says Wyndham a little moodily when it is over. 'I envy you; I often think I too should like to break off the threads of society that bind one in, and start on a career that would leave civilization and—its worries behind.'

'Its worries?'

'Well, gossip for one thing, and that delicate espionage that so often leads to the damning of a man.'

'Poor old boy! Got into deep water,' thinks Crosby whilst toying with his champagne.

'Once in it, one never gets out of civilization,' says he. 'It sticks to one like a burr. Don't hope for that when you start on the wild career you speak of. For myself, I like civilization. It's clean, for one thing—savages don't do much in the way of washing. But I confess I like wandering for wandering's sake. It's a mania with me. Here to-day and gone to-morrow—that's the motto that suits me. Yet, I dare say, in time I shall get tired of it.'

'Not you. Where are you going next?'

'Not made up my mind yet. But I'll tell you where I've been last—right into Arcadia! A difficult place to find nowadays, the savants tell you; but the savants, like the Cretans, are all liars. And in my Arcadia I fell in with an adventure, and met——'

He pauses, and, leaning back in his chair, clasps his hands behind his head and gives way to silent laughter. Evidently some memory is amusing him.

'Someone who apparently was kind to you,' says Wyndham indifferently, breaking off from the stem, but not eating, the purple grapes before him.

'Kind!' says Crosby. 'Hardly that.'

'Unkind?'

'More than that.'

'She told you——'

'That I was a thief.' Wyndam's indifference ceases for a moment.

'Strong language,' says he.

'True, I assure you. Do I look like one? Ever since that terrible denunciation I have often asked myself whether so much knocking about as I have known has not ruffianized me in appearance, at all events.'

'Where on earth is the Arcadia you speak of?' asks Wyndham.

'Well, to tell you everything, I went down to Curraghcloyne this morning to have a look at the old place.'

'What! There! Why, I was there to-day, too,' says Wyndham, and then pauses, as if suddenly sorry he had spoken.

'We must have missed each other, then, and come up by different trains.'

'I suppose so,' says Wyndham slowly. 'And so your Arcadia is Curraghcloyne? Fancy an adventure there!' He shrugs his shoulders, and leans back in his chair. 'You have had so many real adventures that I expect you like to revel in imagining one now and then.'

'Perhaps so,' says Crosby. 'Still, even in Arcadia one doesn't like to be called a thief. I say, it is getting late, isn't it? Your aunt spoke of ten. It is now well after eleven. Buck up, my child, and let us on.'

CHAPTER XV.

> 'The web of our life is of mingled yarn,
> Good and ill together.'

THE rooms are crowded to excess, and it is with difficulty that Crosby and Wyndham make their way to the place where someone has told them their hostess is to be found. They have arrived very late, in spite of Crosby's attempt at haste, so late, indeed, that already some of the guests are leaving —a fact that has somewhat embarrassed their journey up the staircase. The heat is intense, and the perfume of the many roses makes the air heavy.

Quite at the end of the music-room Wyndham sees his aunt, and presently she, seeing him and Crosby in the doorway, makes them a faint salutation. The Hon. Mrs. Prior is a tall woman, with a high, aristocratic nose, fair hair, and blue eyes, now a little pale. She was the handsomest of the three daughters of Sir John Burke, and, what is not always the case, had made the best marriage. Her youngest sister, Kate, had, however, done very well, too, when she married James Wyndham, but the eldest sister had made a distinct fiasco of her life. She had run away with a ne'er-do-weel, a certain Robert Haines, who came from no one knew where, and went no one knew where, either, taking Sir John's favourite daughter with him. It was hushed up at the time, but the old man had caused ceaseless secret inquiries to be made for the missing daughter, always, however, without result. It was for a time a blot upon the family history, but it was forgotten after awhile, and Mrs. Prior and her daughter have for some time taken leading parts in Dublin society.

A tall, thin woman is singing very beautifully as the two young men enter, and Mrs. Prior's slight movement of recognition to her nephew conveys with it a desire that he should not seek her until the song has come to an end. And presently the last quivering note dies away upon the air, and the crowd is once more in motion. Lady H—— is being congratulated on the beauties of her voice by many people, and Mrs. Prior, having done her part, is now able to receive her nephew and Crosby without having to pause and wonder who she is to speak to next.

Indeed, Lady H——'s singing has virtually wound up the evening. Few would care to sing after her, and now the rooms are beginning to look deserted.

'Always a laggard, Paul,' says his aunt, who, having bidden good-bye to her principal guests, has left the rest to her daughter. 'But I suppose something of it must be put down to to-night.' She smiles at Crosby, whom she has known since he was a little boy. 'You should have been here earlier, you two; she sang even better in the beginning of the evening. It was "Allan Water," and you know how that would suit her voice. But now that you have come so late, you must stay a little later and have supper with Josephine and me.'

She talks on to them in her cultivated yet somewhat hard voice, rising now and then to say good-bye to someone, until the rooms are quite cleared and her daughter is able to join them.

Josephine Prior comes across the polished floor of the music-room to where they are sitting in a curtained recess; she is as tall as her mother, and as fair, and a little harder. Miss Prior is undoubtedly the handsomest girl in Dublin this season (now all but over), and has been for the past two or three. Tall, *distinguée* and with irreproachable manners, there are very few who can outdo her. She sweeps up to them now, her pretty silken skirts falling gracefully around her, and her mother, rising, motions her into her own seat, that next to Wyndham's, while she sinks into a chair on Crosby's left.

It had been a settled thing with Mrs. Prior for years that Josephine, her only child, should marry Paul Wyndham, who, though only a barrister, is still a very rising one, and heir to his grand-uncle, Lord Shangarry. To know Josephine a countess! There lay all the hope, all the ambition, of Mrs. Prior's life, and the fact that old Lord Shangarry shared her hopes about this matter naturally led to the idea that in time it must be accomplished. If Paul were to offend his uncle, then—well, then, the title would be his indeed; but the enormous income now attached to it, not being entailed, could be left as Lord Shangarry wished. Few people fly in the face of Providence where thousands a year are concerned, and Mrs. Prior depended upon Wyndham's common-sense to secure him as a husband for her daughter. As for Wyndham, though up to this not a syllable has passed between him and Josephine to bind him to her in any way, he has of late brought himself to believe that a marriage with her, considering the stakes, is not out of the question. She is a handsome girl, too, and as a countess would look the part.

Now, as she seats herself beside him, he again acknowledges the beauty of her chiselled nose and chin. But——yes; there is a but. All at once it occurs to him that beauty is very seldom to be found in perfect features. The really artistic face has always one feature quite beyond the bounds of art. Strange that it had not occurred to him before! Still, Josephine is undoubtedly handsome.

Josephine's voice is like her mother's —clear and very hard. She is talking now.

'Do you know we were down in your part of the world the other day?' says she. 'We were lunching with dear Lady Millbank, and then went on to your cottage. We wanted to get some flowers. You know how mean Lady Millbank is about her roses, so we decided on saying nothing to her, and trusting to your place. But when we got there'—with an elephantine attempt at playfulness—'the cupboard was bare, at all events to us, because we could not get in.'

'Yes, so odd!' says Mrs. Prior. 'We rang, and rang, and rang, but no one came for quite a long time. At last your housekeeper appeared, a most disagreeable person, my dear Paul. She was, indeed, almost rude, and said she had your orders to admit nobody.'

She looks back at Wyndham, who looks back at her with an immovable countenance.

'Not my orders, certainly,' says he calmly. 'I was abroad until the other day, you know, so I can hardly be responsible for Mrs. Moriarty's manœuvres.'

His voice is perfectly even, though a perfect storm of rage against Mrs. Denis is rendering him furious. Confound the woman! what does she mean by seeking to create a scandal out of a mere nothing—a mountain out of a mole-hill?

Crosby, glancing at him steadily for a moment, turns his eyes away again, and breaks into the discussion.

'I am sorry you did not go up to my place,' says he, addressing Miss Prior. 'It is quite a terrible thing to contemplate, your having been in want of flowers.'

'Ah, but you weren't there!' says Josephine, with a mild attempt at coquetry. 'If you had been, we might have made a raid on you.'

'Well, I'm at home now,' says Crosby cheerfully. 'You must come down some day soon, and help me to gather my roses.'

'You mean to stay, then?' says Josephine, leaning a little towards him across her mother. She is quite bent on marrying her cousin, though she is as indifferent to him as he is to her; but in the meantime she is not above a slight flirtation with Crosby. To tell the truth, this big, good-humoured, handsome man appeals to her far more than Paul has ever done.

'Until the autumn, at all events,' says he.

As for Wyndham, he is still sitting mute, apparently listening to his aunt's diatribes about society, and Dublin society in particular, but in reality raging over Mrs. Denis's shortcomings, and the deplorable Irish sympathetic nature that has led her to sacrifice everything—even the excellent situation she has at the Cottage—to a mere passing fancy for a girl whom she has known at the longest for four or five weeks.

Crosby, noting his abstraction, is still rattling along.

'Now, it's a promise, Mrs. Prior, isn't it? You'—here he glances deliberately at Josephine—'you will come and look round my place soon, won't you? I'm thinking of making up a little house-party in September or August, and I hope you and Miss Prior will leave a week open for me.' He throws a look over his shoulder. 'You too, Wyndham?'

'Thank you,' says Paul absently.

'What a charming idea!' cries Josephine ecstatically. Here she decides upon clapping her hands, and she does it in her perfectly well-bred way. The result is deadly. 'To stay with a bachelor! Mamma, you will consent?'

Mamma consents. Josephine, again leaning towards Crosby, says something delightful to him. It has seemed to her since Crosby's coming that to have two strings to your bow is a very desirable thing. Paul is well enough, and in the end, of course, she will marry him, though at times she has thought that he—— But, of course, that is nonsense. He would be afraid to marry anyone else — afraid of his uncle. What a pity he is not Mr. Crosby, or Mr. Crosby Paul! Well, one can't have everything one's own way, after all, and there is the title. Lady Shangarry—Mrs. Crosby. Yes; the title counts. But really Paul is so very dull, and Mr. Crosby, though he has no title, so infinitely better off than Paul will ever be, and the Crosbys are an old family, dating back to — goodness knows when! Still, a title!

Finally she gets back to the title, and stays there.

'But yes, really, dear Paul,' Mrs. Prior is saying, 'I think that housekeeper of yours, or caretaker, or whatever she is, takes too much upon her. I tried to explain to her I was your aunt, and, indeed, she has seen me several times, but I could not shake her determination to let no one in. Anyone might be excused for imagining that she was concealing something.'

'Garden-party for her own friends, no doubt,' says Crosby. He has cast a half-amused, half-inquiring glance at Wyndham; but the latter's face is impassive.

'I think it a little serious,' says Mrs. Prior. 'Young men, as a rule, are always imposed upon by women of her class—caretakers, of course, I mean,' with a careful glance at the innocent Josephine. 'Landladies and that. Do you think, dear Paul, that she is quite honest?'

'Quite, I think.'

'Then why this extraordinary step on her

part—this locking out your very nearest and'—with an open glance at Josephine—'dearest? No, no, George,' to Crosby, 'you really must not jest on this subject. I feel it is quite important where Paul is concerned. You really know of no reason, Paul, why she should have forbidden us an entrance?'

Is there meaning in the question? Wyndham looks at her steadily before replying.

'I was in France at the time,' says he carelessly. 'If she had a motive, how could I know it?'

Crosby leans back and crosses his arms negligently. 'What an idiotic equivocation!' thinks he.

'You certainly ought to speak to her about it.'

'Of course I shall speak to her.'

Crosby smiles.

'I really think you ought,' says Mrs. Prior. 'You can'—severely—'mention me if you wish. I consider she behaved extremely badly. And I quite tremble for the dear little old place. You know it was an uncle of ours—a grand-uncle of yours—who left the place to your mother, and as girls we—that is, your aunts and I—used to be very fond of running up from your grandfather's place in Kerry to spend a few weeks in it. We were all girls then—your mother, and I, and your —— ' She stops, and sneezes most opportunely behind her lace handkerchief. The innocent Josephine had touched her foot under cover of her gown. Of course the aunt who had disappeared so unpleasantly had better not be mentioned.

'I hope, Paul, you will see that this woman keeps the dear old place in order,' says Mrs. Prior rather hastily.

'To confess a dreadful truth,' says Wyndham, smiling somewhat briefly, 'I have almost made up my mind to let the Cottage. It has been rather a burden to me of late. And——'

'To let it. But why?'

'Well, as you see yourself,' says Wyndham desperately, 'Mrs. Moriarty does not seem capable of looking after it. It is an awful bore, you know, and'—with a rush of affection hitherto unborn—'the idea of her having kept you out of the place seems to put an end to my trust in her for ever.'

Crosby flicks a little point of dust off his coat-sleeve. 'Oh, the handsome liar!' thinks he.

'But, my dear boy, you must not be too precipitate. A word to her would perhaps——'

'I've quite made up my mind,' says Wyndham steadfastly. 'I shall look out for a tenant.'

'Dear Paul!' says Mrs. Prior, touched by this nephew-like act, 'I of course appreciate your sweetness in this matter. It is very dear of you to be so angry about the woman's incivility to me, and if you have made up your mind about getting a tenant for the dear old Cottage, I think I can help you.'

Here Crosby leans forward. It is proving very interesting.

'You mustn't take any trouble,' says Wyndham; 'I couldn't allow you.'

'It will be no trouble — for you,' says Josephine, breaking into the conversation very affectionately.

'Thanks awfully, but I think I've got a desirable tenant in my eye,' says Wyndham —'one suitable in every respect.'

'The real thing is to know if he is solvent,' says Mrs. Prior.

'Oh, I think so—I think so,' says Wyndham thoughtfully.

'Is he young or old?' asks Josephine, who feels she ought to show some interest in his affairs.

Wyndham remains wrapt up in thought for a moment, then apparently wakes up.

'Oh, the tenant,' says he dreamily. 'Not old; no, not old!'

'At that rate you must introduce us to him,' says Mrs. Prior, with quite surprising archness. 'Solvent and not old! Quite a desirable acquaintance! What is his name, Paul?'

'I don't know,' says Wyndham.

'Not know? But, my dear Paul!'

'I positively don't,' says Wyndham, in quite a loud voice. It occurs to Crosby that now at last he is telling the truth, and that he is wildly glad at being able to do so. But the truth! Where does it come in? Crosby grows curious. 'Strange as it may sound, the name is unknown to me. And for the matter of that nothing is settled. There have been only preliminaries. There must always be preliminaries, you know,' talking briskly to his aunt.

'Well, be careful,' says Mrs. Prior. 'And whatever you do, Paul, don't take a lady tenant. They are so difficult. Now promise me, Paul, you won't take a lady as a tenant.'

Providentially, at this moment the very late supper is announced, and Paul, rising, gives his arm to Josephine, after which the conversation drifts into other channels.

CHAPTER XVI.

'This is the short and long of it.'

THE moon is streaming brilliantly over the silent streets as the two men leaving Fitzwilliam Square turn presently into Stephen's Green and then down Dawson Street. Crosby's footsteps are bound for the Gresham Hotel, and Wyndham, who should have gone the other way, considering his rooms are in Elgin Road, walks with him silently, and so mechanically that it becomes at once plain to Crosby that he has lost himself a little in a world of troublous thought.

Determining to let him find his way out of his mind's labyrinth by himself, Crosby maintains a discreet silence, refraining even from good words and the whistle that has come to be part of him during his strange wanderings by sea and land, and is difficult to discard when in the midst of civilization.

It is not until they have reached the railings that run round Trinity College, where the glorious light of the moon is lighting up the old and splendid pile, that Wyndham speaks.

'I've had the deuce of a time,' says he.

'Well, I could see that,' says Crosby, turning his cigar in his fingers. 'I'm rather disappointed in you, do you know, Paul. How you are to make a fortune out of your profession is to me a mystery. Throw it up. You are certainly not a liar born.'

'I'm in a tight place,' says Wyndham disgustedly, 'but I dare say I'll get out of it. Well'—reluctantly—'good-night.'

'Not a bit of it,' says Crosby, tucking his arm into his; 'come and have a pipe with me, and—if you can bring yourself to it—give voice to this worry of yours, and get it off your mind.'

A pipe is a great help; soothed by it, and the influence of the society of his old chum, Wyndham, seated comfortably in a huge armchair in Crosby's room, tells the latter the whole of his remarkable acquaintance with his unknown guest at the Cottage.

It is, to confess the truth, a rather lame story, very lamely told; and at the close of it Wyndham looks at his friend, at least at as much of him as he can see, Crosby being now enclouded in smoke. He had been smoking very vigorously, indeed, all through the recital, and there had been moments when he had seemed to be choking, but whether altogether from the smoke Wyndham felt uncertain.

'Well, that's the story,' says he at last, flinging himself back in his chair.

There is a short silence.

'Then I suppose you could not think of a better one?' says Crosby, beginning to choke again.

'Oh, I knew how you'd take it—how any fellow would take it,' says Wyndham wrathfully. 'I can see that there isn't a soul in the world who would believe such an idiotic story as mine. But there it is, and you can take it or leave it as you like. But for all that, Crosby, you ought to know me well enough to understand that I should not trouble myself to lie to you unless there was occasion for it.'

At this Crosby gives way to a roar.

'Well, I honestly believe there's no occasion now,' says he; 'and for the rest, dear old chap! of course I believe every word you have said. You must be thoroughly hipped, or you'd have seen how I was enjoying the joke. Come, it seems we have both had adventures in Arcadia, and that we have both come in rather sorry fashion out of them.'

'Oh, you—you can afford to speak of adventures,' says Wyndham ruefully. 'You're accustomed to them, but I—I confess this last and first has been enough for me. You who have faced lions——'

'Not so many, after all,' interrupts Crosby,

laughing. 'Don't magnify them like that. I've shot a few, I confess, but I only seem to remember seven. One does remember them when one's face to face with them. But there is not such a lot to remember, after all.'

'It would serve, so far as I am concerned,' says Wyndham frankly. 'Indeed, I think I could do with one—always supposing he was dead. As for how I feel now, it is as though I were in a den of them, and I doubt if I'll come as well out of it as Daniel did.'

Crosby regards him with an amused eye.

'Apropos your tenant,' says he, 'when are you going to introduce your aunt to your young man?'

'Oh, get out!' says Wyndham.

'That's a lion if you like,' says Crosby.

'Which—my aunt or my tenant?'

'I haven't seen the tenant. Still, it strikes me that she will be a lion, too. I'd get out of that den if I were you.'

'Well, I want to. But what's one to do? I can't get rid of either of my lions.'

'Not even of the tenant?'

'I don't see how I can, now I have given my promise.'

'Well, introduce them to each other; that's a capital suggestion if you will only look into it. Whilst they claw each other, you may be able to make your escape.'

'Introduce them?' Wyndham pauses, as if sounding the proposition, then gives way to wrath. 'Hang it!' says he; 'you are worse than Job's three comforters all rolled into one.'

CHAPTER XVII.

'No hinge nor loop
To hang a doubt on.'

To-day is Sunday—the first Sunday since that eventful day when Susan had tackled and disarmed the thief, and certainly the warmest day that has come this season. In here in the church the heat is almost intolerable; and Susan, when the Litany begins, feels her devotion growing faint.

She has, indeed, up to this had a good deal of troublous excitement. To keep one eye on Jacky, who had left home in a distinctly resentful mood, and the other on Tommy, who doesn't believe in churches as a satisfactory playground, is a task to which few would be equal; and even now, when Tommy has been reduced to silence by Betty and lemon-drops, the excessive warmth of the day leaves Susan too tired to follow the beautiful service.

Mechanically she says, 'We beseech Thee to hear us, good Lord'; but her mind is wandering, and presently her eyes begin to wander too.

The curate, how hideous he is, poor little man! and what a pity he is so painfully conscious of the loss of his front tooth! and what a lovely light that is from the window falling on his gown! It must be nice outside now. How the flies are buzzing on the panes, just like the organ! Maria Tanner should not be laughing like that; if father saw her he would be so angry, and Maria is such a nice girl, and so clever—took all the prizes at the diocesan examination last year—and her sister is considered quite an excellent housemaid by Lady Millbank. What a pretty bonnet Lady Millbank has on! Those violets suit her. Who is the man in the pew behind her? Why, that is the Crosby pew, and——

For one awful minute Susan feels the walls of the church closing in upon her; a sensation of faintness, a trembling of the knees, oppress her. She is conscious of all this, and then the mist fades away.

No, no; of course it is not true. It is impossible. A remarkable likeness, no more. She could laugh almost at her own folly, and very nearly does so in her nervous state; but providentially the sight of a gloomy black and white tablet, erected to the memory of a dead and gone Crosby, that stands out from the wall right before her, prevents this act of desecration.

She—she will look again, if only to assure herself of her own folly. Slowly, slowly she lifts her eyes—the eyes that now are standing in a very white face—and looks with a desperate courage at the Crosby pew. Her eyes meet full the eyes of its one occupant, and then Susan tells herself that it is all over, and death alone is to be looked for.

For the eyes of the Crosby pew man are the eyes of Susan's thief. There can be no mistake about it any longer. The man who sits in Mr. Crosby's pew and Susan's repentant thief are one and the same.

Her eyes seem to cling to his. In the fever of horror that has overtaken her, she feels as if she could never remove them. For a full minute the man in the Crosby pew and Susan kneel, staring at each other; and then suddenly something happens. Lady Millbank, who is sitting in the pew before that of the Crosbys, turns round and hands Susan's thief a Prayer-book. That in itself would be very well—everyone should give a thief a Prayer-book—but Lady Millbank has accompanied her gift with a friendly nod of recognition, a charming smile—the smile that Susan so well knows, the smile that is only given to those whom Lady Millbank desires to honour or to be in with.

It is all quite plain now. The thief is Mr. Crosby, and Susan with a groan lets her face fall upon her clasped hands, and hopes vainly for the earth to open and swallow her up quick.

But the earth is a stupid thing, and never does anything nowadays. Not a single earthquake appears for Susan's accommodation, and the good old church is not conscious of even a quiver. The service goes on. The Litany is done. They all rise from their knees, and the curate gives out a hymn:

'"O Paradise! O Paradise!"'

Poor Susan feels as if 'O Purgatory!' would be much nearer it, so far as she is concerned. She would have stopped the hymn there and then if she could, feeling utterly upset and nervous. But it would take a great many feelings to stop a church service when it is once in full swing; and the hymn goes on gaily in spite of Susan's despair. It reaches, indeed, a most satisfactory ending, in spite of a slight contretemps occasioned by the one unlucky Protestant maid belonging to the Rectory, called Sarah.

Poor Sarah has this day for the first time put on a hat of which a brilliant magenta feather is the principal feature. Hitherto it has not caught Miss Barry's eye—a wonder in itself even greater than the magenta feather, as this estimable spinster, with a view to keeping the servants' moral conduct perfect, has elected that they shall sit on a bench in the big square Rectory pew right before her and her nephew and nieces.

It is at the beginning of the first verse that Miss Barry's eye lights on the monstrosity in Sarah's hat. Feathers and flowers are abominations in Miss Barry's eyes when worn by the 'common people,' as she calls those beneath her in the social scale. How dare that impertinent girl come to church with such an immodest ornament on her head! What on earth is the world coming to? She must, she will, speak to her; impossible to let her enjoy that feather another second.

If she can't speak, she can at all events sing at her.

She darts across the pew, and, leaning over Sarah's shoulder, sings piercingly into her ear:

THE PROFESSOR'S EXPERIMENT

"'O Paradise! O Paradise." Sarah, what do you mean?' (Rising note.) 'How dare' (prolonged shriek on top note) 'you wear that feather, girl! Where did you get that hat?'

She is simply screaming this to the hymn-tune. You all know the hymn, of course, and can understand how Miss Barry's voice rose to a shrill yell in the 'dare.' Sarah, with a convulsive start, turns round. It seems to her that this loud voice shouting in her ear must be heard by every other soul in the church; and frightened, ashamed, she sinks down into her seat, and prepares to hide herself and the magenta feather behind her Prayer-book. But at this breach of church etiquette Miss Barry grows even more incensed, and proceeds to rouse the wretched girl to a sense of her further iniquity by well-directed and vigorous punches and prods of her Prayer-book on her back. Whereon Sarah, dissolved in tears, rises to her feet once more. She is evidently on the verge of hysterics, and would have undoubtedly given way to them, but that at this moment Betty, who is afraid of nothing under heaven, lays her hand on Miss Barry's arm, and forcibly pulls her back to her accustomed place.

The hymn has now come to an end, and only Sarah's stifled groanings are heard upon the air. Most people take these to be the buzzing of the innumerable bluebottles collected in the window-panes, so that the whole affair goes off better than might have been expected.

Slowly, slowly, go the minutes; slower and slower still is the voice of the curate, as he intones the Commandments. The bluebottles, as if invigorated by it, buzz louder than ever, until poor Sarah's sobs are completely drowned.

The heat grows more and more intense. Jacky, beneath its pressure, has fallen sound asleep, and is now giving forth loud and handsome snorings. Miss Barry, horrified, makes frantic signs to Dominick, who is next to the culprit, to stop this unsolicited addition to the church music that Jacky has so 'kindly consented' to give, and Dom waves back at her wildly. No, no, of course. He quite understands; he will see that no one interferes with the dear boy's slumbers on any account whatever. The wavings backwards and forwards grow fast and furious—furious on the part of Miss Barry, and really as fast as lightning on the part of Mr. Fitzgerald, who is having a thoroughly *bon quart d'heure;* but Carew ends it.

He has been trying mentally to get through one of his papers for his next examination, and finding Jacky's snores a deadly interruption to his thoughts, he fetches that resounding hero a telling kick on a part that shall be nameless, which brings him not only to his senses, but the floor.

There is a momentary confusion in the Rectory pew; but as every member of the congregation is more or less drowsing, Jacky is picked up and restored to his seat before the real meaning of the confusion is known. And, indeed, when anyone does look, all the Barrys are sitting so demure and innocent that no one could connect them with anything out of the way. Susan, alone flushed and unnerved, in spite of her determination not to do it, looks quickly at the Crosby pew, to find the thief looking at her with a singular intensity of regard. It is at this moment that Susan, for the first time in her young, happy life, wakes to sympathy with those unfortunate people who sometimes wish that they were dead.

The curate, a short, squat little man—a man so short, indeed, that a footstool has had to be placed in the pulpit for him to let the congregation see him as he preaches—is now droning away like the flies, 'shooting out shafts of eloquence to the bucolic mind' is how he puts it when writing to his people; but even his people, if here, could hardly catch the shafts to-day. The fact is, he has not yet had time to get in the teeth he lost by his fall last week; and, however admirable his discourse may be, the beauties of it are known to him alone.

The farmers who are awake are leaning

forward, their hands to their ears to catch the Gospel words that never reach them. Lady Millbank has fallen gracefully asleep. Sarah is still weeping copiously, but now, thank Heaven, quietly. The curate, vainly striving to pronounce his 'this' and his 'that,' grows more and more nervous. He leans over the pulpit, and thunders at the sleeping farmers and at the leading families around, in whose pews, too, Somnus is holding a full court. Farther and farther he leans, striving with his parishioners as much as with his teeth; a very passion of anxiety grows upon him. He lifts his arms from the desk before him—the desk that is supporting him—and waves them frantically.

'Hear—hear, my brethren,' cries he. 'Hear and see——'

His cry, like the 'Excelsior' young man's clarion, rings loud and clear. It wakes some of the sleepy members, who look up to see what it is all about. But when they do look up there is nothing to see.

Most unexpectedly and disgracefully—considering its relation to the Church—the footstool has given way with a crash, and Mr. Haldane, the curate, has given way with it, and disappeared, holus bolus, into the big old pulpit.

For quite a minute, though no doubt 'to memory dear,' the curate is certainly 'lost to sight;' and when at last he ventures once more to mount the offending stool, and look down at his parishioners, it is to find that the far larger half of them are gladly streaming down the aisle to the fresh air outside, under the fond delusion that 'church is over.'

These are the specially drowsy ones. The crash caused by the curate's unpremeditated descent had roused them from their happy dreams, and, on opening their eyes, seeing no preacher in the pulpit, they had naturally come to the conclusion that the performance was at an end.

Vain to call them back. Mr. Haldane spreads out his arms to heaven in a mournful appeal, but, hearing some unmistakable tittering to his left, turns, and incontinently flies.

CHAPTER XVIII.

' Life is thorny, and youth is vain !'

NOT so quickly as Susan, however. He could hardly have flown with the fleetness of that heart-troubled nympth. She—at the first chance, when her father, rising hurriedly at the flight of his curate, had breathed the blessing—had flown down the side-aisle and through the small oak door into the golden air outside ; and from there into a small lane filled with flowering weeds, that led straight homewards.

Running—racing, indeed—goes Susan, with her heart on fire, as her cheeks, and her lovely, child-like eyes darkened and bright with the sense of coming disaster.

She does not draw breath until she finds

herself safe in her own little room, with just five precious minutes (precious, unusual five minutes, gained only by that swift run that has left them all behind) in which to think out as calmly as she can what has befallen her.

A thief! She had called him a thief! He—Mr. Crosby—the distinguished traveller! Oh! what is to become of her? Not even now, at this last gasp, does she try to persuade herself that the man in the Crosby pew was a fraud—that he wasn't Mr. Crosby. She knows as positively as though she had been introduced to him that he is Mr. Crosby.

Introduced to him! As if—— She covers her face with her hands. No, no; there need be no fear of that. He will go away soon—at once. People say he cannot bear civilized life; that he always hankers after savages, and lions, and things. He will go away, of course. Oh, if only he will go away soon enough, and never come back! Susan, with her hands before her gentle eyes, has sudden dreams of people who have been devoured by lions, and for the first time fails to see the extreme horror of it.

Yes, he will go away soon; and in the meantime—well, in the meantime it is very unlikely that she will come face to face with him.

'Susan, Susan! are you there?'

'Yes,' says Susan. She goes to the door, and finds Jacky on the threshold of it.

'Dinner is ready,' says that solemn youth; 'and they sent me up for you.'

'I can't come down,' says Susan. 'I have a headache. Jacky—dear, dear Jacky, say I have a headache. And I have, too—I have indeed. There won't be any lie. The heat —you must have felt the heat in church—you fell asleep——'

'Yes, I know,' says Jacky, in his queer way, that always expresses anger with difficulty suppressed. 'You won't come down, then?'

'No; I can't—I——' She lifts her hand to her head.

Jacky hesitates, turns slowly, and then throws a glance at her.

'Susan, did you see that man in the Crosby pew?'

Susan's nerves being a little overwrought, she almost jumps at this.

'Yes, yes,' says she in a hurried way.

'He was very like the thief, wasn't he?' says Jacky anxiously. Susan colours hotly.

'Nonsense, Jacky'—with a very poor attempt at scorn. 'That gentleman in Mr. Crosby's pew was, I think, Mr. Crosby himself, or, at all events, some friend of his.'

'Well, the thief was the image of him,' says Jacky slowly. That's the worst of Jacky, he is always so abominably slow. 'I looked at him, and I said to myself, "That's Susan's thief," and,' with awful obstinacy, 'I think it was, too.'

'No, no, no!' says Susan. 'It was Mr. Crosby, I tell you. I saw Lady Millbank nod and smile at him.'

Jacky considers.

'Very well,' says he, in a thoroughly unconvinced tone. He moves away a bit and then looks back. 'If that is true,' says he, 'Mr. Crosby looks like a thief.'

* * * * *

At half-past three Susan, having come to the conclusion that sitting up here won't help her out of her difficulty, wanders downstairs and into the schoolroom, where Betty makes much of her, and makes her sandwiches out of the still warm mutton, which, in spite of their nastiness and her headache, Susan devours with avidity. Hunger is a great sauce; no one has ever yet invented one to beat it. And perhaps, if all were known, Susan's ache belongs more to the heart than the head. When the sandwiches are finished, she declares herself much better, and Jane coming to say that Lady Millbank is in the drawing-room, she rises, and expresses a desire to see her.

Lady Millbank, or 'the Sack,' as the irreverent young Barrys always call her, thinks it the correct thing to be in with, and civil to, her Rector—without giving herself any unnecessary trouble. The drive from Millbank to the parish church is five good miles, so she always makes a point of lunching with some of her friends and taking afternoon tea at the Rectory. Even so far she would not have condescended, but that the Rector, poor as he is, has sprung from a good old stock, and that his wife was a connection of the late Sir Geoffrey Millbank.

'So sorry to hear you have been ill,' says she, as Susan enters. Susan is a favourite of hers. 'The heat, eh?' She speaks exactly as she looks. She is one of those people who can be very gracious when they like, and perfectly abominable on other occasions. She is ugly and shapeless, and careless about her dress, but no one can mistake for a minute that she is well born.

'It was very warm,' says Susan.

'You look pale, my dear. I think, Miss Barry, she ought not to go to church this evening.'

'No, no, of course not, Susan,' says Miss Barry severely; she is sitting behind a wonderfully battered old teapot that has certainly seen service, and must have been pure at heart to have come out of the trial thus victoriously, though maimed and wounded. It is the pride of Miss Barry's life, and has come down to the Rector after many days.

'I suppose you saw that George Crosby has come home?' says Lady Millbank. 'I had heard a rumour of his coming a week or so ago, but thought nothing of it. Such a man as he is can never be relied upon, and when he turned up actually alive last week, I was more surprised than I can tell you.'

Last week! She had seen him, had talked with him. Had he told her? Susan's heart sinks within her. Positive despair makes her raise her eyes and look at Lady Millbank. Oh, if——

But Lady Millbank is still chatting on, and in her eyes, as they meet Susan's, there is no *arrière-pensée*. No; he had not betrayed her.

'I don't suppose we shall see much of him; he is always on the stampede,' Lady Millbank is saying. 'One would think from his habits that he was a criminal running before the law. I told him so. Ah'—rising suddenly and looking out of the window—'there he is! And coming here! Of course, to call upon Mr. Barry. Your brother was a great friend of George Crosby's father, I think. Eh?'

'There was a friendship,' says Miss Barry. 'Susan, how pale you are! Come out of that dark corner, child, and sit near the window. The air will do you good.'

'I like being here,' says Susan quickly.

There is no time to say any more. Susan's 'thief' is in the room.

CHAPTER XIX.

'A secret is in my custody if I keep it; but if I blab it, it is I that am prisoner.'

THE Rector has come in, and has stayed to have a cup of tea with Mr. Crosby. Lady Millbank declares herself charmed and very jealous. He never leaves his beloved books to see her! Mr. Barry smiles, and then falls back upon the memories of Crosby's father that are always so dear to him. He is a tall, gaunt man, severe, with a far-away look, and the indifferent air of those who live with dead authors, and who are, besides, a little worried by the money transactions of life.

To have to think of the daily needs is hateful to Mr. Barry, who ought to have been a bachelor, with nothing but his notes to worry him, living in a world in which he could sit loosely. Even now he sometimes forgets how time flies, and to tell him that Susan is almost a woman grown would have roused him to quite an extraordinary wonder. The world goes on whilst he stands still, and to-day the dragging of him out of his shell, even to the ordinary business of a drawing-room conversation, has bewildered him. After a little while he retires.

His sermons, his visits to the sick, the poor (he never visits the rich unless they specially send for him)—all these things concern him. But when he knows himself happiest is when his study-door is shut for the night to all intruders, and he can read, read, read, until the little hours begin to chime.

As Crosby entered the drawing-room, Susan felt her heart stand still. She rose mechanically, and held out her hand to him as he came up to her, but she did not lift her eyes. She felt vaguely conscious that she had flushed over cheek and brow. Such a blush! So quick! so deep! Oh, he must have seen it, and known the meaning of it!

If he did, he made no sign whatever; and until the departure of Lady Millbank he devoted himself to the Rector.

When Lady Millbank rose to say good-bye, Susan told herself that now at last the ordeal was at an end, and that he would go too. But, apparently, he had no intention whatever of stirring. And the climax came when Dom and Carew asked him to come out into the garden and have a cigarette. The cigarettes were Dom's. Mr. Crosby seemed only too willing to accept this lively invitation, and Dom, thrusting his arm through Betty's, asked her to come along with him.

'And you, Miss Barry,' says Crosby, now walking up deliberately to Susan, who is still sitting in her shady corner. The elder Miss Barry had gone out into the hall to bid Lady Millbank a last adieu, and tell her of the latest misdoings of the young women of the Christian Association in Curraghcloyne. 'I hope you will come too.'

'Oh yes, Susan, come on,' says Betty. 'It's lovely outside to-day, and father won't be able to see the smoke through the beech hedge.' The Rector objects to smoking, so that Dom and Carew have quite a time of it keeping their pipes and cigarettes out of his way.

'I hope you will come,' says Crosby. He is bending over Susan now, and he has distinctly lowered his tone. 'Do you know, I have come over to-day to see and thank you. I felt it quite my duty to do it.'

'To thank me?' For the first time during the afternoon Susan looks straight at him. Her large and lovely eyes are full of wonderment. 'To thank me?'

'Yes, indeed; I have great cause to be grateful to you,' says Mr. Crosby, with such extreme earnestness and gravity that she rises. What if, after all, she was wrong, and the thief was not really Mr. Crosby?

A cousin perhaps—a disagreeable one: cousins are very often disagreeable, and often, too, more like one than one's own brothers are. Of course, if he was a kinsman, Mr. Crosby would be very grateful to her for hushing up the whole affair, and telling nobody. And yet——

Again she lifts her eyes and studies his face. No, not even twins were ever so alike as this man and the man that stole the cherries.

'Are you coming?' calls Betty impatiently, and Susan moves forward. In a moment she is stepping from the low sill of the Rectory drawing-room on to the little plot of grass beneath, disregarding Mr. Crosby's hand as he holds it out to help her.

She and he are well behind the others now, and Crosby speaks again.

'You don't ask me why I am grateful,' says he reproachfully. 'Don't you care to know? I care to tell you. I have had it on my mind since that day in the garden. You remember?'

'Yes,' says Susan. She stops short, and confronts him with flushed cheeks and nervous eyes, but a little touch of courage that sits most charmingly upon her. 'I do remember. You — you were the man who——' She hesitates.

'Stole the cherries?' suggests he.

'No'—coldly—'who sat on the top of the ladder and made fun of me.'

There is a little silence.

'That is a most unkind speech,' says Crosby at last. 'After all, I don't feel as grateful now as I did a minute ago. I came here to-day to thank you for looking so kindly after my property, and you meet me with an accusation that absolutely strikes me dumb.'

At this Susan cannot refrain from bitter jest.

'True,' says she scornfully; 'one can see how silent you are.'

Mr. Crosby regards her with apparent awe, tempered with grief.

'If you persist in your present course,' says he, 'I shall commit suicide. There will be nothing else left for me to do.'

'In the meantime,' says Susan, with

astonishing spirit, 'you had better come into the garden. They are expecting you.'

Not so very much, after all. Betty, Carew, and Dom Fitzgerald are engaged in a lively discussion on Miss Barry's wild attack on the unoffending Sarah in church this morning, and, in the delights of it, have almost forgotten Mr. Crosby. The children are playing about on the tennis-ground below, and Crosby's eyes fall on Bonnie, as with great difficulty, and with the help of a stick, he tries to follow little Tom. Jacky, in the distance, is stretched on his stomach reading.

'Those are your brothers?' asks Crosby, looking more deliberately at Bonnie, whose charming little face, though pale and emaciated, attracts him.

'Yes, I have four brothers and one sister.'

'Five brothers, I thought.'

'Oh no; Dominick Fitzgerald is our cousin. He lives with us nearly altogether, and father is coaching him for the Indian Civil.'

'Oh, I see. That little brother'—gently indicating Bonnie—'does not look very strong.'

'No, he had rheumatic fever, and he has not been'—correcting herself hastily, as though it is impossible to her to say the more terrible word—'very strong since.'

'What a beautiful face!' says Crosby involuntarily. And, indeed, the loveliest flower of all this handsome Barry family is the little suffering cripple child.

Susan is conscious for a moment of a choking in her throat. Oh, her little lovely darling brother! To hear him praised is a great joy to her, but with the joy follows pain unutterable. If only she had looked more closely after him! And poor, poor mamma, who had told her to be a mother to him! Then, all at once, she remembers the cherries, and how he had enjoyed them, and a queer passion of feeling, arising first of all from the fact that Crosby had admired the child, makes her turn to him.

'Mr. Crosby, I want to tell you something,' says she timidly; 'those cherries that you sent me'—he is about to tease her again, to pretend he knows nothing of the gift, but her face, pale now and filled with a strange but carefully-held-back emotion, keeps him silent—' they gave Bonnie a happy half-hour. No matter how I am feeling towards you, about your pretending to be—you know— still, if only for the pleasure your cherries gave Bonnie, I feel intensely thankful to you. He is not strong, as you see. They say he will never be strong again, and it was my fault; for I forgot him one day—one day —and mamma was dead too. I was cross to you about your pretending to be a thief—I hope you won't mind me?'

It is such a childish speech, and there is such tragedy in the dark eyes! She has not broken down at all. There is not a suspicion of tears in her low, clear young voice, but that the child's ill-health is a constant grief to her is not to be doubted for a moment.

'If it comes to that,' says he slowly, 'it is I who ought to apologize. And the worst of it is, I haven't an apology ready. The plain truth is that I couldn't resist the situation. If I could hope that you would try to forgive me——'

He breaks off. Susan has looked at him, and through the deep gloom of a minute ago a smile has broken on her face. Such a smile! It makes her look about twelve years old, and is indescribably pretty. 'What a lovely child!' says Crosby to himself. She holds out her hand to him frankly.

'But don't tell anybody,' says she, in an eager little whisper.

'Tell! "Is thy servant——" But the brother over there catching cold on the grass with a book before him—he was with you, I think.'

'Ah, Jacky and I are chums!' says she. This seems to settle the question. It occurs to Mr. Crosby that it would be rather nice to be chums with Susan, and he vaguely wonders if she would accept a chum who was not one of the family. Is Dominick a chum? But, then, he is one of the family. When Susan has chums, does she trust them—

have little secrets with them? If so, he may clearly rise to the desired position in time. He is conscious of a sense of exhilaration as he tells himself that Susan once regarded him as a thief, and that he is bound by her to keep that regard a secret.

'Oh, there you are, Mr. Crosby!' says Carew, stopping in his discussion with Betty; 'come here and sit down.'

'Don't sit on Betty, whatever you do,' says Dominick from his place beside her on the grass; 'she'd be sure to resent it. She takes after our own particular auntie in the way of temper. Susan, my darling'—making a grab at Susan's ankle, which she has learned from long practice to avoid—'come and sit down by me. No? Your brainpower must be weak. Have a cigarette, Mr. Crosby. You need not mind the girls. It is all we can do to keep our "baccy" from them.'

'If I wanted your nasty "baccy,"' says Betty, 'it isn't likely you would be able to keep it from me. Give Mr. Crosby a match.'

'Thanks, I have one,' says Crosby. He had accepted Dom's offer of a cigarette without hesitation, and, indeed, would have smoked it to the bitter end rather than offend any member of the little group around him. They all please him; they all seem in unison with him—frank, happy, rollicking youngsters, without a scrap of real harm amongst them. Perhaps the secret of their success with Crosby lies in the fact that, in spite of his being well in the thirties, he is still a boy himself at heart, with a spice of mischief in him not to be controlled. The cigarette, however, proves very tolerable, and Susan having seated herself where he can distinctly see her, he feels that he is going to spend an uncommonly pleasant afternoon.

'It's a shame to say Betty's got a temper,' says Susan. 'I'm sure she hasn't—not a bad one, any way.'

'You needn't defend me, Susan,' says Betty, clasping her long, lean arms behind her head. 'I prefer to do it for myself, and'—with a fell glance at the doomed Dominick—'I think I know where revenge lies.'

'I give in!' cries Mr. Fitzgerald frantically. 'Betty, pax!'

'Never,' says Betty.

'If you burn my fly-book a second time, I warn you that there will be murder,' says Dom; and then Betty has mercy.

'A public retractation, then!' demands she viciously.

'A hundred of them. I swear to you, Mr. Crosby, that I wronged her, and that her temper is like that of an angel, and not a bit like our Aunt Jemima's'—softly, 'May I be forgiven!'

'Did you hear her in church?' asks Carew, turning to Crosby. 'Aunt Jemima, I mean, not Betty. She was mad with Sarah this morning——'

Crosby looks rather helplessly round him.

'Another sister?' asks he.

'No, no,' says Susan, whilst the others explode; and Crosby, unable to resist their gaiety, joins in the merriment. 'A servant——'

'Had a magenta feather in her hat!' cries Betty, roaring with laughter, 'and Aunt Jemima hates feathers, and——'

'This is my story, Betty,' interrupts Carew; 'I insist on telling it. When the Paradise hymn began, Aunt Jemima saw the feather——'

'Pounced upon Sarah!' cries Susan, who is nearly in hysterics. 'Oh, did you see her? She sang the most dreadful things at her until the poor girl nearly fainted, and——'

'And then our only auntie punched her in the back with her Prayer-book,' puts in Dom. 'Really, Betty, I did wrong you! You aren't in it with her. She cussed and swore like anything, but worse than all, Susan, was her ribald rendering of music-hall songs within the sainted precincts of the church.'

'Nonsense, Dom! you spoil the story by exaggeration.'

'Exaggeration! My dear girl, didn't you hear her? Why, she was shouting it! She got rather mixed up in the music—I'm bound to say the two times are not the same—but she managed it wonderfully. You heard her, Carew, didn't you?

'"Where did you get that hat?"

I waited for the rest, but I suppose her courage failed her, or else the organ drowned it; at all events, the second line,

'"Where did you get that tile?"

did not come in. But I think we ought to speak to our auntie, Susan, don't you? That sort of thing is very well outside, but in a church! Betty, you look as if you'd love to speak to somebody. We'll put you on for this job. You shall expostulate with Aunt Jemima on her deplorable weakness for low-class comic songs.'

'I shall leave you to interview her on the subject,' says Betty.

'Interview! What a splendid word!' says

Dom. 'What'll you sell it for?' But Betty very properly decides on not hearing him.

Softly, sweetly, the sun is going down, topping the distant hills, and now falling behind them. A golden colour is lighting all around. Overhead the swallows are darting here and there, and from the beds of mignonette in the old-fashioned garden exquisite perfumes are wafted; and now 'at shut of evening flowers' faint breezes rise, and corners grow rich in shadows, and from the stream below comes a song that makes musical the happy hours.

Crosby, with a sigh of distinct regret, rises to his feet.

'I fear I must go,' says he.

'What, not so soon?' cries Carew, getting up too. Indeed, as Crosby persists, though evidently with reluctance, in his determination to leave them, they all get up, the innate courtesy of this noisy group being their best point.

'Have another cigarette for the walk home?' says Dom hospitably.

'We'll all go with you to the gate!' cries Betty.

'I suppose a big traveller like you doesn't play tennis?' says Carew diffidently, but with an essence of hope in his tone.

'Oh, don't I!' says Crosby; 'I'm quite a dab at it, I can tell you! If I were to come down to-morrow afternoon, would there be any chance that any of you would be here to play a game with me?'

He looks at Susan.

'We'll all be here!' cries Betty ecstatically. To have a new element thrown into their daily games seems too enchanting for anything. 'You will come?'

'May I?' says Crosby. Susan has not answered, and now he purposely addresses her.

'Oh, I hope you will!' says she cordially. She had been thinking hurriedly if it would be possible to ask him to luncheon—to their early dinner. But with the children and Jane's attendance! Oh no—a thousand times no! Yet it seems so inhospitable.

'Thank you, I should very much like to come. It is quite taking pity on an unfortunate bachelor,' says he. And this being settled, they all in a body prepare to accompany him to the gate. Even little Tom runs up to them, and Bonnie, with uneven steps, hurries as fast as the poor mite can. Susan turns to help him, and Crosby, watching her for a moment, follows her, and, taking the child in his arms, without a word swings him to his shoulder.

At the gate, having bidden them good-bye, and Dom having taken Bonnie on his back for a race home, Crosby looks at Susan.

'Are you fond of cherries?' asks he. His face is profoundly grave, but she can see the twinkle in his eyes, and her own give him back a reproachful glance.

This playing with fire is hardly prudent.

'Sometimes,' says she demurely.

'And you, Bonnie?' asks Crosby, pinching gently the child's pale pretty cheek as he rests on Dominick's back. 'You like them,

I'm sure. Well, I'll send you some to-morrow and every day while they last, and perhaps the red of their cheeks will run into yours. See that it does, now.'

The child laughs shyly, and Crosby turns to Susan again.

'Good-bye, Miss Barry.'

'Oh, don't call her that!' cries Betty. 'That makes her sound like Aunt Jemima. Susan, tell him he can call you by your own name.'

This handsome advice ought, thinks Crosby, to fill Susan with angry confusion. But it doesn't.

'You may—you may indeed!' says she, quite sweetly and naturally, looking him fair in the eyes. 'I should like you to call me Susan, and I am very much obliged to you for promising the cherries to Bonnie.'

She gives him her hand; he presses it, and goes up the road towards his home. A little thorn in his heart goes with him. If he had been her own age, would she so readily have permitted him to call her Susan? No doubt she regards him as quite a middle-aged old fellow, and truly, next to her youth, that promises to be eternal, he is nothing less.

CHAPTER XX.

> 'Fear oftentimes restraineth words,
> But makes not thoughts to cease.'

THE weather since the beginning of the summer has been exceptionally warm, and to-day has outdone itself.

Here in the Cottage garden, surrounded by its ivied walls, the heat is excessive, and there is a certain languor in the lithe figure of the girl as she comes forward, the dog beside her, to greet Wyndham, that meets his eye. Perhaps nervousness has conduced to the pallor that is whitening her lips and brow, and is making even more striking the darkness of her appealing eyes. There is something about her so full of grief suppressed that he hastens to allay it.

'I have come, you see,' says he—he holds out his hand, and she lays hers in it; he holds it a moment—'to speak about our rent.' He smiles at her. The smile, to tell the truth, is a little grim, and hardly reassures her. 'I have come to the conclusion that, as you wish to become my tenant, you must pay me a huge rent.'

'Ah! and I have been thinking,' says she very sadly, with the mournful air of one who is giving up all that is worth having in this world, 'that I shall not be your tenant at all, and shall never pay you any rent.'

'Do you mean to say,' says Wyndham, reading her like a book, but humouring her mood, 'that you've found another house more suited to you?'

'Oh no, it isn't that. There is no house I shall ever like so well as this.'

'Then, let me tell you beforehand that I shall charge you a very handsome rent,' persists Wyndham, trying to be genial. He smiles at her, but the smile is a dismal failure.

'I can't accept your offer—I can't indeed,' says the girl, who, in spite of her protests, has brightened considerably beneath his apparent determination to let the Cottage to her. 'This is your own house. Your mother gave it to you. Mrs. Denis has told me all about it, and if you give it to me you will never come here again.'

'I shall indeed—to collect my rent,' says Wyndham, a little touched by her evident earnestness, and assuming a more natural air of lightness.

'Ah, that,' says she. She pauses a moment, and then: 'If'—timidly—'you would promise to come here sometimes to see your dog and the flowers, I might think of it. . . . I could keep out of your way when you came. I could sit in my own room, and you could——'

'What a cheerful prospect for you!' says he. 'I'm not a very agreeable fellow, I know, when all is told; but I believe I am so far on the road to respectability as to be incapable of enjoying myself at the expense of another fellow-creature's comfort. Fancy my taking the joys of the country with the knowledge that you were stifling in some cellar downstairs with a view to saving me from the annoyance of your presence!'

'It wouldn't be a cellar, and it isn't downstairs,' says the girl anxiously. 'It is a pretty little room upstairs.'

'It's all the same,' says Wyndham. 'The prettiest little room in the world is a bore if one is imprisoned in it.'

Silence follows upon this. Wyndham, going forward, stoops down to a bed of seedlings that he had ordered to be planted a month ago. They are in a very promising condition, and the regret he feels for this little home of his that is slipping through his fingers increases. And yet to thrust her out —he knows quite well now that he will never do that.

'Mr. Wyndham,' says the girl—she is at his elbow now—'don't be so sorry about it; I shall go—to-morrow, if possible.'

He is not prepared for this, nor for the soft

breathings of her voice in his ear. He turns abruptly.

'All that is arranged,' says he peremptorily. 'You cannot go; you have nowhere to go to, as'—pointedly—'you tell me. In the meantime, it is absolutely necessary that you should have someone to live with you.'

'There is Mrs. Denis,' says she nervously.

'Not good enough for an heiress like you,' returns he, smiling. Now that he has finally, most unwillingly and most ungraciously, given in to the fact that she is to be his tenant, he feels more kindly towards her, and more human. 'You will want a lady companion to read with you—you say you wish to go on with your studies—and to go out with you.'

'Go out!' She regards him with quick horror. 'I shall never go out of this—never!' cries she.

The extraordinary passion of her manner checks him. She has sunk upon a garden-chair, as if incapable of supporting herself any longer; and from this she looks up at him with a sad and frightened face.

'I will leave,' says she at last. It is a most mournful surrender of hope, and all things that make life still dear to her.

'There is no necessity for that,' says Wyndham hurriedly. 'If I knew more—if I knew how to help you—but'—breaking off abruptly—' you yourself have decided against that. You must pardon me. You have already told me that you do not wish to tell me of yourself, your past——'

She makes a little gesture with her hand. Wyndham, standing still upon the gravelled path, looks at her.

'I have been thinking about that,' says she, 'and'—with growing agitation—'it has seemed very ungrateful of me to distrust you—you who have done so much for me, who are now giving up your lovely home for me. Mr. Wyndham'—rising and coming towards him—'I have made up my mind; I will tell you all.'

END OF VOL. I.

BILLING AND SONS, PRINTERS, GUILDFORD.

[July, 1895.

A List of Books Published by

CHATTO & WINDUS
214, Piccadilly, London, W.

ABOUT (EDMOND).—THE FELLAH: An Egyptian Novel. Translated by Sir RANDAL ROBERTS. Post 8vo, illustrated boards, **2s.**

ADAMS (W. DAVENPORT), WORKS BY.
A DICTIONARY OF THE DRAMA: The Plays, Playwrights, Players, and Playhouses of the United Kingdom and America. Cr. 8vo, half-bound, **12s. 6d.** [*Preparing.*
QUIPS AND QUIDDITIES. Selected by W. D. ADAMS. Post 8vo, cloth limp, **2s. 6d.**

AGONY COLUMN (THE) OF "THE TIMES," from 1800 to 1870. Edited, with an Introduction, by ALICE CLAY. Post 8vo, cloth limp, **2s. 6d.**

AIDE (HAMILTON), WORKS BY. Post 8vo, illustrated boards, **2s.** each.
CARR OF CARRLYON. | CONFIDENCES.

ALBERT (MARY).—BROOKE FINCHLEY'S DAUGHTER. Post 8vo, picture boards, **2s.**; cloth limp, **2s. 6d.**

ALDEN (W. L.).—A LOST SOUL. Fcap. 8vo, cloth boards, **1s. 6d.**

ALEXANDER (MRS.), NOVELS BY. Post 8vo, illustrated boards, **2s.** each.
MAID, WIFE, OR WIDOW? | VALERIE'S FATE.

ALLEN (F. M.).—GREEN AS GRASS. Crown 8vo, cloth, **3s. 6d.**

ALLEN (GRANT), WORKS BY.
THE EVOLUTIONIST AT LARGE. Crown 8vo, cloth extra, **6s.**
POST-PRANDIAL PHILOSOPHY. Crown 8vo, art linen, **3s. 6d.**
Crown 8vo, cloth extra, **3s. 6d.** each ; post 8vo, illustrated boards, **2s.** each.

PHILISTIA.	THE DEVIL'S DIE.	THE DUCHESS OF POWYSLAND.
BABYLON.	THIS MORTAL COIL.	BLOOD ROYAL.
STRANGE STORIES.	THE TENTS OF SHEM.	IVAN GREET'S MASTERPIECE.
BECKONING HAND.	THE GREAT TABOO.	
FOR MAIMIE'S SAKE.	DUMARESQ'S DAUGHTER.	THE SCALLYWAG.
IN ALL SHADES.		

DR. PALLISER'S PATIENT. Fcap. 8vo, cloth extra, **1s. 6d.**
AT MARKET VALUE. Two Vols., crown 8vo, cloth, **10s.** net.
UNDER SEALED ORDERS. Three Vols., crown 8vo, cloth, **15s.** net.

ANDERSON (MARY).—OTHELLO'S OCCUPATION. Cr. 8vo, cl., **3s. 6d.**

ARNOLD (EDWIN LESTER), STORIES BY.
THE WONDERFUL ADVENTURES OF PHRA THE PHŒNICIAN. With 12 Illusts. by H. M. PAGET. Crown 8vo, cloth extra, **3s. 6d.**; post 8vo, illust. boards, **2s.**
THE CONSTABLE OF ST. NICHOLAS. With Front. by S. WOOD. Cr. 8vo, cl., **3s. 6d.**

ARTEMUS WARD'S WORKS. With Portrait and Facsimile. Crown 8vo, cloth extra, **7s. 6d.**—Also a POPULAR EDITION, post 8vo, picture boards, **2s.**
THE GENIAL SHOWMAN: Life and Adventures of ARTEMUS WARD. By EDWARD P. HINGSTON. With a Frontispiece. Crown 8vo, cloth extra, **3s. 6d.**

ASHTON (JOHN), WORKS BY. Crown 8vo, cloth extra, **7s. 6d.** each.
HISTORY OF THE CHAP-BOOKS OF THE 18th CENTURY. With 334 Illusts.
SOCIAL LIFE IN THE REIGN OF QUEEN ANNE. With 85 Illustrations.
HUMOUR, WIT, AND SATIRE OF SEVENTEENTH CENTURY. With 82 Illusts.
ENGLISH CARICATURE AND SATIRE ON NAPOLEON THE FIRST. 115 Illusts.
MODERN STREET BALLADS. With 57 Illustrations.

BACTERIA, YEAST FUNGI, AND ALLIED SPECIES, A SYNOPSIS OF. By W. B. GROVE, B.A. With 87 Illustrations. Crown 8vo, cloth extra, 3s. 6d.

BARDSLEY (REV. C. W.), WORKS BY.
ENGLISH SURNAMES: Their Sources and Significations. Cr. 8vo, cloth, 7s. 6d.
CURIOSITIES OF PURITAN NOMENCLATURE. Crown 8vo, cloth extra, 6s.

BARING GOULD (S., Author of "John Herring," &c.), NOVELS BY.
Crown 8vo, cloth extra, 3s. 6d. each; post 8vo, illustrated boards, 2s. each.
RED SPIDER. | EVE.

BARR (ROBERT: LUKE SHARP), STORIES BY. Cr. 8vo, cl., 3s. 6d. ea.
IN A STEAMER CHAIR. With Frontispiece and Vignette by DEMAIN HAMMOND.
FROM WHOSE BOURNE, &c. With 47 Illustrations.

BARRETT (FRANK), NOVELS BY.
Post 8vo, illustrated boards, 2s. each; cloth, 2s. 6d. each.
FETTERED FOR LIFE.
THE SIN OF OLGA ZASSOULICH.
BETWEEN LIFE AND DEATH.
FOLLY MORRISON. | HONEST DAVIE.
LITTLE LADY LINTON.
A PRODIGAL'S PROGRESS.
JOHN FORD; and HIS HELPMATE.
A RECOILING VENGEANCE.
LIEUT. BARNABAS. | FOUND GUILTY.
FOR LOVE AND HONOUR.
THE WOMAN OF THE IRON BRACELETS. Crown 8vo, cloth. 3s. 6d.

BEACONSFIELD, LORD. By T. P. O'CONNOR, M.P. Cr. 8vo, cloth, 5s.

BEAUCHAMP (S).—GRANTLEY GRANGE. Post 8vo, illust. boards, 2s.

BEAUTIFUL PICTURES BY BRITISH ARTISTS: A Gathering from the Picture Galleries, engraved on Steel. Imperial 4to, cloth extra, gilt edges, 21s.

BECHSTEIN (LUDWIG).—AS PRETTY AS SEVEN, and other German Stories. With Additional Tales by the Brothers GRIMM, and 98 Illustrations by RICHTER. Square 8vo, cloth extra, 6s. 6d.; gilt edges, 7s. 6d.

BESANT (Sir WALTER), NOVELS BY.
Cr. 8vo, cl. ex., 3s. 6d. each; post 8vo, illust. bds., 2s. each; cl. limp, 2s. 6d. each.
ALL SORTS AND CONDITIONS OF MEN. With Illustrations by FRED. BARNARD.
THE CAPTAINS' ROOM, &c. With Frontispiece by E. J. WHEELER.
ALL IN A GARDEN FAIR. With 6 Illustrations by HARRY FURNISS.
DOROTHY FORSTER. With Frontispiece by CHARLES GREEN.
UNCLE JACK, and other Stories. | CHILDREN OF GIBEON.
THE WORLD WENT VERY WELL THEN. With 12 Illustrations by A. FORESTIER.
HERR PAULUS: His Rise, his Greatness, and his Fall.
FOR FAITH AND FREEDOM. With Illustrations by A. FORESTIER and F. WADDY.
TO CALL HER MINE, &c. With 9 Illustrations by A. FORESTIER.
THE BELL OF ST. PAUL'S.
THE HOLY ROSE, &c. With Frontispiece by F. BARNARD.
ARMOREL OF LYONESSE: A Romance of To-day. With 12 Illusts. by F. BARNARD.
ST. KATHERINE'S BY THE TOWER. With 12 page Illustrations by C. GREEN.
VERBENA CAMELLIA STEPHANOTIS, &c. | THE IVORY GATE: A Novel.
THE REBEL QUEEN.
BEYOND THE DREAMS OF AVARICE. Crown 8vo, cloth extra, 6s.
IN DEACON'S ORDERS, &c. With Frontispiece. Crown 8vo, cloth, 6s.
FIFTY YEARS AGO. With 144 Plates and Woodcuts. Crown 8vo, cloth extra, 5s.
THE EULOGY OF RICHARD JEFFERIES. With Portrait. Cr. 8vo, cl. extra, 6s.
LONDON. With 125 Illustrations. New Edition. Demy 8vo, cloth extra, 7s. 6d.
SIR RICHARD WHITTINGTON. Frontispiece. Crown 8vo, art linen, 3s. 6d.
GASPARD DE COLIGNY. With a Portrait. Crown 8vo, art linen, 3s. 6d.
AS WE ARE: AS WE MAY BE: Social Essays. Crown 8vo, linen, 6s. [Shortly.

BESANT (Sir WALTER) AND JAMES RICE, NOVELS BY.
Cr. 8vo, cl. ex., 3s. 6d. each; post 8vo, illust. bds., 2s. each; cl. limp, 2s. 6d. each.
READY-MONEY MORTIBOY.
MY LITTLE GIRL.
WITH HARP AND CROWN.
THIS SON OF VULCAN.
THE GOLDEN BUTTERFLY.
THE MONKS OF THELEMA.
BY CELIA'S ARBOUR.
THE CHAPLAIN OF THE FLEET.
THE SEAMY SIDE.
THE CASE OF MR. LUCRAFT, &c.
'TWAS IN TRAFALGAR'S BAY, &c.
THE TEN YEARS' TENANT, &c.

** There is also a LIBRARY EDITION of the above Twelve Volumes, handsomely set in new type on a large crown 8vo page, and bound in cloth extra, 6s. each; and a POPULAR EDITION of THE GOLDEN BUTTERFLY, medium 8vo, 6d.; cloth, 1s.; and a NEW EDITION, printed in large type, crown 8vo, figured cloth binding, 3s. 6d.

CHATTO & WINDUS, PUBLISHERS, PICCADILLY. 3

BEERBOHM (JULIUS).—WANDERINGS IN PATAGONIA; or, Life among the Ostrich Hunters. With Illustrations. Crown 8vo, cloth extra, **3s. 6d.**

BELLEW (FRANK).—THE ART OF AMUSING: A Collection of Graceful Arts, Games, Tricks, Puzzles, and Charades. 300 Illusts. Cr. 8vo, cl. ex, **4s. 6d.**

BENNETT (W. C., LL.D.)—SONGS FOR SAILORS. Post 8vo, cl. limp **2s.**

BEWICK (THOMAS) AND HIS PUPILS. By AUSTIN DOBSON. With 95 Illustrations. Square 8vo, cloth extra, **6s.**

BIERCE (AMBROSE).—IN THE MIDST OF LIFE: Tales of Soldiers and Civilians. Crown 8vo, cloth extra, **6s.**; post 8vo, illustrated boards, **2s.**

BILL NYE'S HISTORY OF THE UNITED STATES. With 146 Illustrations by F. OPPER. Crown 8vo, cloth extra, **3s. 6d.**

BLACKBURN'S (HENRY) ART HANDBOOKS.
ACADEMY NOTES, 1875, 1877-86, 1889, 1890, 1892-1895. Illustrated, each **1s.**
ACADEMY NOTES, 1875-79. Complete in One Vol., with 600 Illusts. Cloth, **6s.**
ACADEMY NOTES, 1880-84. Complete in One Vol., with 700 Illusts. Cloth, **6s.**
ACADEMY NOTES, 1890-94. Complete in One Vol., with 800 Illusts. Cloth, **7s. 6d.**
GROSVENOR NOTES, 1877. **6d.**
GROSVENOR NOTES, separate years, from 1878-1890, each **1s.**
GROSVENOR NOTES, Vol. I., 1877-82. With 300 Illusts. Demy 8vo, cloth, **6s.**
GROSVENOR NOTES, Vol. II., 1883-87. With 300 Illusts. Demy 8vo, cloth, **6s.**
GROSVENOR NOTES, Vol. III., 1888-90. With 230 Illusts. Demy 8vo, cloth, **3s. 6d.**
THE NEW GALLERY, 1888-1895. With numerous Illustrations, each **1s.**
THE NEW GALLERY, Vol. I., 1888-1892. With 250 Illustrations. Demy 8vo, cloth, **6s.**
ENGLISH PICTURES at the NATIONAL GALLERY. With 114 Illustrations. **1s.**
OLD MASTERS AT THE NATIONAL GALLERY. With 128 Illustrations. **1s. 6d.**
ILLUSTRATED CATALOGUE TO THE NATIONAL GALLERY. 242 Illusts., cl., **3s.**
THE PARIS SALON, 1894. With Facsimile Sketches. **3s.**

BLIND (MATHILDE). POEMS BY.
THE ASCENT OF MAN. Crown 8vo cloth, **5s.**
DRAMAS IN MINIATURE. With a Frontispiece by F. MADOX BROWN. Cr. 8vo, **5s.**
SONGS AND SONNETS. Fcap. 8vo, vellum and gold, **5s.**
BIRDS OF PASSAGE: Songs. Crown 8vo. linen **6s.** net.

BOURNE (H. R. FOX), WORKS BY.
ENGLISH MERCHANTS: Memoirs in Illustration of the Progress of British Commerce. With numerous Illustrations. Crown 8vo, cloth extra, **7s. 6d.**
ENGLISH NEWSPAPERS: The History of Journalism. Two Vols., demy 8vo, cl., **25s.**
THE OTHER SIDE OF THE EMIN PASHA RELIEF EXPEDITION. Cr. 8vo, **6s.**

BOWERS (GEORGE).—LEAVES FROM A HUNTING JOURNAL. Oblong folio, half-bound. **21s.**

BOYLE (FREDERICK), WORKS BY. Post 8vo, illustrated boards, **2s.** each.
CHRONICLES OF NO-MAN'S LAND. | CAMP NOTES. | SAVAGE LIFE.

BRAND (JOHN).—OBSERVATIONS ON POPULAR ANTIQUITIES; chiefly illustrating the Origin of our Vulgar Customs, Ceremonies, and Superstitions. With the Additions of Sir HENRY ELLIS, and Illusts. Cr. 8vo, cloth extra, **7s. 6d.**

BREWER (REV. DR.), WORKS BY.
THE READER'S HANDBOOK OF ALLUSIONS, REFERENCES, PLOTS, AND STORIES. Seventeenth Thousand. Crown 8vo, cloth extra, **7s. 6d.**
AUTHORS AND THEIR WORKS, WITH THE DATES: Being the Appendices to "The Reader's Handbook," separately printed. Crown 8vo, cloth limp, **2s.**
A DICTIONARY OF MIRACLES. Crown 8vo, cloth extra, **7s. 6d.**

BREWSTER (SIR DAVID), WORKS BY. Post 8vo, cl. ex., **4s. 6d.** each.
MORE WORLDS THAN ONE: Creed of Philosopher and Hope of Christian. Plates.
THE MARTYRS OF SCIENCE: GALILEO, TYCHO BRAHE, and KEPLER. With Portraits.
LETTERS ON NATURAL MAGIC. With numerous Illustrations.

BRILLAT-SAVARIN.—GASTRONOMY AS A FINE ART. Translated by R. E. ANDERSON, M.A. Post 8vo. half-bound, **2s.**

BURTON (RICHARD F.).—THE BOOK OF THE SWORD. With over 400 Illustrations. Demy 4to, cloth extra, **32s.**

BURTON (ROBERT).—THE ANATOMY OF MELANCHOLY. With Translations of the Quotations. Demy 8vo, cloth extra, **7s. 6d.**
MELANCHOLY ANATOMISED. Abridgment of BURTON'S ANAT. Post 8vo, **2s. 6d.**

CHATTO & WINDUS, PUBLISHERS, PICCADILLY.

BRET HARTE'S COLLECTED WORKS. Revised by the Author.
LIBRARY EDITION. In Eight Volumes, crown 8vo, cloth extra, **6s.** each.
Vol. I. COMPLETE POETICAL AND DRAMATIC WORKS. With Steel Portrait.
Vol. II. LUCK OF ROARING CAMP—BOHEMIAN PAPERS—AMERICAN LEGENDS.
Vol. III. TALES OF THE ARGONAUTS—EASTERN SKETCHES.
Vol. IV. GABRIEL CONROY. | Vol. V. STORIES—CONDENSED NOVELS, &c.
Vol. VI. TALES OF THE PACIFIC SLOPE.
Vol. VII. TALES OF THE PACIFIC SLOPE—II. With Portrait by JOHN PETTIE, R.A.
Vol.VIII. TALES OF THE PINE AND THE CYPRESS.
THE SELECT WORKS OF BRET HARTE, in Prose and Poetry. With Introductory Essay by J. M. BELLEW, Portrait of Author, and 50 Illusts. Cr.8vo, cl. ex., **7s. 6d.**
BRET HARTE'S POETICAL WORKS. Hand-made paper & buckram. Cr.8vo, **4s. 6d.**
THE QUEEN OF THE PIRATE ISLE. With 28 original Drawings by KATE GREENAWAY, reproduced in Colours by EDMUND EVANS. Small 4to, cloth, **5s.**

Crown 8vo, cloth extra, **3s. 6d.** each; post 8vo, picture boards, **2s.** each.
A WAIF OF THE PLAINS. With 60 Illustrations by STANLEY L. WOOD.
A WARD OF THE GOLDEN GATE. With 59 Illustrations by STANLEY L. WOOD.

Crown 8vo, cloth extra, **3s. 6d.** each.
A SAPPHO OF GREEN SPRINGS, &c. With Two Illustrations by HUME NISBET.
COLONEL STARBOTTLE'S CLIENT, AND SOME OTHER PEOPLE. Frontisp.
SUSY: A Novel. With Frontispiece and Vignette by J. A. CHRISTIE.
SALLY DOWS, &c. With 47 Illustrations by W. D. ALMOND, &c.
A PROTÉGÉE OF JACK HAMLIN'S. With 26 Illustrations by W. SMALL, &c.
THE BELL-RINGER OF ANGEL'S, &c. 39 Illusts. by DUDLEY HARDY, &c.
CLARENCE: A Story of the War. With Illustrations. [Shortly.

Post 8vo, illustrated boards, **2s.** each.
GABRIEL CONROY. | **THE LUCK OF ROARING CAMP**, &c.
AN HEIRESS OF RED DOG, &c. | **CALIFORNIAN STORIES.**

Post 8vo, illustrated boards, **2s.** each; cloth limp, **2s. 6d.** each.
FLIP. | **MARUJA.** | **A PHYLLIS OF THE SIERRAS.**

Fcap. 8vo. picture cover, **1s.** each.
SNOW-BOUND AT EAGLE'S. | **JEFF BRIGGS'S LOVE STORY.**

BRYDGES (HAROLD).—UNCLE SAM AT HOME. Post 8vo, illustrated boards, **2s.**; cloth limp, **2s. 6d.**

BUCHANAN (ROBERT), WORKS BY. Crown 8vo, cloth extra, **6s.** each.
SELECTED POEMS OF ROBERT BUCHANAN. With Frontispiece by T. DALZIEL.
THE EARTHQUAKE; or, Six Days and a Sabbath.
THE CITY OF DREAM: An Epic Poem. With Two Illustrations by P. MACNAB.
THE WANDERING JEW: A Christmas Carol. Second Edition.
THE OUTCAST: A Rhyme for the Time. With 15 Illustrations by RUDOLF BLIND PETER MACNAB, and HUME NISBET. Small demy 8vo, cloth extra, **8s.**
ROBERT BUCHANAN'S COMPLETE POETICAL WORKS. With Steel-plate Portrait. Crown 8vo, cloth extra, **7s. 6d.**

Crown 8vo, cloth extra, **3s. 6d.** each; post 8vo, illustrated boards, **2s.** each.
THE SHADOW OF THE SWORD. | LOVE ME FOR EVER. Frontispiece.
A CHILD OF NATURE. Frontispiece. | ANNAN WATER. | FOXGLOVE MANOR.
GOD AND THE MAN. With 11 Illustrations by FRED. BARNARD. | THE NEW ABELARD.
 | MATT: A Story of a Caravan. Frontisp.
THE MARTYRDOM OF MADELINE. | THE MASTER OF THE MINE. Front.
With Frontispiece by A. W. COOPER. | THE HEIR OF LINNE.

Crown 8vo, cloth extra, **3s. 6d.** each.
WOMAN AND THE MAN. | RED AND WHITE HEATHER.
RACHEL DENE. Crown 8vo, cloth extra, **3s. 6d.** [Sept
LADY KILPATRICK. Crown 8vo, cloth extra, **6s.** [Shortly.
THE CHARLATAN. By ROBERT BUCHANAN and H. MURRAY. Two Vols., **10s.** net.

CAINE (T. HALL), NOVELS BY. Crown 8vo, cloth extra, **3s. 6d.** each; post 8vo, illustrated boards, **2s.** each; cloth limp, **2s. 6d.** each.
SHADOW OF A CRIME. | A SON OF HAGAR. | THE DEEMSTER.

CAMERON (COMMANDER V. LOVETT).—THE CRUISE OF THE "BLACK PRINCE" PRIVATEER. Post 8vo. picture boards, **2s.**

CAMERON (MRS. H. LOVETT), NOVELS BY. Post 8vo, illust. bds., **2s.** each.
JULIET'S GUARDIAN. | DECEIVERS EVER.

CARRUTH (HAYDEN).—THE ADVENTURES OF JONES. With 17 Illustrations. Fcap. 8vo, cloth. **2s.**

CARLYLE (JANE WELSH), LIFE OF. By Mrs. ALEXANDER IRELAND. With Portrait and Facsimile Letter. Small demy 8vo, cloth extra, **7s. 6d.**

CARLYLE (THOMAS) on the CHOICE of BOOKS. Post 8vo, 1s. 6d.
CORRESPONDENCE OF THOMAS CARLYLE AND R. W. EMERSON, 1834 to 1872.
Edited by C. E. NORTON. With Portraits. Two Vols., crown 8vo. cloth, 24s.
CHAPMAN'S (GEORGE) WORKS.—Vol. I., Plays.—Vol. II., Poems and Minor Translations, with Essay by A. C. SWINBURNE.—Vol. III., Translations of the Iliad and Odyssey. Three Vols., crown 8vo. cloth, 6s. each.
CHAPPLE (J. M.).—THE MINOR CHORD: Story of Prima Donna. 3s. 6d.
CHATTO (W. A.) AND J. JACKSON.— A TREATISE ON WOOD ENGRAVING. With 450 fine Illustrations. Large 4to, half-leather, 28s.
CHAUCER FOR CHILDREN: A Golden Key. By Mrs. H. R. HAWEIS. With 8 Coloured Plates and 30 Woodcuts. Small 4to, cloth extra, 3s. 6d.
CHAUCER FOR SCHOOLS. By Mrs. H. R. HAWEIS. Demy 8vo. cloth limp, 2s. 6d.
CHESS, THE LAWS AND PRACTICE OF. With Analysis of Openings. By HOWARD STAUNTON. Edited by R. B. WORMALD. Crown 8vo, cloth, 5s.
THE MINOR TACTICS OF CHESS: A Treatise on the Deployment of the Forces. By F. K. YOUNG and E. C. HOWELL. Long fcap. 8vo, cloth, 2s. 6d.
CLARE (A.).—FOR THE LOVE OF A LASS. Post 8vo, 2s.; cl., 2s. 6d.
CLIVE (MRS. ARCHER), NOVELS BY. Post 8vo, illust. boards 2s. each.
PAUL FERROLL. | WHY PAUL FERROLL KILLED HIS WIFE.
CLODD (EDWARD, F.R.A.S.).—MYTHS AND DREAMS. Cr. 8vo, 3s. 6d.
COBBAN (J. MACLAREN), NOVELS BY.
THE CURE OF SOULS. Post 8vo, illustrated boards, 2s.
THE RED SULTAN. Crown 8vo, cl. extra, 3s. 6d.; post 8vo, illustrated bds., 2s.
THE BURDEN OF ISABEL. Crown 8vo, cloth extra, 3s. 6d.
COLEMAN (JOHN).—PLAYERS AND PLAYWRIGHTS I HAVE KNOWN. Two Vols., demy 8vo, cloth, 24s.
COLERIDGE (M. E.)—SEVEN SLEEPERS OF EPHESUS. 1s. 6d.
COLLINS (C. ALLSTON).—THE BAR SINISTER. Post 8vo, 2s.
COLLINS (JOHN CHURTON, M.A.), BOOKS BY.
ILLUSTRATIONS OF TENNYSON. Crown 8vo, cloth extra, 6s.
JONATHAN SWIFT: A Biographical and Critical Study. Crown 8vo, cloth extra, 8s.
COLLINS (MORTIMER AND FRANCES), NOVELS BY.
Crown 8vo, cloth extra, 3s. 6d. each; post 8vo, illustrated boards, 2s. each.
FROM MIDNIGHT TO MIDNIGHT. | BLACKSMITH AND SCHOLAR.
TRANSMIGRATION. | YOU PLAY ME FALSE. | A VILLAGE COMEDY.
Post 8vo, illustrated boards, 2s. each.
SWEET ANNE PAGE. | FIGHT WITH FORTUNE. | SWEET & TWENTY. | FRANCES.
COLLINS (WILKIE), NOVELS BY.
Cr. 8vo, cl. ex., 3s. 6d. each; post 8vo, illust. bds., 2s. each; cl. limp, 2s. 6d. each.
ANTONINA. With a Frontispiece by Sir JOHN GILBERT, R.A.
BASIL. Illustrated by Sir JOHN GILBERT, R.A., and J. MAHONEY.
HIDE AND SEEK. Illustrated by Sir JOHN GILBERT, R.A., and J. MAHONEY.
AFTER DARK. Illustrations by A. B. HOUGHTON. | THE TWO DESTINIES.
THE DEAD SECRET. With a Frontispiece by Sir JOHN GILBERT, R.A.
QUEEN OF HEARTS. With a Frontispiece by Sir JOHN GILBERT, R.A.
THE WOMAN IN WHITE. With Illusts. by Sir J. GILBERT, R.A., and F. A. FRASER.
NO NAME. With Illustrations by Sir J. E. MILLAIS, R.A., and A. W. COOPER.
MY MISCELLANIES. With a Steel-plate Portrait of WILKIE COLLINS.
ARMADALE. With Illustrations by G. H. THOMAS.
THE MOONSTONE. With Illustrations by G. DU MAURIER and F. A. FRASER.
MAN AND WIFE. With Illustrations by WILLIAM SMALL.
POOR MISS FINCH. Illustrated by G. DU MAURIER and EDWARD HUGHES.
MISS OR MRS.? With Illusts. by S. L. FILDES, R.A., and HENRY WOODS, A.R.A.
THE NEW MAGDALEN. Illustrated by G. DU MAURIER and C. S. REINHARDT.
THE FROZEN DEEP. Illustrated by G. DU MAURIER and J. MAHONEY.
THE LAW AND THE LADY. Illusts. by S. L. FILDES, R.A., and SYDNEY HALL.
THE HAUNTED HOTEL. Illustrated by ARTHUR HOPKINS.
THE FALLEN LEAVES. | HEART AND SCIENCE. | THE EVIL GENIUS.
JEZEBEL'S DAUGHTER. | "I SAY NO." | LITTLE NOVELS.
THE BLACK ROBE. | A ROGUE'S LIFE. | THE LEGACY OF CAIN.
BLIND LOVE. With Preface by Sir WALTER BESANT. Illusts. by A. FORESTIER.
Popular Editions. Medium 8vo, 6d. each; cloth 1s. each.
THE WOMAN IN WHITE. | THE MOONSTONE.

COLMAN'S (GEORGE) HUMOROUS WORKS: "Broad Grins," "My Nightgown and Slippers," &c. With Life and Frontis. Cr. 8vo, cl. extra, **7s. 6d.**

COLQUHOUN (M. J.)—EVERY INCH A SOLDIER. Post 8vo, bds., **2s.**

CONVALESCENT COOKERY: A Family Handbook. By CATHERINE RYAN. Crown 8vo, **1s.**; cloth limp **1s. 6d.**

CONWAY (MONCURE D.), WORKS BY.
DEMONOLOGY AND DEVIL-LORE. 65 Illustrations. Two Vols. 8vo, cloth, **28s.**
GEORGE WASHINGTON'S RULES OF CIVILITY. Fcap. 8vo, Jap. vellum, **2s. 6d.**

COOK (DUTTON), NOVELS BY.
PAUL FOSTER'S DAUGHTER. Cr. 8vo, cl. ex., **3s. 6d.**; post 8vo, illust. boards, **2s.**
LEO. Post 8vo, illustrated boards, **2s.**

COOPER (EDWARD H.)—GEOFFORY HAMILTON. Cr. 8vo, **3s. 6d.**

CORNWALL.—POPULAR ROMANCES OF THE WEST OF ENGLAND; or, The Drolls, Traditions, and Superstitions of Old Cornwall. Collected by ROBERT HUNT, F.R.S. Two Steel-plates by GEO. CRUIKSHANK. Cr. 8vo, cl., **7s. 6d.**

COTES (V. CECIL).—TWO GIRLS ON A BARGE. With 44 Illustrations by F. H. TOWNSEND. Post 8vo, cloth, **2s. 6d.**

CRADDOCK (C. EGBERT), STORIES BY.
PROPHET OF THE GREAT SMOKY MOUNTAINS. Post 8vo, illustrated boards, **2s.**
HIS VANISHED STAR. Crown 8vo, cloth extra, **3s. 6d.**

CRELLIN (H. N.), BOOKS BY.
ROMANCES of the OLD SERAGLIO. 28 Illusts. by S. L. WOOD. Cr. 8vo, cl., **3s. 6d.**
TALES OF THE CALIPH. Crown 8vo, cloth **2s.**
THE NAZARENES: A Drama. Crown 8vo, **1s.**

CRIM (MATT.).—ADVENTURES OF A FAIR REBEL. Crown 8vo, cloth extra, with a Frontispiece, **3s. 6d**; post 8vo, illustrated boards, **2s.**

CROKER (MRS. B. M.), NOVELS BY. Crown 8vo, cloth extra, **3s. 6d.** each; post 8vo, illustrated boards, **2s.** each; cloth limp, **2s. 6d.** each.
PRETTY MISS NEVILLE. | DIANA BARRINGTON.
A BIRD OF PASSAGE. | PROPER PRIDE.
A FAMILY LIKENESS. | "TO LET."
MR. JERVIS. Three Vols., crown 8vo, cloth **15s.** net.
VILLAGE TALES AND JUNGLE TRAGEDIES. Crown 8vo, cloth, **3s. 6d.**

CRUIKSHANK'S COMIC ALMANACK. Complete in Two SERIES: The FIRST from 1835 to 1843; the SECOND from 1844 to 1853. A Gathering of the BEST HUMOUR of THACKERAY, HOOD, MAYHEW, ALBERT SMITH, A'BECKETT, ROBERT BROUGH, &c. With numerous Steel Engravings and Woodcuts by CRUIKSHANK, HINE, LANDELLS, &c. Two Vols., crown 8vo, cloth gilt, **7s. 6d.** each.
THE LIFE OF GEORGE CRUIKSHANK. By BLANCHARD JERROLD. With 84 Illustrations and a Bibliography. Crown 8vo, cloth extra, **6s.**

CUMMING (C. F. GORDON), WORKS BY. Demy 8vo, cl. ex., **8s. 6d.** each.
IN THE HEBRIDES. With Autotype Facsimile and 23 Illustrations.
IN THE HIMALAYAS AND ON THE INDIAN PLAINS. With 42 Illustrations.
TWO HAPPY YEARS IN CEYLON. With 28 Illustrations.
VIA CORNWALL TO EGYPT. With Photogravure Frontis. Demy 8vo, cl., **7s. 6d.**

CUSSANS (JOHN E.)—A HANDBOOK OF HERALDRY; with Instructions for Tracing Pedigrees and Deciphering Ancient MSS., &c.; 408 Woodcuts and 2 Coloured Plates. Fourth edition, revised. crown 8vo, cloth extra, **6s.**

CYPLES (W.)—HEARTS of GOLD. Cr. 8vo, cl, **3s. 6d.**; post 8vo, bds., **2s.**

DANIEL (GEORGE).—MERRIE ENGLAND IN THE OLDEN TIME. With Illustrations by ROBERT CRUIKSHANK. Crown 8vo, cloth extra, **3s. 6d.**

DAUDET (ALPHONSE).—THE EVANGELIST; or, Port Salvation. Crown 8vo, cloth extra, **3s. 6d.**; post 8vo, illustrated boards, **2s.**

DAVIDSON (HUGH COLEMAN).—MR. SADLER'S DAUGHTERS. With a Frontispiece by STANLEY WOOD. Crown 8vo, cloth extra, **3s. 6d.**

DAVIES (DR. N. E. YORKE-), WORKS BY. Cr. 8vo, **1s.** ea.; cl., **1s. 6d.** ea.
ONE THOUSAND MEDICAL MAXIMS AND SURGICAL HINTS.
NURSERY HINTS: A Mother's Guide in Health and Disease.
FOODS FOR THE FAT: A Treatise on Corpulency, and a Dietary for its Cure.
AIDS TO LONG LIFE. Crown 8vo, **2s.**; cloth limp, **2s. 6d.**

DAVIES' (SIR JOHN) COMPLETE POETICAL WORKS. Collected and Edited, with Memorial-Introduction and Notes, by the Rev. A. B Grosart, D.D. Two Vols., crown 8vo, cloth boards, **12s.**

DAWSON (ERASMUS, M.B.).—THE FOUNTAIN OF YOUTH. Crown 8vo, cloth extra, **3s. 6d.**; post 8vo, illustrated boards, **2s.**

DE GUERIN (MAURICE), THE JOURNAL OF. Edited by G. S. TREBUTIEN. With a Memoir by SAINTE-BEUVE. Translated from the 20th French Edition by JESSIE P. FROTHINGHAM. Fcap. 8vo, half-bound, **2s. 6d.**

DE MAISTRE (XAVIER).—A JOURNEY ROUND MY ROOM. Translated by Sir HENRY ATTWELL. Post 8vo, cloth limp, **2s. 6d.**

DE MILLE (JAMES).—A CASTLE IN SPAIN. With a Frontispiece. Crown 8vo, cloth extra, **3s. 6d.**; post 8vo, illustrated boards, **2s.**

DERBY (THE).—THE BLUE RIBBON OF THE TURF. With Brief Accounts of THE OAKS. By LOUIS HENRY CURZON. Cr. 8vo, cloth limp, **2s. 6d.**

DERWENT (LEITH), NOVELS BY. Cr.8vo,cl., **3s.6d.** ea.; post 8vo,bds.,**2s.**ea.
OUR LADY OF TEARS. | CIRCE'S LOVERS.

DEWAR (T. R.).—A RAMBLE ROUND THE GLOBE. With 220 Illustrations. Crown 8vo, cloth extra, **7s. 6d.**

DICKENS (CHARLES), NOVELS BY. Post 8vo, illustrated boards, **2s.** each.
SKETCHES BY BOZ. | NICHOLAS NICKLEBY. | OLIVER TWIST.
THE SPEECHES OF CHARLES DICKENS, 1841-1870. With a New Bibliography Edited by RICHARD HERNE SHEPHERD. Crown 8vo, cloth extra, **6s.**
ABOUT ENGLAND WITH DICKENS. By ALFRED RIMMER. With 57 Illustrations by C. A. VANDERHOOF, ALFRED RIMMER, and others. Sq. 8vo, cloth extra, **7s. 6d.**

DICTIONARIES.
A DICTIONARY OF MIRACLES: Imitative, Realistic, and Dogmatic. By the Rev. E. C. BREWER, LL.D. Crown 8vo, cloth extra, **7s. 6d.**
THE READER'S HANDBOOK OF ALLUSIONS, REFERENCES, PLOTS, AND STORIES. By the Rev. E. C. BREWER. LL.D. With an ENGLISH BIBLIOGRAPHY. Seventeenth Thousand. Crown 8vo cloth extra **7s. 6d.**
AUTHORS AND THEIR WORKS, WITH THE DATES. Cr. 8vo, cloth limp, **2s.**
FAMILIAR SHORT SAYINGS OF GREAT MEN. With Historical and Explanatory Notes. By SAMUEL A. BENT, A.M. Crown 8vo, cloth extra, **7s. 6d.**
SLANG DICTIONARY: Etymological, Historical, and Anecdotal. Cr. 8vo, cl., **6s. 6d.**
WOMEN OF THE DAY: A Biographical Dictionary. By F. HAYS. Cr. 8vo, cl., **5s.**
WORDS, FACTS, AND PHRASES: A Dictionary of Curious, Quaint, and Out-of-the-Way Matters. By ELIEZER EDWARDS. Crown 8vo, cloth extra, **7s. 6d.**

DIDEROT.—THE PARADOX OF ACTING. Translated, with Notes, by WALTER HERRIES POLLOCK. With a Preface by HENRY IRVING. Crown 8vo, parchment, **4s. 6d.**

DOBSON (AUSTIN), WORKS BY.
THOMAS BEWICK & HIS PUPILS. With 95 Illustrations. Square 8vo, cloth, **6s.**
FOUR FRENCHWOMEN. With 4 Portraits. Crown 8vo, buckram, gilt top, **6s.**
EIGHTEENTH CENTURY VIGNETTES. Two SERIES. Cr. 8vo, buckram, **6s.** each.

DOBSON (W. T.)—POETICAL INGENUITIES AND ECCENTRICITIES. Post 8vo, cloth limp, **2s. 6d.**

DONOVAN (DICK), DETECTIVE STORIES BY.
Post 8vo, illustrated boards, **2s.** each; cloth limp, **2s. 6d.** each.
THE MAN-HUNTER. | WANTED! | A DETECTIVE'S TRIUMPHS.
CAUGHT AT LAST! | IN THE GRIP OF THE LAW.
TRACKED AND TAKEN. | FROM INFORMATION RECEIVED.
WHO POISONED HETTY DUNCAN? | LINK BY LINK. | DARK DEEDS.
SUSPICION AROUSED. | THE LONG ARM OF THE LAW. [Shortly.

Crown 8vo, cloth, **3s. 6d.** each; post 8vo, boards, **2s.** each; cloth, **2s. 6d.** each.
THE MAN FROM MANCHESTER. With 23 Illustrations.
TRACKED TO DOOM. With 6 full-page Illustrations by GORDON BROWNE.

DOYLE (A. CONAN).—THE FIRM OF GIRDLESTONE: A Romance of the Unromantic. Crown 8vo, cloth extra, **3s. 6d.**

DRAMATISTS, THE OLD. With Vignette Portraits. Cr. 8vo, cl. ex., **6s.** per Vol.
  BEN JONSON'S WORKS. With Notes Critical and Explanatory, and a Biographical Memoir by WM. GIFFORD. Edited by Col. CUNNINGHAM. Three Vols.
  CHAPMAN'S WORKS. Complete in Three Vols. Vol. I. contains the Plays complete; Vol. II., Poems and Minor Translations, with an Introductory Essay by A. C. SWINBURNE; Vol. III., Translations of the Iliad and Odyssey.
  MARLOWE'S WORKS. Edited, with Notes, by Col. CUNNINGHAM. One Vol.
  MASSINGER'S PLAYS. From GIFFORD's Text. Edit by Col. CUNNINGHAM. One Vol.

DUNCAN (SARA JEANNETTE: Mrs. EVERARD COTES), **WORKS BY.**
  Crown 8vo, cloth extra, **7s. 6d.** each.
  A SOCIAL DEPARTURE: How Orthodocia and I Went round the World by Ourselves. With 111 Illustrations by F. H. TOWNSEND.
  AN AMERICAN GIRL IN LONDON. With 80 Illustrations by F. H. TOWNSEND.
  THE SIMPLE ADVENTURES OF A MEMSAHIB. Illustrated by F. H. TOWNSEND.
  Crown 8vo, cloth extra, **3s. 6d.** each.
  A DAUGHTER OF TO-DAY. | **VERNON'S AUNT.** 47 Illusts. by HAL HURST.

DYER (T. F. THISELTON, M.A.).—FOLK-LORE OF PLANTS. 6s.

EARLY ENGLISH POETS. Edited, with Introductions and Annotations, by Rev. A. B. GROSART, D.D. Crown 8vo, cloth boards, **6s.** per Volume.
  FLETCHER'S (GILES) COMPLETE POEMS. One Vol.
  DAVIES' (SIR JOHN) COMPLETE POETICAL WORKS. Two Vols.
  HERRICK'S (ROBERT) COMPLETE COLLECTED POEMS. Three Vols.
  SIDNEY'S (SIR PHILIP) COMPLETE POETICAL WORKS. Three Vols.

EDGCUMBE (Sir E. R. PEARCE).—ZEPHYRUS: A Holiday in Brazil and on the River Plate. With 41 Illustrations. Crown 8vo, cloth extra, **5s.**

EDISON, THE LIFE & INVENTIONS OF THOMAS A. By W. K. L. and A. DICKSON. With 200 Illustrations by R. F. OUTCALT, &c. Demy 4to, cloth gilt, **18s.**

EDWARDES (MRS. ANNIE), NOVELS BY.
  A POINT OF HONOUR. Post 8vo, illustrated boards, **2s.**
  ARCHIE LOVELL. Crown 8vo, cloth extra, **3s. 6d.**; post 8vo, illust. boards, **2s.**

EDWARDS (ELIEZER).—WORDS, FACTS, AND PHRASES: A Dictionary of Quaint Matters. Crown 8vo, cloth, **7s. 6d.**

EDWARDS (M. BETHAM-), NOVELS BY.
  KITTY. Post 8vo, **2s.**; cloth, **2s. 6d.** | **FELICIA.** Post 8vo, **2s.**

EGERTON (REV. J. C.).—SUSSEX FOLK AND SUSSEX WAYS. With Introduction by Rev. Dr. H. WACE, and 4 Illustrations. Cr. 8vo, cloth ex., **5s.**

EGGLESTON (EDWARD).—ROXY: A Novel. Post 8vo, illust. bds., **2s.**

ENGLISHMAN'S HOUSE, THE: A Practical Guide to all interested in Selecting or Building a House; with Estimates of Cost, Quantities, &c. By C. J. RICHARDSON. With Coloured Frontispiece and 600 Illusts. Crown 8vo, cloth, **7s. 6d.**

EWALD (ALEX. CHARLES, F.S.A.), WORKS BY.
  THE LIFE AND TIMES OF PRINCE CHARLES STUART, Count of Albany (THE YOUNG PRETENDER). With a Portrait. Crown 8vo, cloth extra, **7s. 6d.**
  STORIES FROM THE STATE PAPERS. With an Autotype. Crown 8vo, cloth, **6s.**

EYES, OUR: How to Preserve Them. By JOHN BROWNING. **1s.**

FAMILIAR SHORT SAYINGS OF GREAT MEN. By SAMUEL ARTHUR BENT, A.M. Fifth Edition, Revised and Enlarged. Crown 8vo, cloth extra, **7s. 6d.**

FARADAY (MICHAEL), WORKS BY. Post 8vo, cloth extra, **4s. 6d.** each.
  THE CHEMICAL HISTORY OF A CANDLE: Lectures delivered before a Juvenile Audience. Edited by WILLIAM CROOKES, F.C.S. With numerous Illustrations.
  ON THE VARIOUS FORCES OF NATURE, AND THEIR RELATIONS TO EACH OTHER. Edited by WILLIAM CROOKES, F.C.S. With Illustrations.

FARRER (J. ANSON), WORKS BY.
  MILITARY MANNERS AND CUSTOMS. Crown 8vo, cloth extra, **6s.**
  WAR: Three Essays, reprinted from "Military Manners." Cr. 8vo, **1s.**; cl., **1s. 6d.**

FENN (G. MANVILLE), NOVELS BY.
  Crown 8vo, cloth extra, **3s. 6d.** each; post 8vo, illustrated boards, **2s.** each.
  THE NEW MISTRESS. | **WITNESS TO THE DEED.**
  Crown 8vo, cloth extra, **3s. 6d.** each.
  THE TIGER LILY: A Tale of Two Passions. | **THE WHITE VIRGIN.**

FIN-BEC.—THE CUPBOARD PAPERS: Observations on the Art of Living and Dining. Post 8vo, cloth limp, **2s. 6d.**

FIREWORKS, THE COMPLETE ART OF MAKING; or, The Pyrotechnist's Treasury. By THOMAS KENTISH. With 267 Illustrations. Cr. 8vo. cl., **5s.**

FIRST BOOK, MY. By WALTER BESANT, JAMES PAYN, W. CLARK RUSSELL, GRANT ALLEN, HALL CAINE, GEORGE R. SIMS, RUDYARD KIPLING, A. CONAN DOYLE, M. E. BRADDON, F. W ROBINSON, H. RIDER HAGGARD, R. M. BALLANTYNE, I. ZANGWILL, MORLEY ROBERTS, D. CHRISTIE MURRAY, MARIE CORELLI, J. K. JEROME, JOHN STRANGE WINTER, BRET HARTE, "Q.," ROBERT BUCHANAN, and R. L. STEVENSON. With a Prefatory Story by JEROME K. JEROME, and 185 Illustrations. Small demy 8vo, cloth extra, **7s. 6d.**

FITZGERALD (PERCY), WORKS BY.
THE WORLD BEHIND THE SCENES. Crown 8vo, cloth extra, **3s. 6d.**
LITTLE ESSAYS: Passages from Letters of CHARLES LAMB. Post 8vo, cl., **2s. 6d.**
A DAY'S TOUR: Journey through France and Belgium. With Sketches. Cr. 4to, **1s.**
FATAL ZERO. Crown 8vo, cloth extra, **3s. 6d.**; post 8vo, illustrated boards, **2s.**

Post 8vo, illustrated boards, **2s.** each.
BELLA DONNA. | LADY OF BRANTOME. | THE SECOND MRS. TILLOTSON.
POLLY. | NEVER FORGOTTEN. | SEVENTY-FIVE BROOKE STREET
LIFE OF JAMES BOSWELL (of Auchinleck). Two Vols., demy 8vo, cloth, **24s.**
THE SAVOY OPERA. With 60 Illustrations and Portraits. Cr. 8vo, cloth, **3s. 6d.**

FLAMMARION (CAMILLE), WORKS BY.
POPULAR ASTRONOMY: A General Description of the Heavens. Translated by J. ELLARD GORE, F.R.A.S. With 3 Plates and 288 Illusts. Medium 8vo, cloth, **16s.**
URANIA: A Romance. With 87 Illustrations. Crown 8vo, cloth extra, **5s.**

FLETCHER'S (GILES, B.D.) COMPLETE POEMS: Christ's Victorie in Heaven, Christ's Victorie on Earth, Christ's Triumph over Death, and Minor Poems. With Notes by Rev. A. B. GROSART, D.D. Crown 8vo, cloth boards, **6s.**

FONBLANQUE (ALBANY).—FILTHY LUCRE. Post 8vo, illust. bds., 2s.

FRANCILLON (R. E.), NOVELS BY.
Crown 8vo, cloth extra, **3s. 6d.** each; post 8vo, illustrated boards, **2s.** each.
ONE BY ONE. | A REAL QUEEN. | KING OR KNAVE?
ROPES OF SAND. Illustrated. | A DOG AND HIS SHADOW.

Post 8vo, illustrated boards, **2s.** each.
QUEEN COPHETUA. | OLYMPIA. | ROMANCES OF THE LAW.

JACK DOYLE'S DAUGHTER. Crown 8vo, cloth, **3s. 6d.**
ESTHER'S GLOVE. Fcap. 8vo, picture cover, **1s.**

FREDERIC (HAROLD), NOVELS BY. Post 8vo, illust. bds., 2s. each.
SETH'S BROTHER'S WIFE. | THE LAWTON GIRL.

FRENCH LITERATURE, A HISTORY OF. By HENRY VAN LAUN. Three Vols., demy 8vo, cloth boards, **7s. 6d.** each.

FRISWELL (HAIN).—ONE OF TWO: A Novel. Post 8vo, illust. bds., 2s.

FROST (THOMAS), WORKS BY. Crown 8vo, cloth extra, **3s. 6d.** each.
CIRCUS LIFE AND CIRCUS CELEBRITIES. | LIVES OF THE CONJURERS.
THE OLD SHOWMEN AND THE OLD LONDON FAIRS.

FRY'S (HERBERT) ROYAL GUIDE TO THE LONDON CHARITIES. Edited by JOHN LANE. Published Annually. Crown 8vo, cloth, **1s. 6d.**

GARDENING BOOKS. Post 8vo. **1s.** each; cloth limp, **1s. 6d.** each.
A YEAR'S WORK IN GARDEN AND GREENHOUSE. By GEORGE GLENNY.
HOUSEHOLD HORTICULTURE. By TOM and JANE JERROLD. Illustrated.
THE GARDEN THAT PAID THE RENT. By TOM JERROLD.
MY GARDEN WILD. By FRANCIS G. HEATH. Crown 8vo, cloth extra, **6s.**

GARDNER (MRS. ALAN).—RIFLE AND SPEAR WITH THE RAJPOOTS: Being the Narrative of a Winter's Travel and Sport in Northern India. With numerous Illustrations by the Author and F. H. TOWNSEND. Demy 4to, half-bound, **21s.**

GARRETT (EDWARD).—THE CAPEL GIRLS: A Novel. Crown 8vo, cloth extra, **3s. 6d.**; post 8vo, illustrated boards, **2s.**

GAULOT (PAUL).—THE RED SHIRTS: A Story of the Revolution. Translated by J. A. J. DE VILLIERS. Crown 8vo, cloth, **3s. 6d.**

GENTLEMAN'S MAGAZINE, THE. 1s. Monthly. With Stories, Articles upon Literature, Science, and Art, and **"TABLE TALK"** by SYLVANUS URBAN.
** Bound Volumes for recent years kept in stock, 8s. 6d. each. Cases for binding, 2s.

GENTLEMAN'S ANNUAL, THE. Published Annually in November. 1s.

GERMAN POPULAR STORIES. Collected by the Brothers GRIMM and Translated by EDGAR TAYLOR. With Introduction by JOHN RUSKIN, and 22 Steel Plates after GEORGE CRUIKSHANK. Square 8vo, cloth, 6s. 6d.; gilt edges, 7s. 6d.

GIBBON (CHARLES), NOVELS BY.
Crown 8vo, cloth extra, 3s. 6d. each; post 8vo, illustrated boards, 2s. each.
ROBIN GRAY. | THE GOLDEN SHAFT.
LOVING A DREAM.

Post 8vo, illustrated boards, 2s. each.
THE FLOWER OF THE FOREST. | IN LOVE AND WAR.
THE DEAD HEART. | A HEART'S PROBLEM.
FOR LACK OF GOLD. | BY MEAD AND STREAM.
WHAT WILL THE WORLD SAY? | THE BRAES OF YARROW.
FOR THE KING. | A HARD KNOT. | FANCY FREE. | OF HIGH DEGREE.
QUEEN OF THE MEADOW. | IN HONOUR BOUND.
IN PASTURES GREEN. | HEART'S DELIGHT. | BLOOD-MONEY.

GIBNEY (SOMERVILLE).—SENTENCED! Cr. 8vo, 1s.; cl., 1s. 6d.

GILBERT (WILLIAM), NOVELS BY. Post 8vo, illustrated boards, 2s. each.
DR. AUSTIN'S GUESTS. | JAMES DUKE, COSTERMONGER.
THE WIZARD OF THE MOUNTAIN.

GILBERT (W. S.), ORIGINAL PLAYS BY. Three Series, 2s. 6d. each.
The FIRST SERIES contains: The Wicked World—Pygmalion and Galatea—Charity—The Princess—The Palace of Truth—Trial by Jury.
The SECOND SERIES: Broken Hearts—Engaged—Sweethearts—Gretchen—Dan'l Druce—Tom Cobb—H.M.S. "Pinafore"—The Sorcerer—Pirates of Penzance.
The THIRD SERIES: Comedy and Tragedy—Foggerty's Fairy—Rosencrantz and Guildenstern—Patience—Princess Ida—The Mikado—Ruddigore—The Yeomen of the Guard—The Gondoliers—The Mountebanks—Utopia.

EIGHT ORIGINAL COMIC OPERAS written by W. S. GILBERT. Containing: The Sorcerer—H.M.S. "Pinafore"—Pirates of Penzance—Iolanthe—Patience—Princess Ida—The Mikado—Trial by Jury. Demy 8vo, cloth limp, 2s. 6d.

THE "GILBERT AND SULLIVAN" BIRTHDAY BOOK: Quotations for Every Day in the Year, Selected from Plays by W. S. GILBERT set to Music by Sir A. SULLIVAN. Compiled by ALEX. WATSON. Royal 16mo, Jap. leather, 2s. 6d.

GLANVILLE (ERNEST), NOVELS BY.
Crown 8vo, cloth extra, 3s. 6d. each; post 8vo, illustrated boards, 2s. each.
THE LOST HEIRESS: A Tale of Love, Battle, and Adventure. With 2 Illusts.
THE FOSSICKER: A Romance of Mashonaland. With 2 Illusts. by HUME NISBET.
A FAIR COLONIST.

GLENNY (GEORGE).—A YEAR'S WORK in GARDEN and GREENHOUSE: Practical Advice to Amateur Gardeners as to the Management of the Flower, Fruit and Frame Garden. Post 8vo, 1s.; cloth limp, 1s. 6d.

GODWIN (WILLIAM).—LIVES OF THE NECROMANCERS. Post 8vo, cloth limp, 2s.

GOLDEN TREASURY OF THOUGHT, THE: An Encyclopædia of QUOTATIONS. Edited by THEODORE TAYLOR. Crown 8vo, cloth gilt, 7s. 6d.

GONTAUT, MEMOIRS OF THE DUCHESSE DE (Gouvernante to the Children of France), 1773-1836. With Photogravure Frontispieces. Two Vols., small demy 8vo, cloth extra, 21s.

GOODMAN (E. J.).—FATE OF HERBERT WAYNE. Cr. 8vo, 3s. 6d.

GRAHAM (LEONARD).—THE PROFESSOR'S WIFE: A Story. Fcap. 8vo, picture cover, 1s.

GREEKS AND ROMANS, THE LIFE OF THE, described from Antique Monuments. By ERNST GUHL and W. KONER. Edited by Dr. F. HUEFFER. With 545 Illustrations. Large crown 8vo, cloth extra, 7s. 6d.

GREVILLE (HENRY), NOVELS BY:
NIKANOR. Translated by ELIZA E. CHASE. Post 8vo, illustrated boards, 2s.
A NOBLE WOMAN. Crown 8vo, cloth extra, 5s.; post 8vo, illustrated boards, 2s.

CHATTO & WINDUS, PUBLISHERS, PICCADILLY. 11

GREENWOOD (JAMES), WORKS BY. Cr. 8vo. cloth extra, 3s. 6d. each.
THE WILDS OF LONDON. | LOW-LIFE DEEPS.

GRIFFITH (CECIL).—CORINTHIA MARAZION: A Novel. Crown 8vo, cloth extra, 3s. 6d.; post 8vo, illustrated boards, 2s.

GRUNDY (SYDNEY).—THE DAYS OF HIS VANITY: A Passage in the Life of a Young Man. Crown 8vo, cloth extra, 3s. 6d.; post 8vo, boards, 2s.

HABBERTON (JOHN, Author of "Helen's Babies"), NOVELS BY. Post 8vo, illustrated boards 2s. each; cloth limp, 2s. 6d. each.
BRUETON'S BAYOU. | COUNTRY LUCK.

HAIR, THE: Its Treatment in Health, Weakness, and Disease. Translated from the German of Dr. J. PINCUS. Crown 8vo, 1s.; cloth, 1s. 6d.

HAKE (DR. THOMAS GORDON), POEMS BY. Cr. 8vo, cl. ex., 6s. each.
NEW SYMBOLS. | LEGENDS OF THE MORROW. | THE SERPENT PLAY.
MAIDEN ECSTASY. Small 4to, cloth extra, 8s.

HALL (MRS. S. C.).—SKETCHES OF IRISH CHARACTER. With numerous Illustrations on Steel and Wood by MACLISE, GILBERT, HARVEY, and GEORGE CRUIKSHANK. Small demy 8vo, cloth extra, 7s. 6d.

HALLIDAY (ANDREW).—EVERY-DAY PAPERS. Post 8vo, 2s.

HANDWRITING, THE PHILOSOPHY OF. With over 100 Facsimiles and Explanatory Text. By DON FELIX DE SALAMANCA. Post 8vo, cloth limp, 2s. 6d.

HANKY-PANKY: Easy Tricks, White Magic, Sleight of Hand, &c. Edited by W. H. CREMER. With 200 Illustrations. Crown 8vo, cloth extra, 4s. 6d.

HARDY (LADY DUFFUS).—PAUL WYNTER'S SACRIFICE. 2s.

HARDY (THOMAS).—UNDER THE GREENWOOD TREE. Crown 8vo, cloth extra, with Portrait and 15 Illustrations, 3s. 6d.; post 8vo, illustrated boards, 2s.; cloth limp, 2s. 6d.

HARPER (CHARLES G.), WORKS BY. Demy 8vo, cloth extra, 16s. each.
THE BRIGHTON ROAD. With Photogravure Frontispiece and 90 Illustrations.
FROM PADDINGTON TO PENZANCE: The Record of a Summer Tramp. 105 Illusts.

HARWOOD (J. BERWICK).—THE TENTH EARL. Post 8vo, illustrated boards, 2s.

HAWEIS (MRS. H. R.), WORKS BY. Square 8vo, cloth extra, 6s. each.
THE ART OF BEAUTY. With Coloured Frontispiece and 91 Illustrations.
THE ART OF DECORATION. With Coloured Frontispiece and 74 Illustrations.
THE ART OF DRESS. With 32 Illustrations. Post 8vo, 1s.; cloth, 1s. 6d.
CHAUCER FOR SCHOOLS. Demy 8vo, cloth limp, 2s. 6d.
CHAUCER FOR CHILDREN. 38 Illusts. (8 Coloured). Sm. 4to, cl. extra, 3s. 6d.

HAWEIS (Rev. H. R., M.A.).—AMERICAN HUMORISTS: WASHINGTON IRVING, OLIVER WENDELL HOLMES, JAMES RUSSELL LOWELL, ARTEMUS WARD, MARK TWAIN, and BRET HARTE. Third Edition. Crown 8vo, cloth extra, 6s.

HAWLEY SMART.—WITHOUT LOVE OR LICENCE: A Novel. Crown 8vo cloth extra, 3s. 6d.; post 8vo, illustrated boards, 2s.

HAWTHORNE (JULIAN), NOVELS BY.
Crown 8vo, cloth extra, 3s. 6d. each; post 8vo, illustrated boards, 2s. each.
GARTH. | ELLICE QUENTIN. | BEATRIX RANDOLPH. | DUST.
SEBASTIAN STROME. | DAVID POINDEXTER.
FORTUNE'S FOOL. | THE SPECTRE OF THE CAMERA.
Post 8vo, illustrated boards, 2s. each.
MISS CADOGNA. | LOVE—OR A NAME.
MRS. GAINSBOROUGH'S DIAMONDS. Fcap. 8vo. illustrated cover, 1s.

HAWTHORNE (NATHANIEL).—OUR OLD HOME. Annotated with Passages from the Author's Note-books, and Illustrated with 31 Photogravures Two Vols., crown 8vo, buckram, gilt top, 15s.

HEATH (FRANCIS GEORGE).—MY GARDEN WILD, AND WHAT I GREW THERE. Crown 8vo, cloth extra, gilt edges, 6s.

HELPS (SIR ARTHUR), WORKS BY. Post 8vo, cloth limp, 2s. 6d. each.
ANIMALS AND THEIR MASTERS. | SOCIAL PRESSURE.
IVAN DE BIRON: A Novel. Cr. 8vo, cl. extra, 3s. 6d.; post 8vo, illust. bds., 2s.

HENDERSON (ISAAC).—AGATHA PAGE: A Novel. Crown 8vo, cloth extra, **3s. 6d.**

HENTY (G. A.), NOVELS BY. Crown 8vo, cloth extra, **3s. 6d.** each.
RUJUB THE JUGGLER. 8 Illusts. by STANLEY L. WOOD. PRESENTATION ED., **5s.**
DOROTHY'S DOUBLE.

HERMAN (HENRY).—A LEADING LADY. Post 8vo, illustrated boards, **2s.**; cloth extra, **2s. 6d.**

HERRICK'S (ROBERT) HESPERIDES, NOBLE NUMBERS, AND COMPLETE COLLECTED POEMS. With Memorial-Introduction and Notes by the Rev. A. B. GROSART, D.D.; Steel Portrait, &c. Three Vols., crown 8vo, cl. bds., **18s.**

HERTZKA (Dr. THEODOR).—FREELAND: A Social Anticipation. Translated by ARTHUR RANSOM. Crown 8vo, cloth extra, **6s.**

HESSE-WARTEGG (CHEVALIER ERNST VON).—TUNIS: The Land and the People. With 22 Illustrations. Crown 8vo, cloth extra, **3s. 6d.**

HILL (HEADON).—ZAMBRA THE DETECTIVE. Post 8vo, illustrated boards, **2s.**; cloth, **2s. 6d.**

HILL (JOHN), WORKS BY.
TREASON-FELONY. Post 8vo, **2s.** | THE COMMON ANCESTOR. Cr. 8vo, **3s. 6d.**

HINDLEY (CHARLES), WORKS BY.
TAVERN ANECDOTES AND SAYINGS: Including Reminiscences connected with Coffee Houses, Clubs, &c. With Illustrations. Crown 8vo, cloth, **3s. 6d.**
THE LIFE AND ADVENTURES OF A CHEAP JACK. Cr. 8vo, cloth ex., **3s. 6d.**

HOEY (MRS. CASHEL).—THE LOVER'S CREED. Post 8vo, **2s.**

HOLLINGSHEAD (JOHN).—NIAGARA SPRAY. Crown 8vo, 1s.

HOLMES (GORDON, M.D.).—THE SCIENCE OF VOICE PRODUCTION AND VOICE PRESERVATION. Crown 8vo, **1s.**

HOLMES (OLIVER WENDELL), WORKS BY.
THE AUTOCRAT OF THE BREAKFAST-TABLE. Illustrated by J. GORDON THOMSON. Post 8vo, cloth limp **2s. 6d.**—Another Edition, post 8vo, cloth, **2s.**
THE AUTOCRAT OF THE BREAKFAST-TABLE and THE PROFESSOR AT THE BREAKFAST-TABLE. In One Vol. Post 8vo, half-bound, **2s.**

HOOD'S (THOMAS) CHOICE WORKS, in Prose and Verse. With Life of the Author, Portrait, and 200 Illustrations. Crown 8vo, cloth extra, **7s. 6d.**
HOOD'S WHIMS AND ODDITIES. With 85 Illusts. Post 8vo, half-bound, **2s.**

HOOD (TOM).—FROM NOWHERE TO THE NORTH POLE: A Noah's Arkæological Narrative. With 25 Illustrations by W. BRUNTON and E. C. BARNES. Square 8vo, cloth extra, gilt edges, **6s.**

HOOK'S (THEODORE) CHOICE HUMOROUS WORKS; including his Ludicrous Adventures, Bons Mots, Puns, and Hoaxes. With Life of the Author, Portraits, Facsimiles, and Illustrations. Crown 8vo, cloth extra, **7s. 6d.**

HOOPER (MRS. GEO.).—THE HOUSE OF RABY. Post 8vo, bds., **2s.**

HOPKINS (TIGHE). — "'TWIXT LOVE AND DUTY:" A Novel. Post 8vo, illustrated boards, **2s.**

HORNE (R. HENGIST).—ORION: An Epic Poem. With Photographic Portrait by SUMMERS. Tenth Edition. Crown 8vo, cloth extra, **7s.**

HUNGERFORD (MRS., Author of "Molly Bawn,"), NOVELS BY.
Post 8vo, illustrated boards, **2s.** each; cloth limp, **2s. 6d.** each.
A MAIDEN ALL FORLORN. | IN DURANCE VILE. | A MENTAL STRUGGLE.
MARVEL. | A MODERN CIRCE.
LADY VERNER'S FLIGHT. Cr. 8vo, cloth, **3s. 6d.**; post 8vo, illust. boards, **2s.**
THE RED-HOUSE MYSTERY. Crown 8vo, cloth extra, **3s. 6d.**
THE THREE GRACES. Two Vols., **10s.** nett.

HUNT (MRS. ALFRED), NOVELS BY.
Crown 8vo, cloth extra, **3s. 6d.** each; post 8vo, illustrated boards, **2s.** each.
THE LEADEN CASKET. | SELF-CONDEMNED. | THAT OTHER PERSON.
THORNICROFT'S MODEL. Post 8vo, illustrated boards, **2s.**
MRS. JULIET. Crown 8vo, cloth extra, **3s. 6d.**

HUNT'S (LEIGH) ESSAYS: A TALE FOR A CHIMNEY CORNER, &c. Edited by EDMUND OLLIER. Post 8vo, printed on laid paper and half-bd., **2s.**

HUTCHISON (W. M.).—HINTS ON COLT-BREAKING. With 25 Illustrations. Crown 8vo, cloth extra, 3s. 6d.

HYDROPHOBIA: An Account of M. Pasteur's System; Technique of his Method, and Statistics. By Renaud Suzor, M.B. Crown 8vo, cloth extra, 6s.

HYNE (C. J. CUTCLIFFE).—HONOUR OF THIEVES. Crown 8vo, cloth extra, 3s. 6d.

IDLER (THE): A Monthly Magazine. Profusely Illustr. 6d. Monthly. The first Six Vols. now ready, cl. extra, 5s. each; Cases for Binding, 1s. 6d. each.

INDOOR PAUPERS. By One of Them. Crown 8vo, 1s.; cloth, 1s. 6d.

INGELOW (JEAN).—FATED TO BE FREE. Post 8vo, illustrated bds., 2s.

INNKEEPER'S HANDBOOK (THE) AND LICENSED VICTUALLER'S MANUAL. By J. Trevor-Davies. Crown 8vo, 1s.; cloth, 1s. 6d.

IRISH WIT AND HUMOUR, SONGS OF. Collected and Edited by A. Perceval Graves. Post 8vo, cloth limp, 2s. 6d.

JAMES (C. T. C.).—A ROMANCE OF THE QUEEN'S HOUNDS. Post 8vo, picture cover, 1s.; cloth limp, 1s. 6d.

JAMESON (WILLIAM).—MY DEAD SELF. Post 8vo, illustrated boards, 2s.; cloth, 2s. 6d.

JAPP (ALEX. H., LL.D.).—DRAMATIC PICTURES, &c. Cr. 8vo, 5s.

JAY (HARRIETT), NOVELS BY. Post 8vo, illustrated boards, 2s. each.
THE DARK COLLEEN. | THE QUEEN OF CONNAUGHT.

JEFFERIES (RICHARD), WORKS BY. Post 8vo, cloth limp, 2s. 6d. each.
NATURE NEAR LONDON. | THE LIFE OF THE FIELDS. | THE OPEN AIR.
⁎ Also the Hand-made Paper Edition, crown 8vo, buckram, gilt top, 6s. each.
THE EULOGY OF RICHARD JEFFERIES. By Sir Walter Besant. With a Photograph Portrait. Crown 8vo, cloth extra, 6s.

JENNINGS (HENRY J.), WORKS BY.
CURIOSITIES OF CRITICISM. Post 8vo, cloth limp, 2s. 6d.
LORD TENNYSON: A Biographical Sketch. Post 8vo, 1s.; cloth, 1s. 6d.

JEROME (JEROME K.), BOOKS BY.
STAGELAND. With 64 Illusts. by J. Bernard Partridge. Fcap. 4to, pict. cov., 1s.
JOHN INGERFIELD, &c. With 9 Illusts. by A. S. Boyd and John Gulich. Fcap. 8vo, picture cover, 1s. 6d.

JERROLD (DOUGLAS).—THE BARBER'S CHAIR; and THE HEDGEHOG LETTERS. Post 8vo, printed on laid paper and half-bound, 2s.

JERROLD (TOM), WORKS BY. Post 8vo, 1s. each; cloth limp, 1s. 6d. each.
THE GARDEN THAT PAID THE RENT.
HOUSEHOLD HORTICULTURE: A Gossip about Flowers. Illustrated.

JESSE (EDWARD).—SCENES AND OCCUPATIONS OF A COUNTRY LIFE. Post 8vo, cloth limp, 2s.

JONES (WILLIAM, F.S.A.), WORKS BY. Cr. 8vo, cl. extra, 7s. 6d. each.
FINGER-RING LORE: Historical, Legendary, and Anecdotal. With nearly 300 Illustrations. Second Edition, Revised and Enlarged.
CREDULITIES, PAST AND PRESENT. Including the Sea and Seamen, Miners, Talismans, Word and Letter Divination, Exorcising and Blessing of Animals, Birds, Eggs, Luck, &c. With an Etched Frontispiece.
CROWNS AND CORONATIONS: A History of Regalia. With 100 Illustrations.

JONSON'S (BEN) WORKS. With Notes Critical and Explanatory, and a Biographical Memoir by William Gifford. Edited by Colonel Cunningham. Three Vols., crown 8vo, cloth extra, 6s. each.

JOSEPHUS, THE COMPLETE WORKS OF. Translated by Whiston. Containing "The Antiquities of the Jews" and "The Wars of the Jews." With 52 Illustrations and Maps. Two Vols., demy 8vo, half-bound, 12s. 6d.

KEMPT (ROBERT).—PENCIL AND PALETTE: Chapters on Art and Artists. Post 8vo, cloth limp, 2s. 6d.

KERSHAW (MARK).—COLONIAL FACTS & FICTIONS: Humorous Sketches. Post 8vo, illustrated boards, 2s.; cloth, 2s. 6d.

KEYSER (ARTHUR).—CUT BY THE MESS: A Novel. Crown 8vo, picture cover, 1s.; cloth limp, 1s. 6d.

KING (R. ASHE), NOVELS BY. Cr. 8vo, cl., 3s. 6d. ea.; post 8vo, bds., 2s. ea.
A DRAWN GAME. | "THE WEARING OF THE GREEN."
Post 8vo, illustrated boards, 2s. each.
PASSION'S SLAVE. | BELL BARRY.

KNIGHT (WILLIAM, M.R.C.S., and EDWARD, L.R.C.P.).—THE PATIENT'S VADE MECUM: How to Get Most Benefit from Medical Advice. Crown 8vo, 1s.; cloth limp, 1s. 6d.

KNIGHTS (THE) OF THE LION: A Romance of the Thirteenth Century. Edited, with an Introduction, by the MARQUESS of LORNE, K.T. Cr. 8vo, cl. ex. 6s.

LAMB'S (CHARLES) COMPLETE WORKS, in Prose and Verse, including "Poetry for Children" and "Prince Dorus." Edited, with Notes and Introduction, by R. H. SHEPHERD. With Two Portraits and Facsimile of a page of the "Essay on Roast Pig." Crown 8vo, half-bound, 7s. 6d.
THE ESSAYS OF ELIA. Post 8vo, printed on laid paper and half-bound, 2s.
LITTLE ESSAYS: Sketches and Characters by CHARLES LAMB, selected from his Letters by PERCY FITZGERALD. Post 8vo, cloth limp, 2s. 6d.
THE DRAMATIC ESSAYS OF CHARLES LAMB. With Introduction and Notes by BRANDER MATTHEWS, and Steel-plate Portrait. Fcap. 8vo, hf. bd., 2s. 6d.

LANDOR (WALTER SAVAGE).—CITATION AND EXAMINATION OF WILLIAM SHAKSPEARE, &c., before Sir THOMAS LUCY touching Deer-stealing, 19th September, 1582. To which is added, A CONFERENCE OF MASTER EDMUND SPENSER with the Earl of Essex, touching the State of Ireland, 1595. Fcap. 8vo, half-Roxburghe, 2s. 6d.

LANE (EDWARD WILLIAM).—THE THOUSAND AND ONE NIGHTS, commonly called in England THE ARABIAN NIGHTS' ENTERTAINMENTS. Translated from the Arabic, with Notes. Illustrated by many hundred Engravings from Designs by HARVEY. Edited by EDWARD STANLEY POOLE. With a Preface by STANLEY LANE-POOLE. Three Vols., demy 8vo, cloth extra, 7s. 6d. each.

LARWOOD (JACOB), WORKS BY.
THE STORY OF THE LONDON PARKS. With Illusts. Cr. 8vo, cl. extra, 3s. 6d.
ANECDOTES OF THE CLERGY. Post 8vo, laid paper, half-bound, 2s.
Post 8vo, cloth limp, 2s. 6d. each.
FORENSIC ANECDOTES. | THEATRICAL ANECDOTES.

LEHMANN (R. C.), WORKS BY. Post 8vo, pict. cover, 1s. ea.; cloth, 1s. 6d. ea.
HARRY FLUDYER AT CAMBRIDGE.
CONVERSATIONAL HINTS FOR YOUNG SHOOTERS: A Guide to Polite Talk.

LEIGH (HENRY S.), WORKS BY.
CAROLS OF COCKAYNE. Printed on hand-made paper, bound in buckram, 5s.
JEUX D'ESPRIT. Edited by HENRY S. LEIGH. Post 8vo, cloth limp, 2s. 6d.

LEPELLETIER (EDMOND).—MADAME SANS-GENE. Translated from the French by J. A. J. DE VILLIERS. Crown 8vo, cloth extra, 3s. 6d.

LEYS (JOHN).—THE LINDSAYS: A Romance. Post 8vo, illust. bds., 2s.

LINDSAY (HARRY).—RHODA ROBERTS: A Welsh Mining Story. Crown 8vo, cloth, 3s. 6d.

LINTON (E. LYNN), WORKS BY. Post 8vo, cloth limp, 2s. 6d. each.
WITCH STORIES. | OURSELVES: ESSAYS ON WOMEN.
Crown 8vo, cloth extra, 3s. 6d. each; post 8vo, illustrated boards, 2s. each.
PATRICIA KEMBALL. | IONE. | UNDER WHICH LORD?
ATONEMENT OF LEAM DUNDAS. | "MY LOVE!" | SOWING THE WIND.
THE WORLD WELL LOST. | PASTON CAREW, Millionaire & Miser.
Post 8vo, illustrated boards, 2s. each.
THE REBEL OF THE FAMILY. | WITH A SILKEN THREAD.
THE ONE TOO MANY. Crown 8vo, cloth extra, 3s. 6d.
FREESHOOTING: Extracts from Works of Mrs. LINTON. Post 8vo, cloth, 2s. 6d.

LUCY (HENRY W.).—GIDEON FLEYCE: A Novel. Crown 8vo, cloth extra, 3s. 6d.; post 8vo, illustrated boards, 2s.

MACALPINE (AVERY), NOVELS BY.
TERESA ITASCA. Crown 8vo, cloth extra, 1s.
BROKEN WINGS. With 6 Illusts. by W. J. Hennessy. Crown 8vo, cloth extra, 6s.

McCARTHY (JUSTIN, M.P.), WORKS BY.
A HISTORY OF OUR OWN TIMES, from the Accession of Queen Victoria to the General Election of 1880. Four Vols. demy 8vo, cloth extra, 12s. each.—Also a POPULAR EDITION, in Four Vols., crown 8vo, cloth extra, 6s. each.—And a JUBILEE EDITION, with an Appendix of Events to the end of 1886, in Two Vols., large crown 8vo, cloth extra, 7s. 6d. each.
A SHORT HISTORY OF OUR OWN TIMES. One Vol., crown 8vo, cloth extra, 6s.
—Also a CHEAP POPULAR EDITION, post 8vo, cloth limp, 2s. 6d.
A HISTORY OF THE FOUR GEORGES. Four Vols. demy 8vo, cloth extra, 12s. each. [Vols. I. & II. ready.

Cr. 8vo, cl. extra, 3s. 6d. each; post 8vo, illust. bds., 2s. each; cl. limp, 2s. 6d. each.

THE WATERDALE NEIGHBOURS.	DONNA QUIXOTE.
MY ENEMY'S DAUGHTER.	THE COMET OF A SEASON.
A FAIR SAXON.	MAID OF ATHENS.
LINLEY ROCHFORD.	CAMIOLA: A Girl with a Fortune.
DEAR LADY DISDAIN.	THE DICTATOR.
MISS MISANTHROPE.	RED DIAMONDS.

"THE RIGHT HONOURABLE." By JUSTIN McCARTHY, M.P., and Mrs. CAMPBELL PRAED. Crown 8vo, cloth extra, 6s.

McCARTHY (JUSTIN HUNTLY), WORKS BY.
THE FRENCH REVOLUTION. Four Vols., 8vo, 12s. each. [Vols. I. & II. ready.
AN OUTLINE OF THE HISTORY OF IRELAND. Crown 8vo, 1s.; cloth, 1s. 6d.
IRELAND SINCE THE UNION: Irish History, 1798-1886. Crown 8vo, cloth, 6s.

HAFIZ IN LONDON: Poems. Small 8vo, gold cloth, 3s. 6d.

OUR SENSATION NOVEL. Crown 8vo, picture cover, 1s.; cloth limp, 1s. 6d.
DOOM! An Atlantic Episode. Crown 8vo, picture cover, 1s.
DOLLY: A Sketch. Crown 8vo, picture cover, 1s.; cloth limp, 1s. 6d.
LILY LASS: A Romance. Crown 8vo, picture cover, 1s.; cloth limp, 1s. 6d.
THE THOUSAND AND ONE DAYS. 2 Photogravures. Two Vols., cr. 8vo, 12s.
A LONDON LEGEND. Three Vols., crown 8vo, 15s. net.

MACCOLL (HUGH), NOVELS BY.
MR. STRANGER'S SEALED PACKET. Post 8vo, illustrated boards, 2s.
EDNOR WHITLOCK. Crown 8vo, cloth extra, 6s.

MACDONALD (GEORGE, LL.D.), WORKS BY.
WORKS OF FANCY AND IMAGINATION. Ten Vols., 16mo, cl., gilt edges, in cloth case, 21s. Or the Vols. may be had separately, in grolier cl., at 2s. 6d. each.
Vol. I. WITHIN AND WITHOUT.—THE HIDDEN LIFE.
„ II. THE DISCIPLE.—THE GOSPEL WOMEN.—BOOK OF SONNETS.—ORGAN SONGS.
„ III. VIOLIN SONGS.—SONGS OF THE DAYS AND NIGHTS.—A BOOK OF DREAMS.—ROADSIDE POEMS—POEMS FOR CHILDREN.
„ IV. PARABLES.—BALLADS.—SCOTCH SONGS.
„ V. & VI. PHANTASTES: A Faerie Romance. | Vol. VII. THE PORTENT.
„ VIII. THE LIGHT PRINCESS.—THE GIANT'S HEART.—SHADOWS.
„ IX. CROSS PURPOSES.—THE GOLDEN KEY.—THE CARASOYN.—LITTLE DAYLIGHT.
„ X. THE CRUEL PAINTER.—THE WOW O' RIVVEN.—THE CASTLE.—THE BROKEN SWORDS.—THE GRAY WOLF.—UNCLE CORNELIUS.
POETICAL WORKS OF GEORGE MACDONALD. Collected and arranged by the Author. 2 vols., crown 8vo, buckram, 12s.
A THREEFOLD CORD. Edited by GEORGE MACDONALD. Post 8vo, cloth, 5s.
HEATHER AND SNOW: A Novel. Crown 8vo, cloth extra, 3s. 6d.
PHANTASTES: A Faerie Romance. With 25 Illustrations by J. BELL. Crown 8vo, cloth extra, 3s. 6d.
LILITH: A Romance. Crown 8vo, cloth extra, 6s. [Shortly.

MACDONELL (AGNES).—QUAKER COUSINS. Post 8vo, boards, 2s.

MACGREGOR (ROBERT).—PASTIMES AND PLAYERS: Notes on Popular Games. Post 8vo, cloth limp, 2s. 6d.

MACKAY (CHARLES, LL.D.).—INTERLUDES AND UNDERTONES; or, Music at Twilight. Crown 8vo, cloth extra, 6s.

MACLISE PORTRAIT GALLERY (THE) OF ILLUSTRIOUS LITERARY CHARACTERS: 85 PORTRAITS; with Memoirs — Biographical, Critical, Bibliographical, and Anecdotal—illustrative of the Literature of the former half of the Present Century, by WILLIAM BATES, B.A. Crown 8vo, cloth extra, **7s. 6d.**

MACQUOID (MRS.), WORKS BY. Square 8vo, cloth extra, **6s.** each.
IN THE ARDENNES. With 50 Illustrations by THOMAS R. MACQUOID.
PICTURES AND LEGENDS FROM NORMANDY AND BRITTANY. 34 Illustrations.
THROUGH NORMANDY. With 92 Illustrations by T. R. MACQUOID, and a Map.
THROUGH BRITTANY. With 35 Illustrations by T. R. MACQUOID, and a Map.
ABOUT YORKSHIRE. With 67 Illustrations by T. R. MACQUOID.

Post 8vo, illustrated boards, **2s.** each.
THE EVIL EYE, and other Stories. | LOST ROSE.

MAGICIAN'S OWN BOOK, THE: Performances with Eggs, Hats, &c. Edited by W. H. CREMER. With 200 Illustrations. Crown 8vo, cloth extra, **4s. 6d.**

MAGIC LANTERN, THE, and its Management: including full Practical Directions. By T. C. HEPWORTH. 10 Illustrations. Cr. 8vo, **1s.**; cloth, **1s. 6d.**

MAGNA CHARTA: An Exact Facsimile of the Original in the British Museum. 3 feet by 2 feet, with Arms and Seals emblazoned in Gold and Colours, **5s.**

MALLOCK (W. H.), WORKS BY.
THE NEW REPUBLIC. Post 8vo, picture cover, **2s.**; cloth limp, **2s. 6d.**
THE NEW PAUL & VIRGINIA: Positivism on an Island. Post 8vo, cloth, **2s. 6d.**
POEMS. Small 4to, parchment, **8s.**
IS LIFE WORTH LIVING? Crown 8vo, cloth extra, **6s.**
A ROMANCE OF THE NINETEENTH CENTURY. Crown 8vo, cloth, **6s.**; post 8vo, illustrated boards, **2s.**

MALLORY (SIR THOMAS).—MORT D'ARTHUR: The Stories of King Arthur and of the Knights of the Round Table. (A Selection.) Edited by B. MONTGOMERIE RANKING. Post 8vo, cloth limp, **2s.**

MARK TWAIN, WORKS BY. Crown 8vo, cloth extra, **7s. 6d.** each.
THE CHOICE WORKS OF MARK TWAIN. Revised and Corrected throughout by the Author. With Life, Portrait, and numerous Illustrations.
ROUGHING IT, and INNOCENTS AT HOME. With 200 Illusts. by F. A. FRASER.
MARK TWAIN'S LIBRARY OF HUMOUR. With 197 Illustrations.

Crown 8vo, cloth extra (illustrated), **7s. 6d.** each; post 8vo, illust. boards, **2s.** each.
THE INNOCENTS ABROAD; or, New Pilgrim's Progress. With 234 Illustrations. (The Two-Shilling Edition is entitled MARK TWAIN'S PLEASURE TRIP.)
THE GILDED AGE. By MARK TWAIN and C. D. WARNER. With 212 Illustrations.
THE ADVENTURES OF TOM SAWYER. With 111 Illustrations.
A TRAMP ABROAD. With 314 Illustrations.
THE PRINCE AND THE PAUPER. With 190 Illustrations.
LIFE ON THE MISSISSIPPI. With 300 Illustrations.
ADVENTURES OF HUCKLEBERRY FINN. With 174 Illusts. by E. W. KEMBLE.
A YANKEE AT THE COURT OF KING ARTHUR. With 220 Illusts. by BEARD.

Post 8vo, illustrated boards, **2s.** each.
THE STOLEN WHITE ELEPHANT. | MARK TWAIN'S SKETCHES.

Crown 8vo, cloth extra, **3s. 6d.** each.
THE AMERICAN CLAIMANT. With 81 Illustrations by HAL HURST, &c.
TOM SAWYER ABROAD. With 26 Illustrations by DAN BEARD.
PUDD'NHEAD WILSON. With Portrait and Six Illustrations by LOUIS LOEB.
THE £1,000,000 BANK-NOTE. Cr. 8vo, cloth, **3s. 6d.**; post 8vo, picture bds., **2s.**

MARKS (H. S., R.A.), PEN AND PENCIL SKETCHES BY. With 4 Photogravures and 126 Illustrations. Two Vols., demy 8vo, cloth, **32s.**

MARLOWE'S WORKS. Including his Translations. Edited, with Notes and Introductions, by Col. CUNNINGHAM. Crown 8vo, cloth extra, **6s.**

MARRYAT (FLORENCE), NOVELS BY. Post 8vo, illust. boards, **2s.** each.
A HARVEST OF WILD OATS. | FIGHTING THE AIR.
OPEN! SESAME! | WRITTEN IN FIRE.

MASSINGER'S PLAYS. From the Text of WILLIAM GIFFORD. Edited by Col. CUNNINGHAM. Crown 8vo, cloth extra, **6s.**

CHATTO & WINDUS, PUBLISHERS, PICCADILLY. 17

MASTERMAN (J.).—HALF-A-DOZEN DAUGHTERS: A Novel. Post 8vo, illustrated boards, 2s.

MATTHEWS (BRANDER).—A SECRET OF THE SEA, &c. Post 8vo, illustrated boards, 2s.; cloth limp, 2s. 6d.

MAYHEW (HENRY).—LONDON CHARACTERS & THE HUMOROUS SIDE OF LONDON LIFE. With Illustrations. Crown 8vo, cloth, 3s. 6d.

MEADE (L. T.), NOVELS BY.
A SOLDIER OF FORTUNE. Crown 8vo, cloth, 3s. 6d.
IN AN IRON GRIP. Two Vols., crown 8vo, cloth, 10s. net.
THE VOICE OF THE CHARMER. Three Vols., 15s. net. [Shortly.

MERRICK (LEONARD).—THE MAN WHO WAS GOOD. Post 8vo, illustrated boards, 2s.

MEXICAN MUSTANG (ON A), through Texas to the Rio Grande. By A. E. SWEET and J. ARMOY KNOX. With 265 Illusts. Cr. 8vo, cloth extra, 7s. 6d.

MIDDLEMASS (JEAN), NOVELS BY. Post 8vo, illust. boards, 2s. each.
TOUCH AND GO. | MR. DORILLION.

MILLER (MRS. F. FENWICK).—PHYSIOLOGY FOR THE YOUNG; or, The House of Life. With Illustrations. Post 8vo, cloth limp, 2s. 6d.

MILTON (J. L.), WORKS BY. Post 8vo, 1s. each; cloth, 1s. 6d. each.
THE HYGIENE OF THE SKIN. With Directions for Diet, Soaps, Baths, &c.
THE BATH IN DISEASES OF THE SKIN.
THE LAWS OF LIFE, AND THEIR RELATION TO DISEASES OF THE SKIN.
THE SUCCESSFUL TREATMENT OF LEPROSY. Demy 8vo, 1s.

MINTO (WM.)—WAS SHE GOOD OR BAD? Cr. 8vo, 1s.; cloth, 1s. 6d.

MITFORD (BERTRAM), NOVELS BY. Crown 8vo, cloth extra, 3s. 6d. each.
THE GUN-RUNNER: A Romance of Zululand. With Frontispiece by S. L. WOOD.
THE LUCK OF GERARD RIDGELEY. With a Frontispiece by STANLEY L. WOOD.
THE KING'S ASSEGAI. With Six full-page Illustrations by STANLEY L. WOOD.
RENSHAW FANNING'S QUEST. With a Frontispiece by STANLEY L. WOOD.

MOLESWORTH (MRS.), NOVELS BY.
HATHERCOURT RECTORY. Post 8vo, illustrated boards, 2s.
THAT GIRL IN BLACK. Crown 8vo, cloth, 1s. 6d.

MOORE (THOMAS), WORKS BY.
THE EPICUREAN; and ALCIPHRON. Post 8vo, half-bound, 2s.
PROSE AND VERSE. With Suppressed Passages from the MEMOIRS OF LORD BYRON. Edited by R. H. SHEPHERD. With Portrait. Cr 8vo, cl. ex., 7s. 6d.

MUDDOCK (J. E.), STORIES BY.
STORIES WEIRD AND WONDERFUL. Post 8vo, illust. boards, 2s.; cloth, 2s. 6d.
THE DEAD MAN'S SECRET; or, The Valley of Gold. With Frontispiece by F. BARNARD. Crown 8vo, cloth extra, 5s.; post 8vo, illustrated boards, 2s.
FROM THE BOSOM OF THE DEEP. Crown 8vo, illustrated boards, 2s.
MAID MARIAN AND ROBIN HOOD: A Romance of Old Sherwood Forest. With 12 Illustrations by STANLEY L. WOOD. Crown 8vo, cloth extra, 3s. 6d.

MURRAY (D. CHRISTIE), NOVELS BY.
Crown 8vo, cloth extra, 3s. 6d. each; post 8vo, illustrated boards, 2s. each.
A LIFE'S ATONEMENT. | THE WAY OF THE WORLD. | A BIT OF HUMAN NATURE.
JOSEPH'S COAT. | A MODEL FATHER. | FIRST PERSON SINGULAR.
COALS OF FIRE. | OLD BLAZER'S HERO. | BOB MARTIN'S Little GIRL.
VAL STRANGE. | CYNIC FORTUNE. | TIME'S REVENGES.
HEARTS. | BY THE GATE OF THE SEA. | A WASTED CRIME.
Crown 8vo, cloth extra, 3s. 6d. each.
IN DIREST PERIL.
MOUNT DESPAIR, &c. With Frontispiece by G. GRENVILLE MANTON.
THE MAKING OF A NOVELIST: An Experiment in Autobiography. With a Collotype Portrait and Vignette. Crown 8vo, art linen, 6s.

MURRAY (D. CHRISTIE) & HENRY HERMAN, WORKS BY.
Crown 8vo, cloth extra, 3s. 6d. each; post 8vo, illustrated boards, 2s. each.
ONE TRAVELLER RETURNS. | PAUL JONES'S ALIAS. | THE BISHOPS' BIBLE.

MURRAY (HENRY), NOVELS BY. Post 8vo, illust. bds., 2s. ea.; cl., 2s. 6d. ea.
A GAME OF BLUFF. | A SONG OF SIXPENCE.

CHATTO & WINDUS, PUBLISHERS, PICCADILLY.

NEWBOLT (HENRY).—TAKEN FROM THE ENEMY. Fcap. 8vo, cloth boards, 1s. 6d.

NISBET (HUME), BOOKS BY.
"BAIL UP!" Crown 8vo, cloth extra, 3s. 6d.; post 8vo, illustrated boards, 2s.
DR. BERNARD ST. VINCENT. Post 8vo, illustrated boards, 2s.
LESSONS IN ART. With 21 Illustrations. Crown 8vo, cloth extra, 2s. 6d.
WHERE ART BEGINS. With 27 Illustrations. Square 8vo, cloth extra, 7s. 6d.

NORRIS (W. E.), NOVELS BY.
ST. ANN'S. Cr. 8vo, cl ex., 3s. 6d. | BILLY BELLEW. Two Vols, cr. 8vo, 10s. net

O'HANLON (ALICE), NOVELS BY. Post 8vo, illustrated boards, 2s. each.
THE UNFORESEEN. | CHANCE? OR FATE?

OHNET (GEORGES), NOVELS BY. Post 8vo, illustrated boards, 2s. each.
DOCTOR RAMEAU. | A LAST LOVE.
A WEIRD GIFT. Crown 8vo, cloth, 3s. 6d., post 8vo, picture boards, 2s.

OLIPHANT (MRS.), NOVELS BY. Post 8vo, illustrated boards, 2s. each.
THE PRIMROSE PATH. | WHITELADIES.
THE GREATEST HEIRESS IN ENGLAND.

O'REILLY (HARRINGTON).—LIFE AMONG THE AMERICAN INDIANS: Fifty Years on the Trail. 100 Illusts. by P. FRENZENY. Crown 8vo. 3s. 6d.

O'REILLY (MRS.).—PHŒBE'S FORTUNES. Post 8vo, illust. bds., 2s.

OUIDA, NOVELS BY. Cr. 8vo, cl., 3s. 6d. each; post 8vo, illust. bds., 2s. each.
HELD IN BONDAGE. | FOLLE-FARINE. | MOTHS. | PIPISTRELLO.
TRICOTRIN. | A DOG OF FLANDERS. | A VILLAGE COMMUNE.
STRATHMORE. | PASCAREL. | SIGNA. | IN MAREMMA. | WANDA.
CHANDOS. | TWO WOODEN SHOES. | BIMBI. | SYRLIN.
CECIL CASTLEMAINE. | IN A WINTER CITY. | FRESCOES. | OTHMAR.
UNDER TWO FLAGS. | ARIADNE. | PRINCESS NAPRAXINE.
PUCK. | IDALIA. | FRIENDSHIP. | GUILDEROY. | RUFFINO.

Square 8vo, cloth extra, 5s. each.
BIMBI. With Nine Illustrations by EDMUND H. GARRETT.
A DOG OF FLANDERS, &c. With Six Illustrations by EDMUND H. GARRETT.
SANTA BARBARA, &c. Square 8vo, cloth, 6s.; crown 8vo, cloth, 3s. 6d.; post 8vo, illustrated boards, 2s.
TWO OFFENDERS. Square 8vo, cloth extra, 6s.; crown 8vo, cloth extra, 3s. 6d.
WISDOM, WIT, AND PATHOS, selected from the Works of OUIDA by F. SYDNEY MORRIS. Post 8vo, cloth extra, 5s. CHEAP EDITION, illustrated boards, 2s.

PAGE (H. A.), WORKS BY.
THOREAU: His Life and Aims. With Portrait. Post 8vo, cloth limp, 2s. 6d.
ANIMAL ANECDOTES. Arranged on a New Principle. Crown 8vo, cloth extra, 5s.

PAYN (JAMES), NOVELS BY.
Crown 8vo, cloth extra, 3s. 6d. each; post 8vo, illustrated boards, 2s. each
LOST SIR MASSINGBERD. | FROM EXILE. | HOLIDAY TASKS.
WALTER'S WORD. | THE CANON'S WARD.
LESS BLACK THAN WE'RE PAINTED. | THE TALK OF THE TOWN.
BY PROXY. | FOR CASH ONLY. | GLOW-WORM TALES.
HIGH SPIRITS. | THE MYSTERY OF MIRBRIDGE.
UNDER ONE ROOF. | THE WORD AND THE WILL.
A CONFIDENTIAL AGENT. | THE BURNT MILLION.
A GRAPE FROM A THORN. | SUNNY STORIES. | A TRYING PATIENT.

Post 8vo, illustrated boards, 2s. each.
HUMOROUS STORIES. | FOUND DEAD.
THE FOSTER BROTHERS. | GWENDOLINE'S HARVEST.
THE FAMILY SCAPEGRACE. | A MARINE RESIDENCE.
MARRIED BENEATH HIM. | MIRK ABBEY.
BENTINCK'S TUTOR. | SOME PRIVATE VIEWS.
A PERFECT TREASURE. | NOT WOOED, BUT WON.
A COUNTY FAMILY. | TWO HUNDRED POUNDS REWARD.
LIKE FATHER, LIKE SON. | THE BEST OF HUSBANDS.
A WOMAN'S VENGEANCE. | HALVES.
CARLYON'S YEAR. CECIL'S TRYST. | FALLEN FORTUNES.
MURPHY'S MASTER. | WHAT HE COST HER.
AT HER MERCY. | KIT: A MEMORY.
THE CLYFFARDS OF CLYFFE. | A PRINCE OF THE BLOOD.

IN PERIL AND PRIVATION. 17 Illustrations. Crown 8vo, cloth, 3s. 6d.
NOTES FROM THE "NEWS." Crown 8vo, portrait cover, 1s.; cloth, 1s. 6d.

CHATTO & WINDUS, PUBLISHERS, PICCADILLY. 19

PANDURANG HARI; or, Memoirs of a Hindoo. With Preface by Sir BARTLE FRERE. Crown 8vo, cloth, 3s. 6d.; post 8vo, illustrated boards, 2s.

PASCAL'S PROVINCIAL LETTERS. A New Translation, with Historical Introduction and Notes by T. M'CRIE, D.D. Post 8vo, cloth limp, 2s.

PAUL (MARGARET A.).—GENTLE AND SIMPLE. With Frontispiece by HELEN PATERSON. Crown 8vo, cloth, 3s. 6d.; post 8vo, illust. boards, 2s.

PENNELL (H. CHOLMONDELEY), WORKS BY. Post 8vo, cl., 2s. 6d. each.
PUCK ON PEGASUS. With Illustrations.
PEGASUS RE-SADDLED. With Ten full-page Illustrations by G. DU MAURIER.
THE MUSES OF MAYFAIR. Vers de Société, Selected by H. C. PENNELL.

PHELPS (E. STUART), WORKS BY. Post 8vo 1s. each; cloth 1s. 6d. each.
BEYOND THE GATES. | OLD MAID'S PARADISE. | BURGLARS IN PARADISE.
JACK THE FISHERMAN. Illustrated by C. W. REED. Cr. 8vo, 1s.; cloth, 1s. 6d.

PIRKIS (C. L.), NOVELS BY.
TROOPING WITH CROWS. Fcap. 8vo, picture cover, 1s.
LADY LOVELACE. Post 8vo, illustrated boards, 2s.

PLANCHE (J. R.), WORKS BY.
THE PURSUIVANT OF ARMS. With Six Plates, and 209 Illusts. Cr. 8vo, cl. 7s. 6d.
SONGS AND POEMS, 1819-1879. Introduction by Mrs. MACKARNESS. Cr. 8vo, cl., 6s.

PLUTARCH'S LIVES OF ILLUSTRIOUS MEN. With Notes and Life of Plutarch by J and WM. LANGHORNE. Portraits. Two Vols., demy 8vo, 10s. 6d.

POE'S (EDGAR ALLAN) CHOICE WORKS, in Prose and Poetry. Introduction by CHAS. BAUDELAIRE, Portrait, and Facsimiles. Cr. 8vo, cloth, 7s. 6d.
THE MYSTERY OF MARIE ROGET, &c. Post 8vo, illustrated boards, 2s.

POPE'S POETICAL WORKS. Post 8vo, cloth limp, 2s.

PRAED (MRS. CAMPBELL), NOVELS BY. Post 8vo, illust. bds., 2s. ea.
THE ROMANCE OF A STATION. | THE SOUL OF COUNTESS ADRIAN.
OUTLAW AND LAWMAKER. Crown 8vo, cloth, 3s. 6d.; post 8vo, boards, 2s.
CHRISTINA CHARD. Crown 8vo, cloth extra, 3s. 6d.

PRICE (E. C.), NOVELS BY.
Crown 8vo, cloth extra, 3s. 6d. each; post 8vo, illustrated boards, 2s. each.
VALENTINA. | THE FOREIGNERS. | MRS. LANCASTER'S RIVAL.
GERALD. Post 8vo, illustrated boards, 2s.

PRINCESS OLGA.—RADNA: A Novel. Crown 8vo, cloth extra, 6s.

PROCTOR (RICHARD A., B.A.), WORKS BY.
FLOWERS OF THE SKY. With 55 Illusts. Small crown 8vo, cloth extra, 3s. 6d.
EASY STAR LESSONS. With Star Maps for Every Night in the Year. Cr. 8vo, 6s.
FAMILIAR SCIENCE STUDIES. Crown 8vo, cloth extra, 6s.
SATURN AND ITS SYSTEM. With 13 Steel Plates. Demy 8vo, cloth ex., 10s. 6d.
MYSTERIES OF TIME AND SPACE. With Illustrations. Cr. 8vo, cloth extra, 6s.
THE UNIVERSE OF SUNS. With numerous Illustrations. Cr. 8vo, cloth ex., 6s.
WAGES AND WANTS OF SCIENCE WORKERS. Crown 8vo, 1s. 6d.

PRYCE (RICHARD).—MISS MAXWELL'S AFFECTIONS. Frontispiece by HAL LUDLOW. Crown 8vo, cloth, 3s. 6d.; post 8vo, illust. boards, 2s.

RAMBOSSON (J.).—POPULAR ASTRONOMY. With Coloured Plate and numerous Illustrations. Crown 8vo, cloth extra, 7s. 6d.

RANDOLPH (LIEUT.-COL. GEORGE, U.S.A.).—AUNT ABIGAIL DYKES: A Novel. Crown 8vo, cloth extra, 7s. 6d.

RIDDELL (MRS. J. H.), NOVELS BY.
WEIRD STORIES. Crown 8vo, cloth extra, 3s. 6d.; post 8vo, illustrated bds., 2s.
Post 8vo, illustrated boards, 2s. each.
THE UNINHABITED HOUSE. | FAIRY WATER.
THE PRINCE OF WALES'S GARDEN | HER MOTHER'S DARLING.
PARTY. | THE NUN'S CURSE.
MYSTERY IN PALACE GARDENS. | IDLE TALES.

RIVES (AMELIE).—BARBARA DERING: A Sequel to "The Quick or the Dead." Crown 8vo, cloth extra, 3s. 6d.; post 8vo, illustrated boards, 2s.

READE (CHARLES), NOVELS BY.
Crown 8vo, cloth extra, illustrated, 3s. 6d. each; post 8vo, illust. bds., 2s. each.
PEG WOFFINGTON. Illustrated by S. L. FILDES, R.A.—Also a POCKET EDITION, set in Elzevir style, fcap. 8vo, half-leather, 2s. 6d.—And a LIBRARY EDITION of PEG WOFFINGTON and CHRISTIE JOHNSTONE, in One Vol., cr. 8vo, cloth, 3s. 6d.
CHRISTIE JOHNSTONE. Illustrated by WILLIAM SMALL.—Also a POCKET EDITION, set in New Type, in Elzevir style, fcap. 8vo, half-leather, 2s. 6d.
IT IS NEVER TOO LATE TO MEND. Illustrated by G. J. PINWELL.—Also the Cheap POPULAR EDITION, medium 8vo, portrait cover, 6d.; cloth, 1s.
COURSE OF TRUE LOVE NEVER DID RUN SMOOTH. Illust. HELEN PATERSON.
THE AUTOBIOGRAPHY OF A THIEF, &c. Illustrated by MATT STRETCH.
LOVE ME LITTLE, LOVE ME LONG. Illustrated by M. ELLEN EDWARDS.
THE DOUBLE MARRIAGE. Illusts. by Sir JOHN GILBERT, R.A., and C. KEENE.
THE CLOISTER AND THE HEARTH. Illustrated by CHARLES KEENE.—Also the ELZEVIR EDITION, with Introduction by BESANT, 4 vols., post 8vo, cloth gilt, 14s.
HARD CASH. Illustrated by F. W. LAWSON.
GRIFFITH GAUNT. Illustrated by S. L. FILDES, R.A., and WILLIAM SMALL.
FOUL PLAY. Illustrated by GEORGE DU MAURIER.
PUT YOURSELF IN HIS PLACE. Illustrated by ROBERT BARNES.
A TERRIBLE TEMPTATION. Illustrated by EDWARD HUGHES and A. W. COOPER.
A SIMPLETON. Illustrated by KATE CRAUFURD.
THE WANDERING HEIR. Illust. by H. PATERSON, S. L. FILDES, C. GREEN, &c.
A WOMAN-HATER. Illustrated by THOMAS COULDERY.
SINGLEHEART AND DOUBLEFACE. Illustrated by P. MACNAB.
GOOD STORIES OF MEN AND OTHER ANIMALS. Illust. by E. A. ABBEY, &c.
THE JILT, and other Stories. Illustrated by JOSEPH NASH.
A PERILOUS SECRET. Illustrated by FRED. BARNARD.
READIANA. With a Steel-plate Portrait of CHARLES READE.
    POPULAR EDITIONS, medium 8vo, 6d. each; cloth, 1s. each.
**THE CLOISTER AND THE HEARTH. | IT IS NEVER TOO LATE TO MEND.
PEG WOFFINGTON; and CHRISTIE JOHNSTONE.**
BIBLE CHARACTERS: Studies of David, Paul, &c. Fcap. 8vo, leatherette, 1s.
SELECTIONS FROM THE WORKS OF CHARLES READE. Post 8vo, cloth, 2s. 6d.

RIMMER (ALFRED), WORKS BY. Square 8vo, cloth gilt, 7s. 6d. each.
OUR OLD COUNTRY TOWNS. With 55 Illustrations.
RAMBLES ROUND ETON AND HARROW. With 50 Illustrations.
ABOUT ENGLAND WITH DICKENS. With 58 Illusts. by C. A. VANDERHOOF, &c.

ROBINSON CRUSOE. By DANIEL DEFOE. (MAJOR'S EDITION.) With 37 Illustrations by GEORGE CRUIKSHANK. Post 8vo, half-bound, 2s.

ROBINSON (F. W.), NOVELS BY.
WOMEN ARE STRANGE. Post 8vo, illustrated boards, 2s.
THE HANDS OF JUSTICE. Cr. 8vo, cloth ex., 3s. 6d.; post 8vo, illust. bds., 2s.

ROBINSON (PHIL), WORKS BY. Crown 8vo, cloth extra, 6s. each.
THE POETS' BIRDS. | THE POETS' BEASTS.
THE POETS AND NATURE: REPTILES, FISHES, AND INSECTS.

ROCHEFOUCAULD'S MAXIMS AND MORAL REFLECTIONS. With Notes, and an Introductory Essay by SAINTE-BEUVE. Post 8vo, cloth limp, 2s.

ROLL OF BATTLE ABBEY, THE: A List of the Principal Warriors who came from Normandy with William the Conqueror. Handsomely printed, 5s.

ROSENGARTEN (A.).—HANDBOOK OF ARCHITECTURAL STYLES. Translated by W. COLLETT-SANDARS. With 630 Illusts. Cr. 8vo, cloth extra, 7s. 6d.

ROWLEY (HON. HUGH), WORKS BY. Post 8vo, cloth, 2s. 6d. each.
PUNIANA: RIDDLES AND JOKES. With numerous Illustrations.
MORE PUNIANA. Profusely Illustrated.

RUSSELL (W. CLARK), BOOKS AND NOVELS BY:
Cr. 8vo, cloth extra, 6s. each; post 8vo, illust. boards, 2s. each; cloth limp, 2s. 6d. ea.
ROUND THE GALLEY-FIRE. | A BOOK FOR THE HAMMOCK.
IN THE MIDDLE WATCH. | MYSTERY OF THE "OCEAN STAR."
A VOYAGE TO THE CAPE. | THE ROMANCE OF JENNY HARLOWE.
Cr. 8vo, cl. extra, 3s. 6d. ea.; post 8vo, illust. boards, 2s. ea.; cloth limp, 2s. 6d. ea.
OCEAN TRAGEDY. | SHIPMATE LOUISE. | ALONE ON WIDE WIDE SEA.
ON THE FO'K'SLE HEAD. Post 8vo, illust. boards, 2s.; cloth limp, 2s. 6d.
THE GOOD SHIP "MOHOCK." Two Vols., crown 8vo, 10s. net.
THE PHANTOM DEATH, &c. With Frontispiece. Crown 8vo, 3s. 6d.
THE CONVICT SHIP. Three Vols., crown 8vo, 15s. net.
IS HE THE MAN? Crown 8vo, cloth, 3s. 6d.

RUNCIMAN (JAMES), STORIES BY. Post 8vo, bds., 2s. ea.; cl., 2s. 6d. ea.
SKIPPERS AND SHELLBACKS. | GRACE BALMAIGN'S SWEETHEART.
SCHOOLS AND SCHOLARS.

RUSSELL (DORA), NOVELS BY.
A COUNTRY SWEETHEART. Crown 8vo, cloth extra, 3s. 6d. [Sept.
THE DRIFT OF FATE. Three Vols., crown 8vo, 15s. net.

SAINT AUBYN (ALAN), NOVELS BY.
Crown 8vo, cloth extra, 3s. 6d. each; post 8vo, illust. boards, 2s. each.
A FELLOW OF TRINITY. Note by OLIVER WENDELL HOLMES and Frontispiece.
THE JUNIOR DEAN. | MASTER OF ST. BENEDICT'S. | TO HIS OWN MASTER.
Fcap. 8vo, cloth boards, 1s. 6d. each.
THE OLD MAID'S SWEETHEART. | MODEST LITTLE SARA.
Crown 8vo, cloth extra, 3s. 6d. each.
ORCHARD DAMEREL. | IN THE FACE OF THE WORLD.
THE TREMLETT DIAMONDS. Two Vols., 10s. net.

SALA (G. A.).—GASLIGHT AND DAYLIGHT. Post 8vo, boards, 2s.

SANSON.—SEVEN GENERATIONS OF EXECUTIONERS: Memoirs of the Sanson Family (1688 to 1847). Crown 8vo, cloth extra, 3s. 6d.

SAUNDERS (JOHN), NOVELS BY.
Crown 8vo, cloth extra, 3s. 6d. each; post 8vo, illustrated boards, 2s. each.
GUY WATERMAN. | THE LION IN THE PATH. | THE TWO DREAMERS.
BOUND TO THE WHEEL. Crown 8vo, cloth extra, 3s. 6d.

SAUNDERS (KATHARINE), NOVELS BY.
Crown 8vo, cloth extra, 3s. 6d. each; post 8vo, illustrated boards, 2s. each.
MARGARET AND ELIZABETH. | HEART SALVAGE.
THE HIGH MILLS. | SEBASTIAN.
JOAN MERRYWEATHER. Post 8vo, illustrated boards, 2s.
GIDEON'S ROCK. Crown 8vo, cloth extra, 3s. 6d.

SCOTLAND YARD, Past and Present: Experiences of 37 Years. By Ex-Chief-Inspector CAVANAGH. Post 8vo, illustrated boards, 2s.; cloth, 2s. 6d.

SECRET OUT, THE: One Thousand Tricks with Cards; with Entertaining Experiments in Drawing-room or "White Magic." By W. H. CREMER. With 300 Illustrations. Crown 8vo, cloth extra, 4s. 6d.

SEGUIN (L. G.), WORKS BY.
THE COUNTRY OF THE PASSION PLAY (OBERAMMERGAU) and the Highlands of Bavaria. With Map and 37 Illustrations. Crown 8vo, cloth extra, 3s. 6d.
WALKS IN ALGIERS. With 2 Maps and 16 Illusts. Crown 8vo, cloth extra, 6s.

SENIOR (WM.).—BY STREAM AND SEA. Post 8vo, cloth, 2s. 6d.

SERGEANT (A.).—DR. ENDICOTT'S EXPERIMENT. 2 vols., 10s. net.

SHAKESPEARE FOR CHILDREN: LAMB'S TALES FROM SHAKE-
SPEARE. With Illusts., coloured and plain, by J. MOYR SMITH. Cr. 4to, 3s. 6d.

SHARP (WILLIAM).—CHILDREN OF TO-MORROW: A Novel. Crown 8vo, cloth extra, 6s.

SHELLEY (PERCY BYSSHE), THE COMPLETE WORKS IN VERSE
AND PROSE OF. Edited, Prefaced, and Annotated by R. HERNE SHEPHERD. Five Vols., crown 8vo, cloth boards, 3s. 6d. each.
POETICAL WORKS, in Three Vols.:
  Vol. I. Introduction by the Editor; Posthumous Fragments of Margaret Nicholson; Shelley's Correspondence with Stockdale; The Wandering Jew; Queen Mab, with the Notes; Alastor, and other Poems; Rosalind and Helen; Prometheus Unbound; Adonais, &c.
  Vol. II. Laon and Cythna; The Cenci; Julian and Maddalo; Swellfoot the Tyrant; The Witch of Atlas; Epipsychidion; Hellas.
  Vol. III. Posthumous Poems; The Masque of Anarchy; and other Pieces.
PROSE WORKS, in Two Vols.:
  Vol. I. The Two Romances of Zastrozzi and St. Irvyne; the Dublin and Marlow Pamphlets; A Refutation of Deism; Letters to Leigh Hunt, and some Minor Writings and Fragments.
  Vol. II. The Essays; Letters from Abroad; Translations and Fragments, Edited by Mrs. SHELLEY, With a Bibliography of Shelley, and an Index of the Prose Works.

SHERARD (R. H.).—ROGUES: A Novel. Crown 8vo, 1s.; cloth, 1s. 6d.

SHERIDAN (GENERAL P. H.), PERSONAL MEMOIRS OF. With Portraits and Facsimiles. Two Vols., demy 8vo, cloth, 24s.

SHERIDAN'S (RICHARD BRINSLEY) COMPLETE WORKS. With Life and Anecdotes. Including his Dramatic Writings, his Works in Prose and Poetry, Translations, Speeches and Jokes. 10 Illusts. Cr. 8vo, hf.-bound, **7s. 6d.**
    THE RIVALS, THE SCHOOL FOR SCANDAL, and other Plays. Post 8vo, printed on laid paper and half-bound. **2s.**
    SHERIDAN'S COMEDIES: THE RIVALS and THE SCHOOL FOR SCANDAL. Edited, with an Introduction and Notes to each Play, and a Biographical Sketch, by BRANDER MATTHEWS. With Illustrations. Demy 8vo, half-parchment, **12s. 6d.**

SIDNEY'S (SIR PHILIP) COMPLETE POETICAL WORKS, including all those in "Arcadia." With Portrait, Memorial-Introduction, Notes, &c. by the Rev. A. B. GROSART, D.D. Three Vols., crown 8vo, cloth boards, **18s.**

SIGNBOARDS: Their History. With Anecdotes of Famous Taverns and Remarkable Characters. By JACOB LARWOOD and JOHN CAMDEN HOTTEN. With Coloured Frontispiece and 94 Illustrations. Crown 8vo, cloth extra, **7s. 6d.**

SIMS (GEO. R.), WORKS BY. Post 8vo, illust. bds., **2s.** ea ; cl. limp, **2s. 6d.** ea.
    ROGUES AND VAGABONDS. | TALES OF TO-DAY.
    THE RING O' BELLS. | DRAMAS OF LIFE. With 60 Illustrations.
    MARY JANE'S MEMOIRS. | MEMOIRS OF A LANDLADY.
    MARY JANE MARRIED. | MY TWO WIVES.
    TINKLETOP'S CRIME. | SCENES FROM THE SHOW.
    ZEPH: A Circus Story, &c.
    Crown 8vo, picture cover, **1s.** each ; cloth, **1s. 6d.** each.
    HOW THE POOR LIVE; and HORRIBLE LONDON.
    THE DAGONET RECITER AND READER: being Readings and Recitations in Prose and Verse, selected from his own Works by GEORGE R. SIMS.
    THE CASE OF GEORGE CANDLEMAS. | DAGONET DITTIES.
    DAGONET ABROAD. Crown 8vo, cloth, **3s. 6d.** [Shortly.

SISTER DORA: A Biography. By MARGARET LONSDALE. With Four Illustrations. Demy 8vo, picture cover, **4d.**; cloth, **6d.**

SKETCHLEY (ARTHUR).—A MATCH IN THE DARK. Post 8vo, illustrated boards, **2s.**

SLANG DICTIONARY (THE): Etymological, Historical, and Anecdotal. Crown 8vo, cloth extra, **6s. 6d.**

SMITH (J. MOYR), WORKS BY.
    THE PRINCE OF ARGOLIS. With 130 Illusts. Post 8vo, cloth extra, **3s. 6d.**
    THE WOOING OF THE WATER WITCH. Illustrated. Post 8vo, cloth, **6s.**

SOCIETY IN LONDON. Crown 8vo, 1s. ; cloth, 1s. 6d.

SOCIETY IN PARIS: The Upper Ten Thousand. A Series of Letters from Count PAUL VASILI to a Young French Diplomat. Crown 8vo, cloth, **6s.**

SOMERSET (LORD HENRY).—SONGS OF ADIEU. Small 4to, Japanese vellum, **6s.**

SPALDING (T. A., LL.B.).—ELIZABETHAN DEMONOLOGY: An Essay on the Belief in the Existence of Devils. Crown 8vo, cloth extra, **5s.**

SPEIGHT (T. W.), NOVELS BY.
    Post 8vo, illustrated boards, **2s.** each.
    THE MYSTERIES OF HERON DYKE. | THE GOLDEN HOOP.
    BY DEVIOUS WAYS, &c. | BACK TO LIFE.
    HOODWINKED; and THE SANDY- | THE LOUDWATER TRAGEDY.
    CROFT MYSTERY. | BURGO'S ROMANCE.
    QUITTANCE IN FULL.
    Post 8vo, cloth limp, **1s. 6d.** each.
    A BARREN TITLE. | WIFE OR NO WIFE?
    THE SANDYCROFT MYSTERY. Crown 8vo, picture cover, **1s.**
    A SECRET OF THE SEA. Crown 8vo, cloth extra, **3s. 6d.**
    THE GREY MONK. Three Vols., **15s.** net.

SPENSER FOR CHILDREN. By M. H. TOWRY. With Illustrations by WALTER J. MORGAN. Crown 4to, cloth extra, **3s. 6d.**

STARRY HEAVENS (THE): A POETICAL BIRTHDAY BOOK. Royal 16mo, cloth extra, **2s. 6d.**

STEDMAN (E. C.), WORKS BY. Crown 8vo, cloth extra, **9s.** each.
    VICTORIAN POETS. | THE POETS OF AMERICA.

STERNDALE (R. ARMITAGE).—THE AFGHAN KNIFE: A Novel. Crown 8vo, cloth extra, 3s. 6d.; post 8vo, illustrated boards, 2s.

STEVENSON (R. LOUIS), WORKS BY. Post 8vo, cl. limp, 2s. 6d. each.
TRAVELS WITH A DONKEY. With a Frontispiece by WALTER CRANE.
AN INLAND VOYAGE. With a Frontispiece by WALTER CRANE.
Crown 8vo, buckram, gilt top, 6s. each.
FAMILIAR STUDIES OF MEN AND BOOKS.
THE SILVERADO SQUATTERS. With Frontispiece by J. D. STRONG.
THE MERRY MEN. | UNDERWOODS: Poems.
MEMORIES AND PORTRAITS.
VIRGINIBUS PUERISQUE, and other Papers. | BALLADS. | PRINCE OTTO.
ACROSS THE PLAINS, with other Memories and Essays.
NEW ARABIAN NIGHTS. Crown 8vo, buckram, gilt top, 6s.; post 8vo, illustrated boards, 2s.
THE SUICIDE CLUB; and THE RAJAH'S DIAMOND. (From NEW ARABIAN NIGHTS.) With 8 Illustrations by W. J. HENNESSY. Crown 8vo, cloth, 5s.
FATHER DAMIEN: An Open Letter to the Rev. Dr. Hyde. Crown 8vo, hand-made and brown paper, 1s.
THE EDINBURGH EDITION OF THE WORKS OF ROBERT LOUIS STEVENSON. 20 Vols., demy 8vo. This Edition (which is limited to 1,000 copies) is sold only in Sets, the price of which may be learned from the Booksellers. The Vols. are appearing at the rate of one a month beginning Nov. 1894.

STODDARD (C. WARREN).—SUMMER CRUISING IN THE SOUTH SEAS. Illustrated by WALLIS MACKAY. Crown 8vo, cloth extra, 3s. 6d.

STORIES FROM FOREIGN NOVELISTS. With Notices by HELEN and ALICE ZIMMERN. Crown 8vo, cloth extra, 3s. 6d.; post 8vo, illustrated boards, 2s.

STRANGE MANUSCRIPT (A) FOUND IN A COPPER CYLINDER. Cr. 8vo, cloth extra, with 19 Illusts. by GILBERT GAUL, 5s.; post 8vo, illust. bds., 2s.

STRANGE SECRETS. Told by CONAN DOYLE, PERCY FITZGERALD, FLORENCE MARRYAT, &c. Post 8vo, illustrated boards, 2s.

STRUTT (JOSEPH).—THE SPORTS AND PASTIMES OF THE PEOPLE OF ENGLAND; including the Rural and Domestic Recreations, May Games, Mummeries, Shows, &c., from the Earliest Period to the Present Time. Edited by WILLIAM HONE. With 140 Illustrations. Crown 8vo, cloth extra, 7s. 6d.

SWIFT'S (DEAN) CHOICE WORKS, in Prose and Verse. With Memoir, Portrait, and Facsimiles of the Maps in "Gulliver's Travels." Cr. 8vo. cl., 7s. 6d.
GULLIVER'S TRAVELS, and A TALE OF A TUB. Post 8vo, half-bound, 2s.
JONATHAN SWIFT: A Study. By J. CHURTON COLLINS. Crown 8vo, cloth extra, 8s.

SWINBURNE (ALGERNON C.), WORKS BY.

SELECTIONS FROM POETICAL WORKS OF A. C. SWINBURNE. Fcap. 8vo, 6s.	A NOTE ON CHARLOTTE BRONTE. Cr. 8vo, 6s.
ATALANTA IN CALYDON. Crown 8vo, 6s.	SONGS OF THE SPRINGTIDES. Crown 8vo, 6s.
CHASTELARD: A Tragedy. Crown 8vo, 7s.	STUDIES IN SONG. Crown 8vo, 7s.
POEMS AND BALLADS. FIRST SERIES. Crown 8vo or fcap. 8vo, 9s.	MARY STUART: A Tragedy. Crown 8vo, 8s.
POEMS AND BALLADS. SECOND SERIES. Crown 8vo, 9s.	TRISTRAM OF LYONESSE. Crown 8vo, 9s.
POEMS & BALLADS. THIRD SERIES. Cr. 8vo, 7s.	A CENTURY OF ROUNDELS. Small 4to, 8s.
SONGS BEFORE SUNRISE. Crown 8vo, 10s. 6d.	A MIDSUMMER HOLIDAY. Crown 8vo, 7s.
BOTHWELL: A Tragedy. Crown 8vo, 12s. 6d.	MARINO FALIERO: A Tragedy. Crown 8vo, 6s.
SONGS OF TWO NATIONS. Crown 8vo, 6s.	A STUDY OF VICTOR HUGO. Crown 8vo, 6s.
GEORGE CHAPMAN. (See Vol. II. of G. CHAPMAN'S Works.) Crown 8vo, 6s.	MISCELLANIES. Crown 8vo, 12s.
ESSAYS AND STUDIES. Crown 8vo, 12s.	LOCRINE: A Tragedy. Crown 8vo, 6s.
ERECHTHEUS: A Tragedy. Crown 8vo, 6s.	A STUDY OF BEN JONSON. Crown 8vo, 7s.
	THE SISTERS: A Tragedy. Crown 8vo, 6s.
	ASTROPHEL, &c. Crown 8vo, 7s.
	STUDIES IN PROSE AND POETRY. Crown 8vo, 9s.

SYNTAX'S (DR.) THREE TOURS: In Search of the Picturesque, in Search of Consolation, and in Search of a Wife. With ROWLANDSON'S Coloured Illustrations, and Life of the Author by J. C. HOTTEN. Crown 8vo, cloth extra, 7s. 6d.

TAINE'S HISTORY OF ENGLISH LITERATURE. Translated by HENRY VAN LAUN. Four Vols., small demy 8vo, cl. bds., 30s.—POPULAR EDITION, Two Vols., large crown 8vo, cloth extra, 15s.

TAYLOR (DR. J. E., F.L.S.), WORKS BY. Crown 8vo, cloth, 5s. each.
THE SAGACITY AND MORALITY OF PLANTS: A Sketch of the Life and Conduct of the Vegetable Kingdom. With a Coloured Frontispiece and 100 Illustrations.
OUR COMMON BRITISH FOSSILS, and Where to Find Them. 331 Illustrations.
THE PLAYTIME NATURALIST. With 360 Illustrations.

CHATTO & WINDUS, PUBLISHERS, PICCADILLY.

TAYLOR (BAYARD).—DIVERSIONS OF THE ECHO CLUB : Burlesques of Modern Writers. Post 8vo, cloth limp, 2s.

TAYLOR (TOM).—HISTORICAL DRAMAS. Containing "Clancarty," "Jeanne Darc," "'Twixt Axe and Crown," "The Fool's Revenge," "Arkwright's Wife," "Anne Boleyn," "Plot and Passion." Crown 8vo, cloth extra, 7s. 6d.
*** The Plays may also be had separately, at 1s. each.

TENNYSON (LORD): A Biographical Sketch. By H. J. JENNINGS. Post 8vo, portrait cover, 1s.; cloth, 1s. 6d.

THACKERAYANA : Notes and Anecdotes. Illustrated by Hundreds of Sketches by WILLIAM MAKEPEACE THACKERAY. Crown 8vo, cloth extra, 7s. 6d.

THAMES, A NEW PICTORIAL HISTORY OF THE. By A. S. KRAUSSE. With 340 Illustrations Post 8vo, 1s.; cloth, 1s. 6d.

THIERS (ADOLPHE).—HISTORY of the CONSULATE & EMPIRE of FRANCE UNDER NAPOLEON. Translated by D. FORBES CAMPBELL and JOHN STEBBING. With 36 Steel Plates. 12 vols., demy 8vo, cloth extra, 12s. each.

THOMAS (BERTHA), NOVELS BY. Cr. 8vo, cl., 3s. 6d. ea.; post 8vo, 2s. ea.
THE VIOLIN-PLAYER. | PROUD MAISIE.
CRESSIDA. Post 8vo, illustrated boards, 2s.

THOMSON'S SEASONS, and CASTLE OF INDOLENCE. With Introduction by ALLAN CUNNINGHAM, and 48 Illustrations. Post 8vo, half-bound, 2s.

THORNBURY (WALTER), WORKS BY.
THE LIFE AND CORRESPONDENCE OF J. M. W. TURNER. With Illustrations in Colours. Crown 8vo, cloth extra, 7s. 6d.
Post 8vo, illustrated boards, 2s. each.
OLD STORIES RE-TOLD. | TALES FOR THE MARINES.

TIMBS (JOHN), WORKS BY. Crown 8vo, cloth extra, 7s. 6d. each.
THE HISTORY OF CLUBS AND CLUB LIFE IN LONDON: Anecdotes of its Famous Coffee-houses, Hostelries, and Taverns. With 42 Illustrations.
ENGLISH ECCENTRICS AND ECCENTRICITIES: Stories of Delusions, Impostures, Sporting Scenes, Eccentric Artists, Theatrical Folk, &c. 48 Illustrations.

TROLLOPE (ANTHONY), NOVELS BY.
Crown 8vo, cloth extra, 3s. 6d. each; post 8vo, illustrated boards, 2s. each.
THE WAY WE LIVE NOW. | MR. SCARBOROUGH'S FAMILY.
FRAU FROHMANN. | THE LAND-LEAGUERS.
Post 8vo, illustrated boards, 2s. each.
KEPT IN THE DARK. | THE AMERICAN SENATOR.
THE GOLDEN LION OF GRANPERE. | JOHN CALDIGATE. | MARION FAY.

TROLLOPE (FRANCES E.), NOVELS BY.
Crown 8vo, cloth extra, 3s. 6d. each; post 8vo, illustrated boards, 2s. each.
LIKE SHIPS UPON THE SEA. | MABEL'S PROGRESS. | ANNE FURNESS.

TROLLOPE (T. A.).—DIAMOND CUT DIAMOND. Post 8vo, illust. bds., 2s.

TROWBRIDGE (J. T.).—FARNELL'S FOLLY. Post 8vo, boards, 2s.

TYTLER (C. C. FRASER-).—MISTRESS JUDITH : A Novel. Crown 8vo, cloth extra, 3s. 6d.; post 8vo, illustrated boards, 2s.

TYTLER (SARAH), NOVELS BY.
Crown 8vo, cloth extra, 3s. 6d. each; post 8vo, illustrated boards, 2s. each.
THE BRIDE'S PASS. | BURIED DIAMONDS.
LADY BELL. | THE BLACKHALL GHOSTS.
Post 8vo, illustrated boards, 2s. each.
WHAT SHE CAME THROUGH. | BEAUTY AND THE BEAST.
CITOYENNE JACQUELINE | DISAPPEARED. | NOBLESSE OBLIGE.
SAINT MUNGO'S CITY. | THE HUGUENOT FAMILY.
THE MACDONALD LASS. With Frontispiece. Cr. 8vo, cloth, 3s. 6d.

UPWARD (ALLEN), NOVELS BY.
THE QUEEN AGAINST OWEN. Crown 8vo, cloth, 3s. 6d.; post 8vo, bds., 2s.
THE PRINCE OF BALKISTAN. Crown 8vo, cloth extra, 3s. 6d.

VASHTI AND ESTHER. By the Writer of "Belle's" Letters in *The World*. Crown 8vo, cloth extra, 3s. 6d.

VILLARI (LINDA).—A DOUBLE BOND : A Story. Fcap. 8vo, 1s.

VIZETELLY (ERNEST A.).—THE SCORPION: A Romance of Spain. With a Frontispiece. Crown 8vo, cloth extra, 3s. 6d.

WALFORD (EDWARD, M.A.), WORKS BY.
WALFORD'S COUNTY FAMILIES OF THE UNITED KINGDOM (1895). Containing the Descent, Birth, Marriage, Education, &c., of 12,000 Heads of Families, their Heirs, Offices, Addresses, Clubs, &c. Royal 8vo, cloth gilt, 50s.
WALFORD'S SHILLING PEERAGE (1895). Containing a List of the House of Lords, Scotch and Irish Peers, &c. 32mo, cloth, 1s.
WALFORD'S SHILLING BARONETAGE (1895). Containing a List of the Baronets of the United Kingdom, Biographical Notices, Addresses, &c. 32mo, cloth, 1s.
WALFORD'S SHILLING KNIGHTAGE (1895). Containing a List of the Knights of the United Kingdom, Biographical Notices, Addresses, &c. 32mo, cloth, 1s.
WALFORD'S SHILLING HOUSE OF COMMONS (1895). Containing a List of all the Members of the New Parliament, their Addresses, Clubs, &c. 32mo, cloth, 1s.
WALFORD'S COMPLETE PEERAGE, BARONETAGE, KNIGHTAGE, AND HOUSE OF COMMONS (1895). Royal 32mo, cloth, gilt edges, 5s.
TALES OF OUR GREAT FAMILIES. Crown 8vo, cloth extra, 3s. 6d.

WALTON AND COTTON'S COMPLETE ANGLER; or, The Contemplative Man's Recreation, by IZAAK WALTON; and Instructions how to Angle for a Trout or Grayling in a clear Stream, by CHARLES COTTON. With Memoirs and Notes by Sir HARRIS NICOLAS, and 61 Illustrations. Crown 8vo, cloth antique, 7s. 6d.

WALT WHITMAN, POEMS BY. Edited, with Introduction, by WILLIAM M. ROSSETTI. With Portrait. Cr. 8vo, hand-made paper and buckram, 6s.

WARD (HERBERT).—MY LIFE WITH STANLEY'S REAR GUARD. With a Map by F. S. WELLER. Post 8vo, 1s.; cloth, 1s. 6d.

WARNER (CHARLES DUDLEY).—A ROUNDABOUT JOURNEY. Crown 8vo, cloth extra, 6s.

WARRANT TO EXECUTE CHARLES I. A Facsimile, with the 59 Signatures and Seals. Printed on paper 22 in. by 14 in. 2s.
WARRANT TO EXECUTE MARY QUEEN OF SCOTS. A Facsimile, including Queen Elizabeth's Signature and the Great Seal. 2s.

WASSERMANN (LILLIAS), NOVELS BY.
THE DAFFODILS. Crown 8vo, 1s.; cloth, 1s. 6d.
THE MARQUIS OF CARABAS. By AARON WATSON and LILLIAS WASSERMANN. Post 8vo, illustrated boards, 2s.

WEATHER, HOW TO FORETELL THE, WITH THE POCKET SPECTROSCOPE. By F. W. CORY. With 10 Illustrations. Cr. 8vo, 1s.; cloth, 1s. 6d.

WEBBER (BYRON).—FUN, FROLIC, AND FANCY. With 43 Illustrations by PHIL MAY and CHARLES MAY. Fcap. 4to, picture cover, 1s.

WESTALL (WILLIAM). — TRUST-MONEY. Post 8vo, illustrated boards, 2s.; cloth limp, 2s. 6d.

WHIST, HOW TO PLAY SOLO. By ABRAHAM S. WILKS and CHARLES F. PARDON. Post 8vo, cloth limp, 2s.

WHITE (GILBERT).—THE NATURAL HISTORY OF SELBORNE. Post 8vo, printed on laid paper and half-bound, 2s.

WILLIAMS (W. MATTIEU, F.R.A.S.), WORKS BY.
SCIENCE IN SHORT CHAPTERS. Crown 8vo, cloth extra, 7s. 6d.
A SIMPLE TREATISE ON HEAT. With Illustrations. Crown 8vo, cloth, 2s. 6d.
THE CHEMISTRY OF COOKERY. Crown 8vo, cloth extra, 6s.
THE CHEMISTRY OF IRON AND STEEL MAKING. Crown 8vo, cloth extra, 9s.
A VINDICATION OF PHRENOLOGY. With Portrait and 43 Illustrations. Demy 8vo, cloth extra, 12s. 6d.

WILLIAMSON (MRS. F. H.).—A CHILD WIDOW. Post 8vo, bds., 2s.

WILSON (DR. ANDREW, F.R.S.E.), WORKS BY.
CHAPTERS ON EVOLUTION. With 259 Illustrations. Cr. 8vo, cloth extra, 7s. 6d.
LEAVES FROM A NATURALIST'S NOTE-BOOK. Post 8vo, cloth limp, 2s. 6d.
LEISURE-TIME STUDIES. With Illustrations. Crown 8vo, cloth extra, 6s.
STUDIES IN LIFE AND SENSE. With numerous Illusts. Cr. 8vo, cl. ex., 6s.
COMMON ACCIDENTS: HOW TO TREAT THEM. Illusts. Cr. 8vo, 1s.; cl., 1s. 6d.
GLIMPSES OF NATURE. With 35 Illustrations. Crown 8vo, cloth extra, 3s. 6d.

WISSMANN (HERMANN VON).—MY SECOND JOURNEY THROUGH EQUATORIAL AFRICA. With 92 Illustrations. Demy 8vo, 16s.

WINTER (J. S.), STORIES BY. Post 8vo, illustrated boards, 2s. each; cloth limp, 2s. 6d. each.
    CAVALRY LIFE. | REGIMENTAL LEGENDS.
    A SOLDIER'S CHILDREN. With 34 Illustrations by E. G. THOMSON and E. STUART HARDY. Crown 8vo, cloth extra, 3s. 6d.

WOOD (H. F.), DETECTIVE STORIES BY. Post 8vo, boards, 2s. each.
    PASSENGER FROM SCOTLAND YARD. | ENGLISHMAN OF THE RUE CAIN.

WOOD (LADY).—SABINA: A Novel. Post 8vo, illust. boards, 2s.

WOOLLEY (CELIA PARKER).—RACHEL ARMSTRONG; or, Love and Theology. Post 8vo, illustrated boards, 2s.; cloth, 2s. 6d.

WRIGHT (THOMAS), WORKS BY. Crown 8vo, cloth extra, 7s. 6d. each.
    CARICATURE HISTORY OF THE GEORGES. With 400 Caricatures, Squibs, &c.
    HISTORY OF CARICATURE AND OF THE GROTESQUE IN ART, LITERATURE, SCULPTURE, AND PAINTING. Illustrated by F. W. FAIRHOLT, F.S.A.

WYNMAN (MARGARET).—MY FLIRTATIONS. With 13 Illustrations by J. BERNARD PARTRIDGE. Crown 8vo, cloth extra, 3s. 6d.

YATES (EDMUND), NOVELS BY. Post 8vo, illustrated boards, 2s. each.
    LAND AT LAST. | THE FORLORN HOPE. | CASTAWAY.

ZANGWILL (I.)—GHETTO TRAGEDIES. With Three Illustrations by A. S. BOYD. Fcap. 8vo, picture cover, 1s. net.

ZOLA (EMILE), NOVELS BY. Crown 8vo, cloth extra, 3s. 6d. each.
    THE DOWNFALL. Translated by E. A. VIZETELLY. Fourth Edition, Revised.
    THE DREAM. Translated by ELIZA CHASE. With 8 Illustrations by JEANNIOT.
    DOCTOR PASCAL. Translated by E. A. VIZETELLY. With Portrait of the Author.
    MONEY. Translated by ERNEST A. VIZETELLY.
    LOURDES. Translated by ERNEST A. VIZETELLY.
    EMILE ZOLA: A Biography. By R. H. SHERARD. With Portraits, Illustrations, and Facsimile Letter. Demy 8vo, cloth extra, 12s.

SOME BOOKS CLASSIFIED IN SERIES.

* For fuller cataloguing, see alphabetical arrangement, pp. 1–26.

THE MAYFAIR LIBRARY. Post 8vo, cloth limp, 2s. 6d. per Volume.

A Journey Round My Room. By X. DE MAISTRE. Translated by Sir HENRY ATTWELL.
Quips and Quiddities. By W. D. ADAMS.
The Agony Column of "The Times."
Melancholy Anatomised: Abridgment of Burton.
Poetical Ingenuities. By W. T. DOBSON.
The Cupboard Papers. By FIN-BEC.
W. S. Gilbert's Plays. THREE SERIES.
Songs of Irish Wit and Humour.
Animals and their Masters. By Sir A. HELPS.
Social Pressure. By Sir A. HELPS.
Curiosities of Criticism. By H. J. JENNINGS.
The Autocrat of the Breakfast-Table. By OLIVER WENDELL HOLMES.
Pencil and Palette. By R. KEMPT.
Little Essays: from LAMB'S Letters.
Forensic Anecdotes. By JACOB LARWOOD.
Theatrical Anecdotes. By JACOB LARWOOD.
Jeux d'Esprit. Edited by HENRY S. LEIGH.
Witch Stories. By E. LYNN LINTON.
Ourselves. By E. LYNN LINTON.
Pastimes and Players. By R. MACGREGOR.
New Paul and Virginia. By W. H. MALLOCK.
The New Republic. By W. H. MALLOCK.
Puck on Pegasus. By H. C. PENNELL.
Pegasus Re-saddled. By H. C. PENNELL.
Muses of Mayfair. Edited by H. C. PENNELL.
Thoreau: His Life and Aims. By H. A. PAGE.
Puniana. By Hon. HUGH ROWLEY.
More Puniana. By Hon. HUGH ROWLEY.
The Philosophy of Handwriting.
By Stream and Sea. By WM. SENIOR.
Leaves from a Naturalist's Note-Book. By Dr. ANDREW WILSON.

THE GOLDEN LIBRARY. Post 8vo, cloth limp, 2s. per Volume.

Diversions of the Echo Club. BAYARD TAYLOR.
Songs for Sailors. By W. C. BENNETT.
Lives of the Necromancers. By W. GODWIN.
The Poetical Works of Alexander Pope.
Scenes of Country Life. By EDWARD JESSE.
Tale for a Chimney Corner. By LEIGH HUNT.
The Autocrat of the Breakfast Table. By OLIVER WENDELL HOLMES.
La Mort d'Arthur: Selections from MALLORY.
Provincial Letters of Blaise Pascal.
Maxims and Reflections of Rochefoucauld.

THE WANDERER'S LIBRARY. Crown 8vo, cloth extra, 3s. 6d. each.

Wanderings in Patagonia. By JULIUS BEERBOHM. Illustrated.
Camp Notes. By FREDERICK BOYLE.
Savage Life. By FREDERICK BOYLE.
Merrie England in the Olden Time. By G. DANIEL. Illustrated by CRUIKSHANK.
Circus Life. By THOMAS FROST.
Lives of the Conjurers. By THOMAS FROST.
The Old Showmen and the Old London Fairs. By THOMAS FROST.
Low-Life Deeps. By JAMES GREENWOOD.
Wilds of London. By JAMES GREENWOOD.
Tunis. By Chev. HESSE-WARTEGG. 22 Illusts.
Life and Adventures of a Cheap Jack.
World Behind the Scenes. By P. FITZGERALD.
Tavern Anecdotes and Sayings.
The Genial Showman. By E. P. HINGSTON.
Story of London Parks. By JACOB LARWOOD.
London Characters. By HENRY MAYHEW.
Seven Generations of Executioners.
Summer Cruising in the South Seas. By C. WARREN STODDARD. Illustrated.

CHATTO & WINDUS, PUBLISHERS, PICCADILLY. 27

BOOKS IN SERIES—*continued*.

HANDY NOVELS. Fcap. 8vo, cloth boards, 1s. 6d. each.

The Old Maid's Sweetheart. By A. ST. AUBYN. | Taken from the Enemy. By H. NEWBOLT.
Modest Little Sara. By ALAN ST. AUBYN. | A Lost Soul. By W. L. ALDEN.
Seven Sleepers of Ephesus. M. E. COLERIDGE | Dr. Palliser's Patient. By GRANT ALLEN.

MY LIBRARY. Printed on laid paper, post 8vo, half-Roxburghe, 2s. 6d. each.

Citation and Examination of William Shakspeare | Christie Johnstone. By CHARLES READE.
By W. S. LANDOR. | Peg Woffington. By CHARLES READE.
The Journal of Maurice de Guerin. | The Dramatic Essays of Charles Lamb.

THE POCKET LIBRARY. Post 8vo, printed on laid paper and hf.-bd., 2s. each.

The Essays of Elia. By CHARLES LAMB. | White's Natural History of Selborne.
Robinson Crusoe. Illustrated by G. CRUIKSHANK. | Gulliver's Travels, &c. By Dean SWIFT.
Whims and Oddities. By THOMAS HOOD. With | Plays by RICHARD BRINSLEY SHERIDAN.
85 Illustrations. | Anecdotes of the Clergy. By JACOB LARWOOD.
The Barber's Chair. By DOUGLAS JERROLD. | Thomson's Seasons. Illustrated.
Gastronomy. By BRILLAT-SAVARIN. | The Autocrat of the Breakfast-Table and The
The Epicurean, &c. By THOMAS MOORE. | Professor at the Breakfast-Table. By OLIVER
Leigh Hunt's Essays. Edited by E. OLLIER. | WENDELL HOLMES.

THE PICCADILLY NOVELS.

LIBRARY EDITIONS OF NOVELS, many Illustrated, crown 8vo. cloth extra, 3s. 6d. each.

By F. M. ALLEN.
Green as Grass.

By GRANT ALLEN.
Philistia.
Babylon.
Strange Stories.
Beckoning Hand.
In all Shades.
The Tents of Shem.
For Maimie's Sake.
The Devil's Die.
This Mortal Coil.
The Great Taboo.
Dumaresq's Daughter.
Blood Royal.
Duchess of Powysland.
Ivan Greet's Masterpiece.
The Scallywag.

By MARY ANDERSON.
Othello's Occupation.

By EDWIN L. ARNOLD.
Phra the Phœnician.
The Constable of St. Nicholas.

By ALAN ST. AUBYN.
A Fellow of Trinity.
The Junior Dean
Master of St. Benedict's.
To his Own Master
In Face of the World.
Orchard Damerel.

By Rev. S. BARING GOULD.
Red Spider. | Eve.

By ROBERT BARR.
In a Steamer Chair. | From Whose Bourne.

By FRANK BARRETT.
The Woman of the Iron Bracelets.

By "BELLE."
Vashti and Esther.

Sir W. BESANT & J. RICE.
My Little Girl.
Case of Mr. Lucraft.
This Son of Vulcan.
The Golden Butterfly.
By Celia's Arbour
The Monks of Thelema.
The Seamy Side.
The Ten Years' Tenant.
Ready-Money Mortiboy.
With Harp and Crown.
'Twas in Trafalgar's Bay.
The Chaplain of the Fleet.

By Sir WALTER BESANT.
All Sorts and Conditions of Men.
The Captains' Room.
All in a Garden Fair.
Herr Paulus.
The Ivory Gate.
The World Went Very Well Then.
For Faith and Freedom.
The Rebel Queen.
Dorothy Forster.
Uncle Jack.
Children of Gibeon.
Bell of St. Paul's.
To Call Her Mine.
The Holy Rose.
Armorel of Lyonesse
St. Katherine's by the Tower.
Verbena Camellia Stephanotis.

By ROBERT BUCHANAN.
Shadow of the Sword.
A Child of Nature.
Heir of Linne.
The Martyrdom of Madeline.
God and the Man.
Love Me for Ever.
Annan Water.
Woman and the Man.
The New Abelard.
Foxglove Manor.
Master of the Mine.
Red and White Heather.
Matt. | Rachel Dene.

By J. MITCHELL CHAPPLE.
The Minor Chord.

By HALL CAINE.
The Shadow of a Crime. | The Deemster.
A Son of Hagar.

By MACLAREN COBBAN.
The Red Sultan. | The Burden of Isabel.

MORT. & FRANCES COLLINS.
Transmigration.
Blacksmith & Scholar.
The Village Comedy.
From Midnight to Midnight.
You Play me False.

By WILKIE COLLINS.
Armadale.
After Dark.
No Name.
Antonina.
Basil.
Hide and Seek.
The Dead Secret.
Queen of Hearts.
My Miscellanies.
The Woman in White.
The Moonstone.
Man and Wife.
Poor Miss Finch.
Miss or Mrs.?
The New Magdalen.
The Frozen Deep.
The Two Destinies.
The Law and the Lady
The Haunted Hotel.
The Fallen Leaves.
Jezebel's Daughter.
The Black Robe.
Heart and Science.
"I Say No."
Little Novels.
The Evil Genius.
The Legacy of Cain.
A Rogue's Life.
Blind Love.

By DUTTON COOK.
Paul Foster's Daughter.

By E. H. COOPER.
Geoffory Hamilton.

By V. CECIL COTES.
Two Girls on a Barge.

By C. EGBERT CRADDOCK.
His Vanished Star.

By H. N. CRELLIN.
Romances of the Old Seraglio.

By MATT CRIM.
Adventures of a Fair Rebel.

By B. M. CROKER.
Diana Barrington.
Proper Pride.
A Family Likeness.
Pretty Miss Neville.
A Bird of Passage.
"To Let."
Outcast of the People.

By WILLIAM CYPLES.
Hearts of Gold.

By ALPHONSE DAUDET.
The Evangelist; or, Port Salvation.

By H. COLEMAN DAVIDSON.
Mr. Sadler's Daughters.

By ERASMUS DAWSON.
The Fountain of Youth.

By JAMES DE MILLE.
A Castle in Spain.

By J. LEITH DERWENT.
Our Lady of Tears. | Circe's Lovers.

CHATTO & WINDUS, PUBLISHERS, PICCADILLY.

THE PICCADILLY (3/6) NOVELS—*continued*.

By DICK DONOVAN.
Tracked to Doom. | Man from Manchester

By A. CONAN DOYLE.
The Firm of Girdlestone.

S. JEANNETTE DUNCAN.
A Daughter of To-day. | Vernon's Aunt.

By Mrs. ANNIE EDWARDES.
Archie Lovell.

By G. MANVILLE FENN.
The New Mistress. | The Tiger Lily.
Witness to the Deed. | The White Virgin.

By PERCY FITZGERALD.
Fatal Zero.

By R. E. FRANCILLON.
One by One. | King or Knave?
A Dog and his Shadow. | Ropes of Sand.
A Real Queen. | Jack Doyle's Daughter.

Pref. by Sir BARTLE FRERE.
Pandurang Hari.

By EDWARD GARRETT.
The Capel Girls.

By PAUL GAULOT.
The Red Shirts.

By CHARLES GIBBON.
Robin Gray. | The Golden Shaft.
Loving a Dream. |

By E. GLANVILLE.
The Lost Heiress. | The Fossicker.
A Fair Colonist. |

By E. J. GOODMAN.
The Fate of Herbert Wayne.

By CECIL GRIFFITH.
Corinthia Marazion.

By SYDNEY GRUNDY.
The Days of his Vanity.

By THOMAS HARDY.
Under the Greenwood Tree.

By BRET HARTE.
A Waif of the Plains. | Susy.
A Ward of the Golden | Sally Dows.
 Gate. | A Protégée of Jack
A Sappho of Green | Hamlin's.
 Springs. | Bell-Ringer of Angel's.
Col. Starbottle's Client. | Clarence.

By JULIAN HAWTHORNE.
Garth. | Beatrix Randolph.
Ellice Quentin. | David Poindexter's Dis-
Sebastian Strome. | appearance.
Dust. | The Spectre of the
Fortune's Fool. | Camera

By Sir A. HELPS.
Ivan de Biron.

By I. HENDERSON.
Agatha Page.

By G. A. HENTY.
Rujub the Juggler. | Dorothy's Double.

By JOHN HILL.
The Common Ancestor.

By Mrs. HUNGERFORD.
Lady Verner's Flight. | The Red-House Mystery

By Mrs. ALFRED HUNT.
The Leaden Casket. | Self-Condemned.
That Other Person. | Mrs. Juliet.

By CUTCLIFFE HYNE.
Honour of Thieves.

By R. ASHE KING.
A Drawn Game.
"The Wearing of the Green."

THE PICCADILLY (3/6) NOVELS—*continued*.

By EDMOND LEPELLETIER.
Madame Sans-Gene.

By HARRY LINDSAY.
Rhoda Roberts.

By E. LYNN LINTON.
Patricia Kemball. | Sowing the Wind.
Under which Lord? | The Atonement of Leam
"My Love!" | Dundas.
Ione. | The World Well Lost.
Paston Carew. | The One Too Many.

By H. W. LUCY.
Gideon Fleyce.

By JUSTIN McCARTHY.
A Fair Saxon. | Waterdale Neighbours.
Linley Rochford. | My Enemy's Daughter.
Miss Misanthrope. | Red Diamonds.
Donna Quixote. | Dear Lady Disdain.
Maid of Athens. | The Dictator.
Camiola. | The Comet of a Season.

By GEORGE MACDONALD.
Heather and Snow. | Phantastes.

By L. T. MEADE.
A Soldier of Fortune.

By BERTRAM MITFORD.
The Gun-Runner. | The King's Assegai.
The Luck of Gerard | Renshaw Fanning's
 Ridgeley. | Quest.

By J. E. MUDDOCK.
Maid Marian and Robin Hood.

By D. CHRISTIE MURRAY.
A Life's Atonement. | First Person Singular.
Joseph's Coat. | Cynic Fortune.
Coals of Fire. | The Way of the World.
Old Blazer's Hero. | Bob Martin's Little Girl.
Val Strange. | Hearts. | Time's Revenges.
A Model Father. | A Wasted Crime.
By the Gate of the Sea. | In Direst Peril.
A Bit of Human Nature. | Mount Despair.

By MURRAY & HERMAN.
The Bishops' Bible. | Paul Jones's Alias.
One Traveller Returns. |

By HUME NISBET.
"Bail Up!"

By W. E. NORRIS.
Saint Ann's.

By G. OHNET.
A Weird Gift.

By OUIDA.
Held in Bondage. | Two Little Wooden
Strathmore. | Shoes.
Chandos. | In a Winter City.
Under Two Flags. | Friendship.
Idalia. | Moths.
Cecil Castlemaine's | Ruffino.
 Gage. | Pipistrello.
Tricotrin. | A Village Commune.
Puck. | Bimbi.
Folle Farine. | Wanda.
A Dog of Flanders. | Frescoes. | Othmar.
Pascarel. | In Maremma.
Signa. | Syrlin. | Guilderoy.
Princess Napraxine. | Santa Barbara.
Ariadne. | Two Offenders.

By MARGARET A. PAUL.
Gentle and Simple.

By JAMES PAYN.
Lost Sir Massingberd. | High Spirits.
Less Black than We're | Under One Roof.
 Painted. | From Exile.
A Confidential Agent. | Glow-worm Tales.
A Grape from a Thorn. | The Talk of the Town.
In Peril and Privation. | Holiday Tasks.
The Mystery of Mir- | For Cash Only.
 bridge. | The Burnt Million.
The Canon's Ward. | The Word and the Will.
Walter's Word. | Sunny Stories.
By Proxy. | A Trying Patient.

CHATTO & WINDUS, PUBLISHERS, PICCADILLY. 29

THE PICCADILLY (3/6) NOVELS—*continued.*

By Mrs. CAMPBELL PRAED.
Outlaw and Lawmaker. | Christina Chard.

By E. C. PRICE.
Valentina. | Mrs. Lancaster's Rival.
The Foreigners.

By RICHARD PRYCE.
Miss Maxwell's Affections.

By CHARLES READE.
It is Never Too Late to Mend. | Singleheart and Doubleface.
The Double Marriage. | Good Stories of Men and other Animals.
Love Me Little, Love Me Long. | Hard Cash.
The Cloister and the Hearth. | Peg Woffington.
The Course of True Love. | Christie Johnstone.
The Autobiography of a Thief. | Griffith Gaunt.
Put Yourself in His Place. | Foul Play.
A Terrible Temptation. | The Wandering Heir.
The Jilt. | A Woman-Hater.
 | A Simpleton.
 | A Perilous Secret.
 | Readiana.

By Mrs. J. H. RIDDELL.
Weird Stories.

By AMELIE RIVES.
Barbara Dering.

By F. W. ROBINSON.
The Hands of Justice.

By DORA RUSSELL.
A Country Sweetheart.

By W. CLARK RUSSELL.
Ocean Tragedy. | The Phantom Death.
My Shipmate Louise. | Is He the Man?
Alone on Wide Wide Sea.

By JOHN SAUNDERS.
Guy Waterman. | The Two Dreamers.
Bound to the Wheel. | The Lion in the Path.

By KATHARINE SAUNDERS.
Margaret and Elizabeth | Heart Salvage.
Gideon's Rock. | Sebastian.
The High Mills.

THE PICCADILLY (3/6) NOVELS—*continued.*

By HAWLEY SMART.
Without Love or Licence.

By T. W. SPEIGHT.
A Secret of the Sea.

By R. A. STERNDALE.
The Afghan Knife.

By BERTHA THOMAS.
Proud Maisie. | The Violin-Player.

By ANTHONY TROLLOPE.
The Way we Live Now. | Scarborough's Family.
Frau Frohmann. | The Land-Leaguers.

By FRANCES E. TROLLOPE.
Like Ships upon the Sea. | Anne Furness.
 | Mabel's Progress.

By IVAN TURGENIEFF, &c.
Stories from Foreign Novelists.

By MARK TWAIN.
The American Claimant. | Tom Sawyer Abroad.
The £1,000,000 Bank-note. | Pudd'nhead Wilson.

By C. C. FRASER-TYTLER.
Mistress Judith.

By SARAH TYTLER.
Lady Bell. | The Blackhall Ghosts.
The Bride's Pass. | The Macdonald Lass.
Buried Diamonds.

By ALLEN UPWARD.
The Queen against Owen.
The Prince of Balkistan.

By E. A. VIZETELLY.
The Scorpion: A Romance of Spain.

By J. S. WINTER.
A Soldier's Children.

By MARGARET WYNMAN.
My Flirtations.

By E. ZOLA.
The Downfall. | Dr. Pascal.
The Dream. | Money. | Lourdes.

CHEAP EDITIONS OF POPULAR NOVELS.
Post 8vo, illustrated boards, 2s. each.

By ARTEMUS WARD.
Artemus Ward Complete.

By EDMOND ABOUT.
The Fellah.

By HAMILTON AIDE.
Carr of Carrlyon. | Confidences.

By MARY ALBERT.
Brooke Finchley's Daughter.

By Mrs. ALEXANDER.
Maid, Wife or Widow? | Valerie's Fate.

By GRANT ALLEN.
Strange Stories. | For Maimie's Sake.
Philistia. | The Tents of Shem.
Babylon. | The Great Taboo.
The Devil's Die. | Dumaresq's Daughter.
This Mortal Coil. | The Duchess of Powysland.
In all Shades. | Ivan Greet's Masterpiece.
The Beckoning Hand. | The Scallywag.
Blood Royal.

By E. LESTER ARNOLD.
Phra the Phœnician.

By ALAN ST. AUBYN.
A Fellow of Trinity. | Master of St. Benedict's.
The Junior Dean. | To His Own Master.

By Rev. S. BARING GOULD.
Red Spider. | Eve.

By FRANK BARRETT.
Fettered for Life. | Honest Davie.
Little Lady Linton. | A Prodigal's Progress.
Between Life & Death. | Found Guilty.
The Sin of Olga Zassoulich. | A Recoiling Vengeance.
 | For Love and Honour.
Folly Morrison. | John Ford: and His Helpmate.
Lieut. Barnabas.

SHELSLEY BEAUCHAMP.
Grantley Grange.

By Sir WALTER BESANT.
Dorothy Forster. | For Faith and Freedom.
Children of Gibeon. | To Call Her Mine.
Uncle Jack. | The Bell of St. Paul's.
Herr Paulus. | Armorel of Lyonesse.
All Sorts and Conditions of Men. | The Holy Rose.
 | The Ivory Gate.
The Captains' Room. | St. Katherine's by the Tower.
All in a Garden Fair.
The World Went Very Well Then. | Verbena Camellia.
 | The Rebel Queen.

Sir W. BESANT & J. RICE.
This Son of Vulcan. | The Ten Years' Tenant.
My Little Girl. | Ready-Money Mortiboy.
The Case of Mr. Lucraft. | With Harp and Crown.
The Golden Butterfly. | 'Twas in Trafalgar's Bay.
By Celia's Arbour.
The Monks of Thelema. | The Chaplain of the Fleet.
The Seamy Side.

TWO-SHILLING NOVELS—*continued*.

By AMBROSE BIERCE.
In the Midst of Life.

By FREDERICK BOYLE.
Camp Notes. | Chronicles of No man's
Savage Life. | Land.

By BRET HARTE.
Californian Stories. | Flip. | Maruja.
Gabriel Conroy. | A Phyllis of the Sierras.
The Luck of Roaring | A Waif of the Plains.
Camp. | A Ward of the Golden
An Heiress of Red Dog. | Gate

By HAROLD BRYDGES.
Uncle Sam at Home.

By ROBERT BUCHANAN.
Shadow of the Sword. | The Martyrdom of Ma-
A Child of Nature. | deline.
God and the Man. | Annan Water.
Love Me for Ever. | The New Abelard.
Foxglove Manor. | Matt.
The Master of the Mine | The Heir of Linne.

By HALL CAINE.
The Shadow of a Crime. | The Deemster.
A Son of Hagar.

By Commander CAMERON.
The Cruise of the "Black Prince."

By Mrs. LOVETT CAMERON.
Deceivers Ever. | Juliet's Guardian.

By HAYDEN CARRUTH.
The Adventures of Jones.

By AUSTIN CLARE.
For the Love of a Lass.

By Mrs. ARCHER CLIVE.
Paul Ferroll.
Why Paul Ferroll Killed his Wife.

By MACLAREN COBBAN.
The Cure of Souls. | The Red Sultan.

By C. ALLSTON COLLINS.
The Bar Sinister.

MORT. & FRANCES COLLINS.
Sweet Anne Page. | Sweet and Twenty.
Transmigration. | The Village Comedy.
From Midnight to Mid- | You Play me False.
night. | Blacksmith and Scholar
A Fight with Fortune. | Frances.

By WILKIE COLLINS.
Armadale. | My Miscellanies.
After Dark. | The Woman in White.
No Name. | The Moonstone.
Antonina. | Man and Wife.
Basil. | Poor Miss Finch.
Hide and Seek. | The Fallen Leaves.
The Dead Secret. | Jezebel's Daughter
Queen of Hearts. | The Black Robe.
Miss or Mrs.? | Heart and Science.
The New Magdalen. | "I Say No!"
The Frozen Deep. | The Evil Genius.
The Law and the Lady. | Little Novels.
The Two Destinies. | Legacy of Cain.
The Haunted Hotel. | Blind Love.
A Rogue's Life.

By M. J. COLQUHOUN.
Every Inch a Soldier.

By DUTTON COOK.
Leo. | Paul Foster's Daughter.

By C. EGBERT CRADDOCK.
The Prophet of the Great Smoky Mountains.

By MATT CRIM.
Adventures of a Fair Rebel.

By B. M. CROKER.
Pretty Miss Nevill. | Bird of Passage.
Diana Barrington. | Proper Pride.
"To Let." | A Family Likeness.

By W. CYPLES.
Hearts of Gold.

By ALPHONSE DAUDET.
The Evangelist; or, Port Salvation.

By ERASMUS DAWSON.
The Fountain of Youth.

TWO-SHILLING NOVELS—*continued*.

By JAMES DE MILLE.
A Castle in Spain.

By J. LEITH DERWENT.
Our Lady of Tears. | Circe's Lovers.

By CHARLES DICKENS.
Sketches by Boz. | Nicholas Nickleby.
Oliver Twist.

By DICK DONOVAN.
The Man-Hunter. | From Information Re-
Tracked and Taken. | ceived.
Caught at Last! | Tracked to Doom.
Wanted! | Link by Link
Who Poisoned Hetty | Suspicion Aroused.
Duncan? | Dark Deeds.
Man from Manchester. | The Long Arm of the
A Detective's Triumph | Law.
In the Grip of the Law.

By Mrs. ANNIE EDWARDES.
A Point of Honour. | Archie Lovell.

By M. BETHAM-EDWARDS.
Felicia. | Kitty.

By EDW. EGGLESTON.
Roxy.

By G. MANVILLE FENN.
The New Mistress. | Witness to the Deed.

By PERCY FITZGERALD.
Bella Donna. | Second Mrs. Tillotson.
Never Forgotten. | Seventy-five Brooke
Polly. | Street.
Fatal Zero. | The Lady of Brantome.

By P. FITZGERALD and others.
Strange Secrets.

ALBANY DE FONBLANQUE.
Filthy Lucre.

By R. E. FRANCILLON.
Olympia. | King or Knave?
One by One. | Romances of the Law.
A Real Queen. | Ropes of Sand.
Queen Cophetua. | A Dog and his Shadow

By HAROLD FREDERIC.
Seth's Brother's Wife. | The Lawton Girl.

Pref. by Sir BARTLE FRERE.
Pandurang Hari.

By HAIN FRISWELL.
One of Two.

By EDWARD GARRETT.
The Capel Girls.

By GILBERT GAUL.
A Strange Manuscript.

By CHARLES GIBBON.
Robin Gray. | In Honour Bound.
Fancy Free. | Flower of the Forest.
For Lack of Gold. | The Braes of Yarrow.
What will the World | The Golden Shaft.
Say? | Of High Degree.
In Love and War. | By Mead and Stream.
For the King. | Loving a Dream.
In Pastures Green. | A Hard Knot.
Queen of the Meadow. | Heart's Delight.
A Heart's Problem. | Blood-Money
The Dead Heart.

By WILLIAM GILBERT.
Dr. Austin's Guests. | The Wizard of the
James Duke. | Mountain.

By ERNEST GLANVILLE.
The Lost Heiress. | The Fossicker.
A Fair Colonist.

By HENRY GREVILLE.
A Noble Woman. | Nikanor.

By CECIL GRIFFITH.
Corinthia Marazion.

By SYDNEY GRUNDY.
The Days of his Vanity.

By JOHN HABBERTON.
Brueton's Bayou. | Country Luck.

By ANDREW HALLIDAY.
Every-day Papers.

By Lady DUFFUS HARDY.
Paul Wynter's Sacrifice.

CHATTO & WINDUS, PUBLISHERS, PICCADILLY. 31

Two-Shilling Novels—*continued.*

By THOMAS HARDY.
Under the Greenwood Tree.

By J. BERWICK HARWOOD.
The Tenth Earl.

By JULIAN HAWTHORNE.
Garth.
Ellice Quentin.
Fortune's Fool.
Miss Cadogna.
Sebastian Strome.
Dust.
Beatrix Randolph.
Love—or a Name.
David Poindexter's Disappearance.
The Spectre of the Camera.

By Sir ARTHUR HELPS.
Ivan de Biron.

By HENRY HERMAN.
A Leading Lady.

By HEADON HILL.
Zambra the Detective.

By JOHN HILL.
Treason Felony.

By Mrs. CASHEL HOEY.
The Lover's Creed.

By Mrs. GEORGE HOOPER.
The House of Raby.

By TIGHE HOPKINS.
Twixt Love and Duty.

By Mrs. HUNGERFORD.
A Maiden all Forlorn.
In Durance Vile.
Marvel.
A Mental Struggle.
A Modern Circe.
Lady Verner's Flight.

By Mrs. ALFRED HUNT.
Thornicroft's Model.
That Other Person.
Self-Condemned.
The Leaden Casket.

By JEAN INGELOW.
Fated to be Free.

By WM. JAMESON.
My Dead Self.

By HARRIETT JAY.
The Dark Colleen. | Queen of Connaught.

By MARK KERSHAW.
Colonial Facts and Fictions.

By R. ASHE KING.
A Drawn Game.
"The Wearing of the Green."
Passion's Slave
Bell Barry.

By JOHN LEYS.
The Lindsays.

By E. LYNN LINTON.
Patricia Kemball.
The World Well Lost.
Under which Lord?
Paston Carew.
"My Love!"
Ione.
The Atonement of Leam Dundas.
With a Silken Thread.
The Rebel of the Family.
Sowing the Wind.

By HENRY W. LUCY.
Gideon Fleyce.

By JUSTIN McCARTHY.
Dear Lady Disdain.
Waterdale Neighbours.
My Enemy's Daughter.
A Fair Saxon.
Linley Rochford.
Miss Misanthrope.
Camiola.
Donna Quixote.
Maid of Athens.
The Comet of a Season.
The Dictator.
Red Diamonds.

By HUGH MACCOLL.
Mr. Stranger's Sealed Packet.

By AGNES MACDONELL.
Quaker Cousins.

KATHARINE S. MACQUOID.
The Evil Eye. | Lost Rose.

By W. H. MALLOCK.
A Romance of the Nineteenth Century.
The New Republic.

Two-Shilling Novels—*continued.*

By FLORENCE MARRYAT.
Open! Sesame!
Fighting the Air.
A Harvest of Wild Oats.
Written in Fire.

By J. MASTERMAN.
Half-a-dozen Daughters.

By BRANDER MATTHEWS.
A Secret of the Sea.

By LEONARD MERRICK.
The Man who was Good.

By JEAN MIDDLEMASS.
Touch and Go. | Mr Dorillion.

By Mrs. MOLESWORTH.
Hathercourt Rectory.

By J. E. MUDDOCK.
Stories Weird and Wonderful.
The Dead Man's Secret.
From the Bosom of the Deep.

By MURRAY and HERMAN.
One Traveller Returns. | The Bishops' Bible.
Paul Jones's Alias.

By D. CHRISTIE MURRAY.
A Model Father
Joseph's Coat.
Coals of Fire.
Val Strange.
Old Blazer's Hero.
Hearts.
The Way of the World.
Cynic Fortune.
A Life's Atonement.
By the Gate of the Sea.
A Bit of Human Nature.
First Person Singular.
Bob Martin's Little Girl.
Time's Revenges.
A Wasted Crime.

By HENRY MURRAY.
A Game of Bluff. | A Song of Sixpence.

By HUME NISBET.
"Bail Up!" | Dr. Bernard St. Vincent.

By ALICE O'HANLON.
The Unforeseen. | Chance? or Fate?

By GEORGES OHNET.
Dr. Rameau.
A Last Love.
A Weird Gift.

By Mrs. OLIPHANT.
Whiteladies.
The Primrose Path.
The Greatest Heiress in England.

By Mrs. ROBERT O'REILLY.
Phœbe's Fortunes.

By OUIDA.
Held in Bondage.
Strathmore.
Chandos.
Idalia.
Under Two Flags.
Cecil Castlemaine's Gage
Tricotrin.
Puck.
Folle Farine.
A Dog of Flanders.
Pascarel.
Signa.
Princess Napraxine.
In a Winter City
Ariadne.
Friendship.
Two Little Wooden Shoes.
Moths.
Bimbi.
Pipistrello.
A Village Commune.
Wanda.
Othmar.
Frescoes.
In Maremma.
Guilderoy
Ruffino.
Syrlin.
Santa Barbara.
Ouida's Wisdom, Wit. and Pathos.

MARGARET AGNES PAUL.
Gentle and Simple.

By C. L. PIRKIS.
Lady Lovelace.

By EDGAR A. POE.
The Mystery of Marie Roget.

By Mrs. CAMPBELL PRAED.
The Romance of a Station.
The Soul of Countess Adrian.
Outlaw and Lawmaker.

By E. C. PRICE.
Valentina.
The Foreigners.
Mrs. Lancaster's Rival.
Gerald.

By RICHARD PRYCE.
Miss Maxwell's Affections.

CHATTO & WINDUS, PUBLISHERS, PICCADILLY

TWO-SHILLING NOVELS—*continued*.
By JAMES PAYN.
Bentinck's Tutor.
Murphy's Master.
A County Family.
At Her Mercy.
Cecil's Tryst.
The Clyffards of Clyffe.
The Foster Brothers.
Found Dead.
The Best of Husbands.
Walter's Word.
Halves.
Fallen Fortunes.
Humorous Stories.
£200 Reward.
A Marine Residence.
Mirk Abbey.
By Proxy.
Under One Roof.
High Spirits.
Carlyon's Year.
From Exile.
For Cash Only.
Kit.
The Canon's Ward.
Talk of the Town.
Holiday Tasks.
A Perfect Treasure.
What He Cost Her.
A Confidential Agent.
Glow-worm Tales.
The Burnt Million.
Sunny Stories.
Lost Sir Massingberd.
A Woman's Vengeance.
The Family Scapegrace.
Gwendoline's Harvest.
Like Father, Like Son.
Married Beneath Him.
Not Wooed, but Won.
Less Black than We're Painted.
Some Private Views.
A Grape from a Thorn.
The Mystery of Mirbridge.
The Word and the Will.
A Prince of the Blood.
A Trying Patient.

By CHARLES READE.
It is Never Too Late to Mend.
Christie Johnstone.
The Double Marriage.
Put Yourself in His Place.
Love Me Little, Love Me Long.
The Cloister and the Hearth.
The Course of True Love.
The Jilt.
The Autobiography of a Thief.
A Terrible Temptation.
Foul Play.
The Wandering Heir.
Hard Cash.
Singleheart and Doubleface.
Good Stories of Men and other Animals.
Peg Woffington.
Griffith Gaunt.
A Perilous Secret.
A Simpleton.
Readiana.
A Woman-Hater.

By Mrs. J. H. RIDDELL.
Weird Stories.
Fairy Water.
Her Mother's Darling.
The Prince of Wales's Garden Party.
The Uninhabited House.
The Mystery in Palace Gardens.
The Nun's Curse.
Idle Tales.

By AMELIE RIVES.
Barbara Dering.

By F. W. ROBINSON.
Women are Strange. | The Hands of Justice.

By JAMES RUNCIMAN.
Skippers and Shellbacks.
Grace Balmaign's Sweetheart.
Schools and Scholars.

By W. CLARK RUSSELL.
Round the Galley Fire.
On the Fo'k'sle Head.
In the Middle Watch.
A Voyage to the Cape.
A Book for the Hammock.
The Mystery of the "Ocean Star."
The Romance of Jenny Harlowe.
An Ocean Tragedy.
My Shipmate Louise.
Alone on a Wide Wide Sea.

GEORGE AUGUSTUS SALA.
Gaslight and Daylight.

By JOHN SAUNDERS.
Guy Waterman.
The Two Dreamers.
The Lion in the Path.

By KATHARINE SAUNDERS.
Joan Merryweather.
The High Mills.
Heart Salvage.
Sebastian.
Margaret and Elizabeth.

By GEORGE R. SIMS.
Rogues and Vagabonds.
The Ring o' Bells.
Mary Jane's Memoirs.
Mary Jane Married.
Tales of To-day.
Dramas of Life.
Tinkletop's Crime.
Zeph.
My Two Wives.
Memoirs of a Landlady.
Scenes from the Show.

TWO-SHILLING NOVELS—*continued*.
By ARTHUR SKETCHLEY.
A Match in the Dark.

By HAWLEY SMART.
Without Love or Licence.

By T. W. SPEIGHT.
The Mysteries of Heron Dyke.
The Golden Hoop.
Hoodwinked.
By Devious Ways.
Back to Life.
The Loudwater Tragedy.
Burgo's Romance.
Quittance in Full.

By R. A. STERNDALE.
The Afghan Knife.

By R. LOUIS STEVENSON.
New Arabian Nights. | Prince Otto.

By BERTHA THOMAS.
Cressida.
Proud Maisie.
The Violin-Player.

By WALTER THORNBURY.
Tales for the Marines. | Old Stories Retold.

T. ADOLPHUS TROLLOPE.
Diamond Cut Diamond.

By F. ELEANOR TROLLOPE.
Like Ships upon the Sea.
Anne Furness.
Mabel's Progress.

By ANTHONY TROLLOPE.
Frau Frohmann.
Marion Fay.
Kept in the Dark.
John Caldigate.
The Way We Live Now.
The Land-Leaguers.
The American Senator.
Mr. Scarborough's Family.
The Golden Lion of Granpere.

By J. T. TROWBRIDGE.
Farnell's Folly.

By IVAN TURGENIEFF, &c.
Stories from Foreign Novelists.

By MARK TWAIN.
A Pleasure Trip on the Continent.
The Gilded Age.
Huckleberry Finn.
Mark Twain's Sketches.
Tom Sawyer.
A Tramp Abroad.
Stolen White Elephant.
Life on the Mississippi.
The Prince and the Pauper.
A Yankee at the Court of King Arthur.
The £1,000,000 Banknote.

By C. C. FRASER-TYTLER.
Mistress Judith.

By SARAH TYTLER.
The Bride's Pass.
Buried Diamonds.
St. Mungo's City.
Lady Bell.
Noblesse Oblige.
Disappeared.
The Huguenot Family.
The Blackhall Ghosts.
What She Came Through.
Beauty and the Beast.
Citoyenne Jaqueline.

By ALLEN UPWARD.
The Queen against Owen.

By AARON WATSON and LILLIAS WASSERMANN.
The Marquis of Caratas.

By WILLIAM WESTALL.
Trust-Money.

By Mrs. F. H. WILLIAMSON.
A Child Widow.

By J. S. WINTER.
Cavalry Life. | Regimental Legends.

By H. F. WOOD.
The Passenger from Scotland Yard.
The Englishman of the Rue Cain.

By Lady WOOD.
Sabina.

CELIA PARKER WOOLLEY.
Rachel Armstrong; or, Love and Theology.

By EDMUND YATES.
The Forlorn Hope.
Land at Last.
Castaway.

OGDEN, SMALE AND CO. LIMITED, PRINTERS, GREAT SAFFRON HILL, E.C.

www.ingramcontent.com/pod-product-compliance
Lightning Source LLC
Chambersburg PA
CBHW032058220426
43664CB00008B/1046